The Sociology of the Palestinians

First published in 1980, *The Sociology of the Palestinians* is a comprehensive collection of sociological and demographic studies of the Palestinian people. One paper deals with the Palestinian Arabs in pre-1967 Israel and the various methods of social control adopted by the Zionist regime to co-opt and control the Arab population. A second paper focuses on the Palestinians in the West Bank and Gaza. An analysis of current Palestinian demography with projections for the future is made, and the minority position of the Palestinians in the Arab World is critically assessed. An examination of the role of Palestinian intellectuals is followed by a theoretical discussion on the development of Palestinian class structure. Finally, the role of Palestinian women is examined in the context of traditional social structure and the specific political and economic situation which confront Palestinian society. This book will be of interest to students of history, sociology, and political science.

The Sociology of the Palestinians

Edited by Khalil Nakhleh and Elia Zureik

Routledge
Taylor & Francis Group

First published in 1980
By Croom Helm Ltd.

This edition first published in 2024 by Routledge
4 Park Square, Milton Park, Abingdon, Oxon, OX14 4RN
and by Routledge
605 Third Avenue, New York, NY 10017

Routledge is an imprint of the Taylor & Francis Group, an informa business

Publisher's Note
The publisher has gone to great lengths to ensure the quality of this reprint but points
out that some imperfections in the original copies may be apparent.

Disclaimer
The publisher has made every effort to trace copyright holders and welcomes
correspondence from those they have been unable to contact.

A Library of Congress record exists under ISBN: 0312740735

ISBN: 978-1-032-76945-5 (hbk)
ISBN: 978-1-003-48052-5 (ebk)
ISBN: 978-1-032-76946-2 (pbk)

Book DOI 10.4324/9781003480525

The Sociology of the Palestinians

Edited by Khalil Nakhleh
and Elia Zureik

CROOM HELM LONDON

©1980 Khalil Nakhleh and Elia Zureik
Croom Helm Ltd, 2-10 St John's Road, London SW11

British Library Cataloguing in Publication Data

The sociology of the Palestinians.
  1. Palestinian Arabs
  I. Nakhleh, Khalil
  II. Zureik, Elia T
  301.45'19'275694 DS119.7

ISBN 0-85664-647-4

Reproduced from copy supplied
printed and bound in Great Britain
by Billing and Sons Limited
Guildford, London, Oxford, Worcester

CONTENTS

Dedicated to our children
Michael, Mariam, Osama and
Sharif, and the children of
Palestine, whose Palestine will
become a national reality.

ACKNOWLEDGEMENTS

Khalil Nakhleh would like to express his sincere thanks to the Office of the Vice-President for Academic Affairs at St John's University, Collegeville, Minnesota, for providing generous financial assistance, without which the preparation of the manuscript would have been extremely difficult. Khalil Nakhleh also wishes to thank his friend John Dwyer, of the Liturgical Press, Collegeville, Minnesota, for his continuous, unconditional and able advice. As for the preparation of the chapters in the final form, Khalil Nakhleh wishes to thank his editor, Mark Towmy, and his assistants, Carina and Pam, for typing the many revised drafts with a smile.

Elia Zureik would like to thank the School of Graduate Studies of Queen's University, Ontario, for providing a generous grant which enabled him to finish the research for his contribution to the anthology.

While co-editorship should be a joint enterprise, E. Zureik would like to express his gratitude to K. Nakhleh for being understanding and for looking after the editing, typing and processing of the manuscript so diligently. Needless to say, both editors stand equally responsible for the choice of papers and perspective adopted in this book.

K.N.
E.Z.
Collegeville, Minnesota,
Kingston, Ontario

PREFACE

As a territorial, self-perpetuating entity with autonomous institutions, Palestinian society does not exist today. It was dismembered in 1948. The Palestinian people were reduced to a number of communities, corresponding to the geographical concentrations in which they found themselves. Consequently, Palestinian communities exist in varied and dispersed geographical localities, extending from their historical homeland of Palestine, to the Arab Gulf states, to Europe and the Americas.

This geographical heterogeneity and dispersal, however, are counteracted by shared aspirations for liberation and self-determination. Regardless of geographical boundaries, place of origin, occupation, class interests and religion, Palestinian communities, on the whole, seem to share a cohesive world-view, incubated successfully during the last thirty years. With regard to the shape of their future, they have developed their own self-definition which unites them. While they might (and do) differ concerning the content and final thrust of the self-determination idea, they share in the imperativeness of self-reliance, the precariousness of their state, and they have developed an amazingly uniform perception of self. Their present reality has been moulded by an empirically verifiable set of conditions which can be subjected to sociological analysis. Hence, we speak of a sociology of the Palestinians.

A sociology of the Palestinians may be informed by the Western-generated, 'normal' sociology of minorities. But the underlying premises of such a sociology lack analytic potency when confronted by the Palestinian reality. They are premises generated by the dominant to study the dominated. They emanate from a model of reality which revered a *status quo* of inequality, and which allows for change only as a mechanism for the enhancement of that *status quo*.

The sociology of the Palestinians needs to be organically linked to the sociology of the colonised, the sociology of dominance, and the sociology of settler states. It is a sociology of socio-economic and political realities created by colonial penetration and dominance, and by the implantation of foreign regimes. Unlike Western-generated, 'normal' sociology, a sociology of the Palestinians is a 'native', or indigenous sociology; it must be attached, committed and action-oriented. It is a sociology of the sociology of minorities. A sociology of the Palestinians must be 'reflexive'. It must anchor itself in the persistent re-examination and demystification of Western-generated conceptual frameworks towards groups, communities and societies who do not subscribe to the dominant mode of thought, especially those in the Third World. It is not merely a sociology of domination, but an analysis of methods and theories of dissolving that domination. Thus, a sociology of the Palestinians at this juncture in history must be a sociology of radical socio-cultural change, however violent and abrupt it may prove to be.

The present volume is an attempt in this direction. The various chapters present socio-political analyses of the Palestinian people in their different environments, both in historical Palestine and in the Diaspora. There is a critical examination of the shaping of Palestinian institutions, under military occupation and oppression in mandatory Palestine and under pressure and discrimination in Arab 'host' countries. Furthermore, there is a discussion of the historical and economic processes which explain the occupational shifts within the Palestinian community under Israeli occupation.

Following the guidelines charted above, change in the basic patterns of Palestinian communities is confronted head on: the discussion ranges from a projection of demographic patterns, to changes in the status of women, the ties of economic dependency between occupied Palestinians and the occupying Zionist regime, and finally, processes of ideological change. While the Palestinian social reality emerging from these discussions appears depressed—shaped by forces larger and more powerful than itself—this volume offers an analysis of the conditions under which this reality may be altered. An examination of the role of Palestinian intellectuals in the transformation of this reality is presented.

Even though not all the chapters are informed by the same theoretical framework, two thrusts unite them: the concern with Palestinian socio-economic and political reality, and the concern with the alteration of that reality. What is presented here is *not* another discussion of the Palestine-Zionist conflict, but an analysis of the Palestinian component in this conflict.

1 DEMOGRAPHIC CHARACTERISTICS OF THE ARAB PALESTINIAN PEOPLE*

George Kossaifi

Introduction

We must point out some methodological problems associated with the demographic study of the Arab Palestinian people. These problems reflect, in essence, the social and political history of this people.

After the creation of the state of Israel in 1948, and the subsequent political developments in the Arab East, a large segment of the Palestinian people became dispersed beyond the borders of their country. The Palestinians found themselves distributed in several countries, within and outside the Arab world. Furthermore, this distribution led to social differentiation within the same country, since some Palestinians lived in camps while others lived outside. In addition to the geographical dispersion and the social differentiation, a second and more complicated problem, in relation to demographic research, emerged: some Palestinians were able to obtain citizenship other than their own. Jordan provides the clearest example of this. In the early fifties a series of laws were promulgated which granted Jordanian citizenship to every Palestinian in the West Bank, as well as to those who became refugees in the East Bank of the Jordan.

Two problems therefore complicate the demographic study of the Palestinians: geographical dispersion and naturalisation. The first compounds the difficulties of finding statistical data on the Palestinians in each country, while the second creates difficulties in defining who the Palestinians are in each country.

In this article, we will study and analyse data from each country separately, so that we may estimate as accurately as possible the Palestinians in each country given the quality of the statistical data available.

*This chapter is a summary of a doctoral dissertation in demography which the author presented under the title 'Contribution à l'Etude Démographique de la Population Palestinienne' (Université de Paris I, Pantheon, Sorbonne, Institut de Démographie, Paris, Octobre 1976). It is to be noted, further, that the author is an employee of the United Nations Economic Commission for Western Asia. The views expressed here, however, do not necessarily reflect those of the United Nations, but the author's alone.

The chapter was written originally in Arabic and was translated into English by Khalil Nakhleh.

We will also try to assess whether these estimates encompass all the Palestinians, including the naturalised, or whether they are limited to one category or another.

I. Palestinians in Palestine, 1922-48

1. Method

British Mandate authorities in Palestine conducted two censuses among the settled population in October 1922 and November 1931. All the statistics published after 1931 are based on the second census, since its results were relatively more reliable. The first census was deficient in many ways, largely because of the Arab population's lack of confidence in the British authorities and their fear of military conscription.

In addition to these two censuses, there were the civil registration statistics which recorded births and deaths after 1920. Furthermore, and due to the importance of immigration then (and now), statistics on immigration were also published periodically.

Population estimates of Palestine based on data from the census, the civil registration and migration statistics, appeared annually until 1945. As for the nomadic population, which constituted roughly 10 per cent of the population, a count was taken between May and July 1946, as a prelude to a comprehensive census. But the political events which ensued thereafter prevented the execution of that census.

The statistics divided the population during the Mandate on the basis of religion into Muslims, Christians, Druze and Jews. According to this distribution, and based on the fact that about 87 per cent[1] of the Christians are of Arab origin, we may define the Palestinians as comprising all the Muslims and the Druze, and 87 per cent of the Christians.[2]

2. Population Distribution According to Religion and Geographical Region

Table 1.1 below gives the total of the settled population in Palestine and their percentage distribution by religion. It shows a decrease in the percentage of Muslims, Christians and Druze during the period 1922-45, from 75 to 59 per cent, 11 to 8 per cent, and 1.1 to 0.8 per cent respectively. Contrasted with this is the increase in the Jewish percentage from 13 to 32 per cent for the same period. We shall see later that the differential immigration factor by religion is responsible for this pattern. As for the total Arab settled population of Palestine, their percentage dropped from 85.6 in 1922 to 66.0 in 1946. This shift, in absolute numbers, corresponded to 555,968 in 1922 to 1,218,476 in 1946.

Table 1.1: Distribution of Palestine's Settled Population by Religion
during 1922-45

| Religion | Percentage | | | | | Total Population (in absolute numbers) |
	Muslim	Christian	Druze	Jew	Total	
Date						
23 Oct. 1922	74.90	11.01	1.18	12.91	100.00	649,048
1 July 1926	71.05	9.43	1.08	18.44	100.00	810,885
18 Nov. 1931	71.70	9.20	1.04	18.06	100.00	966,761
31 Dec. 1936	61.24	8.35	0.87	29.54	100.00	1,300,139
31 Dec. 1940	59.63	8.16	0.85	31.36	100.00	1,477,977
31 Dec. 1945	59.37	7.99	0.85	31.79[a]	100.00	1,743,484

a. Based on *de facto* population, this percentage was 32.75.
Sources: Percentages: Palestine Department of Statistics, *Statistical Abstract of Palestine, 1944-1945* (Jerusalem, English edn, 1946), p. 17.
Population Total: Anglo-American Committee of Inquiry, *A Survey of Palestine* (Jerusalem, Dept. of Statistics, 1946), vol. 1, p. 141.

The percentage distribution of the population of Palestine by region and religion for the years 1922, 1931 and 1946[3] makes it clear that the Muslims constituted the vast majority (ranging from 99 to 60 per cent) in most regions and in each of the three years. The Jewish percentage increased in Jaffa, Haifa, Beissan, Ramleh, Toul Karm and Nazareth, especially in 1944. Their percentage in Jaffa, for example, increased from 37 in 1922 to 72 in 1944; from 15 to 46 per cent in Haifa; and from 7 to 30 per cent in Beissan. It is worth noting that in Jerusalem the religious groups maintained constant percentages over time: the Muslims 41 per cent; the Jews 41 per cent, and the Christians 18 per cent for the period 1922-44.

Further, the percentage distribution of each religious group by region (on the basis that each religion constitutes 100 per cent) indicates that the Muslims were distributed in somewhat of a fixed ratio, about 9 per cent (about 13 per cent in Gaza): the Jews concentrated in Jaffa at about 44 per cent, in Jerusalem at 25 per cent, and in Haifa at 16 per cent; the Christians concentrated in Jerusalem at about 33 per cent, in Haifa at 20 per cent, and in Jaffa at 11 per cent; and, finally, the Druze concentrated in Safad where 51 per cent of them lived, and in Tiberias 9 per cent.[4]

If the settled Palestinian population is broken down by religion and by urban-rural residence, we find that over 70 per cent of the Muslims

and Druze were rural dwellers, whereas over 75 per cent of the Jews
and Christians lived in urban areas. We shall see later how this urban-
rural differentiation is reflected in such demographic indicators as fertility
and mortality. The nomadic population was concentrated in *al-Naqab*
desert (70 per cent), and in the Jaffa area (7 per cent).

Two important points emerge from this broad picture of the Palestinian
population according to religion and geographical region: (1) Palestine
was never a land without a people: in 1922 the population density in
Palestine was 72 persons per square mile – a high figure, if compared with
the countries of the region and those outside of it; (2) in spite of intens-
ive Zionist immigration, the Arab population of Palestine still made up
the large majority (66 per cent in 1945) until the creation of the Zionist
state in 1948. Due to the importance of immigration in the creation and
perpetuation of this state, we shall look at its most important characteristics.

3. Some Characteristics of Immigration

Table 1.2 gives the percentages for population growth by natural increase
and immigration. It must be made clear that Palestine had a strong
attraction for all religions, and if we set aside Zionist immigration

Table 1.2:   Factors of Demographic Increase of the Total[a] Population
in Palestine by Religion during 1922-45

Religion	Muslim	Christian	Druze	Jew	Total
Factors of Increase					
23 Oct. 1922	589,177	71,464	7,617	83,790	752,048
31 Dec. 1945	1,101,565	139,285	14,858	554,329	1,810,037
Overall increase	512,388	67,821	7,241	470,539	1,057,989
Natural increase	419,855	48,724	6,493	129,989	677,061
Immigration	20,533	19,097	748	340,550	380,928
Natural increase as percentage of total increase	96	72	90	28	64
Immigration as percentage of total increase	4	28	10	72	36
Total	100.00	100.00	100.00	100.00	100.00

a. With the exclusion of British forces and the inclusion of the nomadic population.
Source: *Statistical Abstract of Palestine, 1944-1945*, p. 17.

because of its clear political motives, we find that Arab immigration to Palestine reflected the flourishing economic situation of the country. This table indicates, further, the importance of immigration for the Jews since it constituted 72 per cent of the overall increase, against only 4 per cent for the Muslims, 28 per cent[5] for the Christians, and 10 per cent for the Druze.

Major Zionist immigration took place during three periods: 1924-6 as a result of an increased Zionist propaganda in the wake of the Balfour Declaration, plus the economic crisis in Europe; 1932-9, because of Fascism and anti-Semitism in Germany; 1943 and after, with the formation of the Jewish Legion in 1944, which became the nucleus of the Israeli army.

Of all the legal immigrants to Palestine between 1920 and 1945, the Arabs constituted only 9 per cent, compared with 91 per cent of Jews.[6] If we break down the immigrants during 1935-45 by age and sex, we find that most of the Jewish immigrants were young males. As for Arab immigrants, the percentage of those from 0-14 years of age ranged from 50 per cent to 37 per cent, whereas the percentage of Arab women immigrants ranged from 120 to 216 per cent.[7] Thus, it is clear that the political motives of Zionist immigration to Palestine reflected themselves in the age and sex composition of the immigrant, since most were young males who were able to carry arms. Arab immigration reflected certain social issues: the large percentage of Arab women indicated that married women were joining their husbands who had preceded them to Palestine. This pattern of immigration also reflected certain economic issues: whole Arab families came there to live, thus the increase in the ratio of children.

What about emigration from Palestine? There was limited emigration before the First World War as Palestinians migrated to Egypt and to the Americas, but it stopped after 1930. It is worth mentioning here that Jewish emigration from Palestine to Egypt and Syria also took place during 1926-8. On the whole, however, this Arab and Jewish emigration from Palestine remained very limited.

We have presented so far the most important characteristics of Palestinian migrations until the eve of the creation of the state of Israel. Since that date, of course, Arab Palestinian people have been subjected to a new form of migration, namely, compulsory emigration which resulted in their expulsion from their country twice in less than twenty years. Israel, in the meantime, has flung open her doors to receive more new Zionists. The most important characteristics of the 1948 refugees will be explored in the following section.

4. Demographic Characteristics of the 1948 Refugees

We based our estimate of the number of Palestinian refugees in 1948 on an estimate of the total Palestinian population before expulsion, the Palestinians who remained in Israel after 1948, and the population of the West Bank and Gaza[8] who lived there before and after the creation of Israel. These estimates indicate that about 714,000[9] Palestinians were expelled from their homes in 1948 and became distributed in the following way: 39 per cent in the West Bank, 26 per cent in Gaza, 14 per cent in Lebanon, 10 per cent in each of Syria and the East Bank, and 1 per cent in Egypt.[10] In so far as their distribution by religion was concerned, it appears that about 93 per cent of the refugees were Muslims and 7 per cent Christians.[11] In other words, 52 per cent of all the Muslims and 35 per cent of all the Christians who lived in Palestine were expelled from their homes, whereas most of the Druze remained.

So, more than thirty years after the Anglo-French Sykes-Picot agreement to divide the Arab East, and the British-Zionist Balfour Declaration, the region was indeed divided. Israel was created at the cost of dispersing of more than one-half of the Arab Palestinian people outside its borders and the Palestinian question became the focus of political development in the Arab world. We shall now examine the demographic characteristics of the Palestinians in each of their major areas of concentration.

II. Geographical Dispersal after 1948

1. Palestinians in Israel, 1948-75

a. Method. The sources for demographic data in Israel are the three population censuses, conducted on 8 November 1948, 21 May 1961 and 19 May 1972. The first census, however, did not cover the Palestinians in all regions of the country for security reasons. In addition to these censuses, there are the civil registration statistics plus specialised socio-demographic studies.

Following the lead of the British authorities during the Mandate, Israeli statistics categorise the population into Jews and non-Jews. The non-Jews are divided, further, into Muslims, Christians and Druze, so that we are able to estimate the ratio of Palestinian Arabs among the non-Jews. They comprise all the Muslims and Druze[12] and between 91 and 96 per cent[13] of the Christians. It must be mentioned here that we did not include the population of East Jerusalem after 1967 with the non-Jews in Israel. Unlike Israeli statistics, we are including it with the population of the West Bank. However, we can conclude that the Pal-

Chart 1: Palestinians in Israel by District in 1975

Districts
1. Northern
2. Haifa
3. Central
4. Southern
5. Tel Aviv
6. Jerusalem

Legend:
International boundary +++
Cease-fire line 1967 _____
District boundary _____
Sub-district boundary − − −

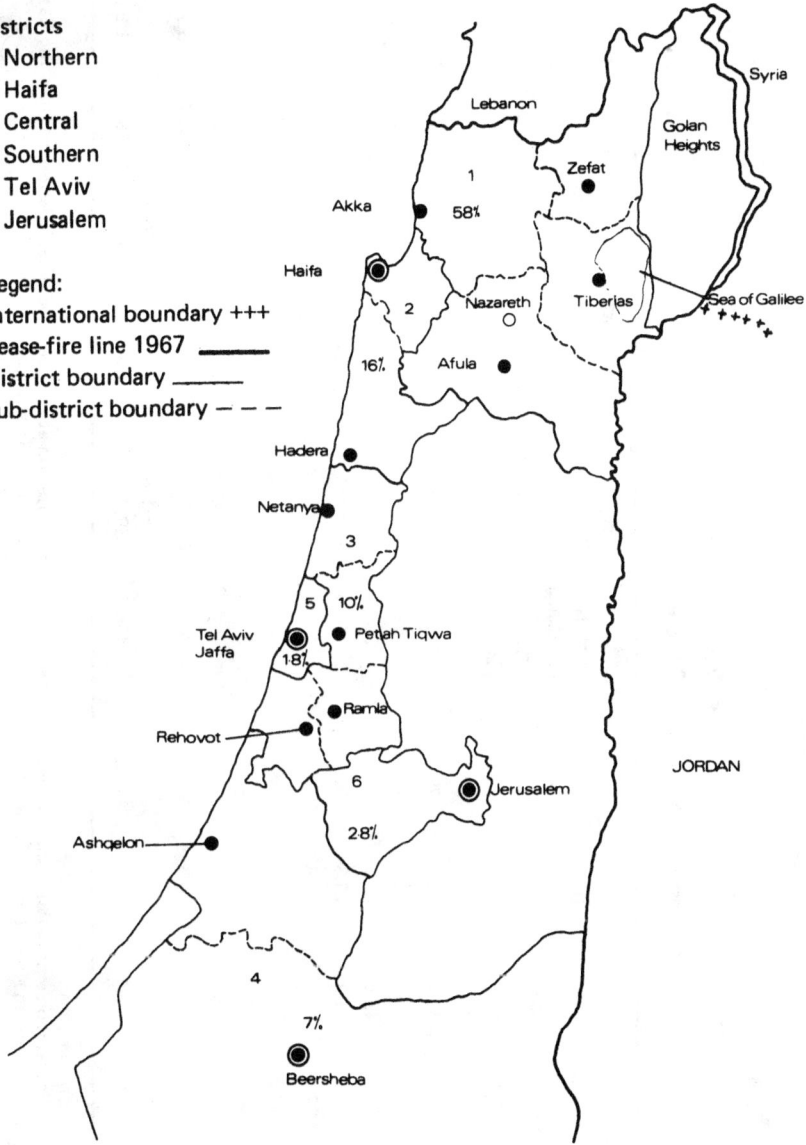

Source: Adapted from Israel's 1972 Census.

Table 1.3: Distribution of Palestinians Resident in Selected Countries/Regions during 1948-75 (in thousands)

Country/ Region Year	Israel					West Bank	Gaza	East Bank		Lebanon	Syria	Kuwait
	Muslims	Christians	Druze	Total Non-Jews	Total Palestinians			Palestinians	Jordanians			
1948	–	–	–	156.0	151.0					100.00	75.0	
1950	116.1	36.0	15.0	167.1	163.8							
1952	122.8	40.4	16.1	179.3	175.7	742.3[a]		184.7	405.1	114.0		
1957	146.9	45.8	20.5	213.2	208.9					152.0		13.5[a]
1960	166.3	49.6	23.3	239.1	234.3					178.0	112.6[a]	
1961	174.9[a]	51.3	26.3	252.5	247.4	801.4[a]		387.8	510.6	183.0		35.4[a]
1964	202.3	55.3	28.6	286.4	280.7		449.0					
1965	212.4	57.1	29.8	299.3	293.3					207.0		73.8[a]
1966	223.0	58.5	31.0	312.5	306.2							
1967	–	–	–			661.8[a]	356.3[a]	467.5	606.5	219.0		
1970	–	–	–	366.6	363.6	683.7	345.6			247.0	155.7[a]	140.3[a]
1972	–	–	–			718.1		612.0	706.8			
1975	–	–	–	440.5	436.1	758.4	390.3	644.2	781.1	288.0	183.0	194.0[a]

a. Based on census reports.

Note: These figures represent Palestinians resident in the designated country/region at the specified date. Palestinians from the East Bank for example, who are now in Kuwait are included in the Kuwaiti figure, and not in the East Bank one.

estinian Arabs constituted 98 per cent of all non-Jews in Israel during 1948-66, and 99 per cent since that date.

b. Population Distribution by Religion and Geographical Region. Table 1.3 shows the distribution of non-Jews and Palestinians in Israel by religion during 1948-75. It is clear from this table that the size of the non-Jewish population increased from 167,100 in 1950 to 440,500[14] in 1975, or from 11.9 per cent (of the total population) to 15.3 per cent respectively. It is also clear from this table that the proportion of the Muslims, among non-Jews, increased from 69.5 per cent to 71.4 per cent during the period from 1950 to 1966. The percentage of the Druze also registered an increase from 9 to 9.9 per cent, whereas the percentage of the Christians decreased from 21.5 to 18.7 per cent for the same period.

As for the areas of concentration of the Arab population in 1974,[15] it is clear that they are highly concentrated in the Northern District (47 per cent), especially in Akka and Yizreel sub-districts. They are also found in Haifa District (16 per cent), Central District (10 per cent), and Southern District (7 per cent). Their presence in the Tel Aviv District, however, is almost non-existent (1.6 per cent).

Since these percentages appear to remain constant for the period 1948-74, one may conclude that there is an absence of internal migration for Arabs in Israel. This is correct only as long as we consider the district or the sub-district as the smallest unit which pulls or pushes migrants. But, if we consider the village as such a unit, the picture changes substantially. Keep in mind that in less than 25 years Israel destroyed 385 Arab villages, whose populations were ejected forcibly in order to make room for Jewish settlements. In fact, the ejection by force of the Arabs from their villages is a form of compulsory internal migration, even though this is not reflected in the statistics because the Arabs remain within the same district or sub-district. We will come back to some of the characteristics of internal migration and settlement in Israel.

The 1961 census shows further that the Muslims are concentrated in the western part of Lower Galilee and the Nazareth mountains (20.8 and 19.8 per cent). There is also a considerable Christian concentration in these two regions (15.5 and 31.7 per cent), and in the Haifa District (14.8 per cent). The Druze are concentrated in the western part of Upper Galilee and the Haifa District (46.1 and 26.1 per cent).[16] Thus, the geographical distribution for Muslims and Christians has changed quite noticeably since before 1948, whereas the Druze have remained in their previous areas of concentration. Yet despite the myth of 'Druze nationality', they, like the rest of the Arabs, have not been spared expropriation of their lands. Examples of this process abound: 2,500 dunums (622 acres) were expropriated from the village of Sajur, 3,000 dunums (750 acres) from Hurfeysh, and 5,000 (1,250 acres) from Beit-Jann. All are Druze villages in Galilee.[17]

By and large, the Arab population maintained its rural style of life; the percentage of rural dwellers ranged from 74 per cent in 1955 to 50.5 per cent in 1974.[18] It must be noted here that the decrease in this percentage is explained by the increase in the percentage of small-town dwellers, which ranged from 0.4 in 1961 to 27.7 per cent in 1974. Furthermore, the nomadic population maintained its ratio among non-Jews (11 per cent), and to a large degree they remained concentrated in the same areas (70 per cent in the Southern District). Most Christians remained concentrated in the urban areas (61 per cent), whereas Muslims and Druze maintained their rural style of life (83 and 91 per cent respectively).[19]

Although we now have a broad picture of the demography of Arabs in Israel during 1948-75, we must examine two important issues to sharpen our analysis: the expropriation of Arab lands and Zionist settlement and internal compulsory migration for the Arabs.

c. Some Characteristics of Zionist Settlement and Compulsory Arab Migration. As we indicated earlier, the destruction of most Arab villages inside Israel resulted in the forcible internal migration of the Arabs. Actually, in his book *The Racism of the State of Israel*, Israel Shahak states that

> from the original 475 Arab villages which existed inside Israel in 1948, only 90 remained at the beginning of the seventies. In the Gaza Strip, for example, the 46 villages which existed there were all destroyed; in Jerusalem only 4 villages remained out of 33; and in Safad 18 out of 75 villages were destroyed.[20]

Sabri Jiryes estimates that Israeli authorities expropriated about 1,000,000 dunums of Arab land within Israel between 1948 and the 1960s. All of this was accomplished, of course, through Israeli legislation and the laws of the military government. For example, the application of the 'Absentee Property Law' resulted in:

the expulsion of more than 20,000 Arabs from their villages, who became refugees in the complete sense of the term, even though most of them remained in Israel only a few kilometers from their original villages which were transformed into places for Jewish immigration.[21]

Naturally, the destruction of villages and the subsequent dispersion of the Arabs are not revealed in the statistics of the distribution of non-Jews by district and sub-district, as long as the overall area of the district or sub-district remains constant, and as long as the statistics are not divided on the basis of the village. Internal migration of the Arabs in Israel cannot be explained in terms of rural-urban migration; it has to be explained in terms of Israel's colonial policy.

After 1948, Zionist settlement focused first on the Southern District and second on the Northern District. The percentage of non-Jews in the Southern District decreased dramatically from 72 per cent in 1948 to 9 per cent in 1974. In the Northern District, the percentage dropped from 63 in 1948 to 47 in 1974. Another drop from 13 to 8 per cent is documented for the same period in the Central District.[22] Why did these areas become the target for Zionist settlement, even though the Southern District, for example, did not show a high density of Arab concentration? Two major reasons explain this policy of settlement: the first is related to the strategy and security of Israel, and the second is political.

Among the major steps which the Israeli government intended to take . . . was its determination to initiate the 'Judaization of Galilee' . . . The reasons for the execution of this project, as explained by the formulators of Israeli policy, were numerous. Some of them see the reason behind the execution of this project as lying in the fact that 'the Jewish settlers in the entire region from Nazareth to the borders of Lebanon constitute a minority . . . and that there is a dangerous regional extension between the Arabs (inside Israel) and the enemy states. This created an additional social-security problem—the Jewish minority in Galilee feels isolated in a hostile Arab majority. Its general feeling is even worse than that of the Arabs of Israel among a Jewish majority.' Others relate the reason to the fact that 'claims are repeated from behind closed, but often transparent doors that Galilee was not a part of Israel in the U.N. Partition Plan, and that the dream of conducting a plebiscite in this region which, in any case, is Arab and not Jewish, is possible.' These policy formulators

emphasize that the problem of Galilee is a Jewish Problem . . . and
this constitutes an Arab empire within the state . . . and those, including the government, who believe that through military government
alone Galilee can be saved are mistaken.[23]

The Judaisation of the Southern District resulted from its proximity
to the Suez Canal and because of its natural resources.

The main demographic characteristics of the Arab population
in Israel are thus peculiar in the Third World. They cannot be explained
only by socio-economic reasons. The causes for internal migration, for
example, do not lie in the lure of the city in terms of health, education
and employment, but in the policy of expropriation of Arab lands. Also,
Zionist settlement is not directed by projects of development and planning as much as by the security of the Israeli state and its consequent
racist policies towards the Arab population there.

2. Palestinians in the West Bank and Gaza, 1948-75

a. Method. Neither the West Bank nor the Gaza Strip fell under Israeli
occupation in 1948. In 1949, the West Bank was annexed to Trans-
Jordan to form the Hashemite Kingdom of Jordan, while the Gaza Strip
came under an Egyptian administration. The sources for demographic
data in the West Bank until 1967 comprise the population count, conducted in Jordan in 1952, and the comprehensive census of population
and housing in November 1961. As for the Gaza Strip, there are some
statistics published by the military governor.

After Israeli occupation of the two areas in June 1967, a population
census was conducted during September of that year. This census remains
the only source for Israeli statistics. But, as we mentioned earlier, the
Arab population of East Jerusalem was lumped with the non-Jewish
population within Israel following Israel's political decision to annex
the area. However, here we shall consider the entire population of the
West Bank and Gaza, including East Jerusalem.

b. Palestinian Demographic Development in the West Bank. The demographic development of the Palestinians in the West Bank reflects the
way they were treated before and after 1967. Before 1967, they suffered from the policy of 'Jordanisation' of Jordan, i.e. the concentration
of investments and development projects in the East Bank, and disregard for the West Bank. Following the Israeli occupation in 1967, they
suffered the brunt of the racist policies of Israel towards the Arab population, as illustrated by deportations and expropiation of lands.

Between 1952 and 1975, the increase in the West Bank population did not exceed 17,000. The absolute numbers went up from 742,000 in 1952 to 758,000 in 1975, or not more than 0.1 per cent.[24] The size of the population in 1952 was, however, larger than that from September 1967 to the end of 1973. On the eve of the June War, 1967, more people lived in the West Bank than at the end of 1975.[25] Over this period the global rate of growth was negative (0.68 per cent).

We estimate the volume of emigration from the West Bank during 1952-61 at 148,000, 139,000 during 1961-May 1967 and 249,000 during June 1967-75. However, in the wake of the June War until the end of 1967, about 178,000 refugees were forced to leave their homes. This continuous 'human attrition' naturally resulted in a lower ratio of West Bank population to the entire population of Jordan (from 55.8 per cent in 1952 to 43.0 per cent on the eve of the June War.)

c. Palestinian Demographic Development in Gaza. After the West Bank, Gaza was the second net exporter of Palestinians, especially after 1967. The global rate of growth during 1952-75 did not exceed 1.1 per cent, whereas it was negative (1.6 per cent) during the period from May 1967 to the end of 1975. The higher rate during 1953-64 (2.7 per cent), however, indicates slower out-migration.

We estimate the volume of refugees from the Strip, following the June War until the end of 1967, at 127,000.

3. Palestinians in the East Bank, 1948-75

a. Method. The East Bank of the Jordan poses the most difficulty for demographic research because of the paucity of demographic data in general, and more importantly, the absence of distinction between Palestinians and Jordanians (meaning East Jordanians)[26] in published statistics. There are only two sources for statistical data for the East Bank: the population count of 1952, and the general population and housing census which was conducted on 18 November 1961. In addition, the Department of General Statistics in Jordan conducted some studies on certain topics, using specialised samples (internal migration, fertility, multi-purpose survey). It is difficult, however, to arrive at an accurate estimate of the total population of the East Bank from such studies, let alone a distinction between Palestinians and Jordanians. Therefore, in this study we have taken the population of Jordan in 1943 as the base,[27] and applied a specific rate of natural increase, and, taking into consideration the migration factor, we have estimated the demographic change of the Jordanian population for the period 1943-75. To determine the size of the Palestinian population, we have subtracted the total population of the East Bank from our estimates of the entire Jordanian population.[28] It is important to note here that our estimates are based upon the following factors: (a) the population of Transjordan in 1943 used as a starting point; (b) the rate of natural increase, and (c) the volume of migrants. We tried to arrive at a working estimation of the Transjordanian population in 1943, based on the British mandate estimation at that time. Rates of natural increase are based on the application of demographic techniques (quasi stable population, Brass methods) to the age structure in the 1961 census, and to the data of the 1972 fertility survey. We have adopted the same rates for both the Palestinian and Transjordanian populations. It has been argued that the Palestinian population had a higher growth rate due to the better medical facilities which prevailed in Palestine before 1948 and to the fact that a large proportion of the Transjordanian population was Bedouin. Such an approach seems to be coherent, but we believe that the poor sanitary conditions existing in the Palestinian camps after 1948 and the rapid decline in mortality in the region in the 1950s, brought the Palestinian and Transjordanian rates back into line with each other. Our estimation of the migration factor is based on the 'departures' and 'arrivals' statistics.

b. Demographic Development. Table 1.3 gives the size of Jordanian and Palestinian population in the East Bank for the period 1952-75. The entire population of the East Bank went up from 590,000 to 1,319,000 in 1972, or at an annual rate of increase of 4.0 per cent. This suggests that the East Bank attracted migrants for the duration of the period. The annual rates of increase for the periods 1952-61, 1961-7 and 1967-72 were 4.7, 3.0 and 4.1 per cent respectively.

A closer study of migration statistics for the East Bank reveals that net migration for the periods 1952-61 and 1967-72 was positive, whereas it was almost non-existent for the period 1961-7.[29]

Since the Palestinians of the West Bank constitute the major source of migrants to the East Bank, it is then expected that the average rate of increase for the Palestinians in the East Bank would follow the same direction of the average rate of increase for the East Bank as a whole. The number of the Palestinians in the East Bank increased from 185,000 in 1952 (equivalent to 31.3 per cent of the total population of the East Bank) to 612,000 in 1972 (46.4 per cent of the total population). This means that the global rate of growth for the entire period was about 6.0 per cent. More specifically, the overall annual rates of increase for 1952-61, 1961-7 and 1967-72 were 8.2, 3.1 and 5.4 per cent respectively.

Chart 2: Distribution of Palestinians by Country/Region in 1975

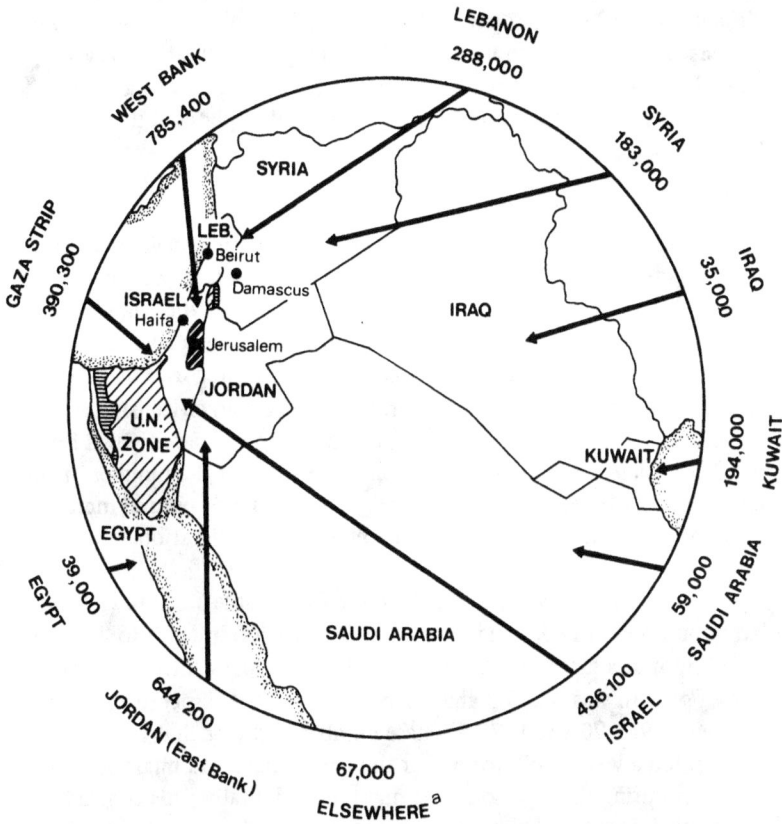

LEBANON
288,000

WEST BANK
785,400

SYRIA
183,000

GAZA STRIP
390,300

IRAQ
35,000

SYRIA

LEB.
Beirut

Damascus

ISRAEL
Haifa

IRAQ

Jerusalem

JORDAN

U.N.
ZONE

KUWAIT

194,000 KUWAIT

EGYPT

EGYPT
39,000

59,000 SAUDI ARABIA

SAUDI ARABIA

644,200

JORDAN (East Bank)

436,100 ISRAEL

67,000
ELSEWHERE[a]

a. Includes: other Gulf countries 29,000; Lybia 10,000; United States 28,000.
Source: Adapted from the *New York Times*, 19 February 1978.

It is perhaps instructive to take a quick look at the numerical development of the Palestinians on both banks of the Jordan. Table 1.3 gives an idea of this development. The shift in numerical importance from the West Bank in 1952 (55.7 per cent of the total population of Jordan) to the East Bank in 1972 (64.7 per cent of the total population) is very clear. It is also clear that the Palestinians constituted all along about two-thirds of the total population of Jordan (69.6 per cent in 1952 and 64.2 per cent in 1975).

4. Palestinians in Lebanon, 1948-75

a. Method. It is also difficult to study the demographic development of Palestinians in Lebanon for similar reasons as in Jordan: the paucity of data on the inhabitants of Lebanon in general, and on the Palestinians in particular,[30] and the fact that some Palestinians were able to obtain Lebanese citizenship. Our estimates include both categories of Palestinians—those who maintained their original Palestinian citizenship and those with Lebanese citizenship. To arrive at approximate figures for the Palestinian population in Lebanon, we estimated the number of the refugees in 1948, and then we applied to it the rate of natural increase which we calculated for Jordan, plus the factor of migration.[31]

b. Demographic Development. As is clear from Table 1.3, the Palestinian population in Lebanon increased from 100,000 in 1948 to 288,000 in 1975, or at a global annual growth rate of 3.9 per cent. This annual rate of growth was 4.8, 3.3 and 3.1 per cent for the respective periods 1948-60, 1961-70 and 1970-5. These numbers indicate that Lebanon constituted a weak 'pull' region for the Palestinians and migration to Lebanon during these periods was slight. (Incidentally, this contradicts the general view that Lebanon attracted large numbers of Palestinians.) But we will see later how Lebanon actually constituted a 'push' region for the Palestinians, especially during 1965-9. In 1977 the Palestinians in camps numbered 94,980, spread in the largest camps as follows: Ein al-Hilweh, Saida (22.0 per cent), al-Rashidiyah, Tyre (13.9 per cent), Burj al-Shamali, Tyre (9.9 per cent) and Burj al-Barajneh, Beirut, and Nahr al-Barid, Tripoli (8.8 per cent).[32]

5. Palestinians in Syria, 1948-75

a. Method. The sources of statistical data on the Palestinians in Syria are the two censuses of 1960 and 1970 and the annual statistical abstracts which publish estimates of the Palestinian population in Syria. It is to be noted here, that it is not difficult to study in this country, since the majority maintained their original Palestinian citizenship.

b. Demographic Development. As is shown in Table 1.3, the Palestinians in Syria increased from 75,000[33] in 1948 to 183,000 in 1975, or at an average annual rate of 3.3 per cent. This means that the migration factor had little impact on the population; Syria constituted neither a 'pull' nor a 'push' region for the Palestinians during this period.

They are clustered in Damascus (66.0 per cent), Dir'a (9.5 per cent), Aleppo (7.8 per cent) and Quneitra (6.8 per cent).[34]

6. Palestinians in Kuwait, 1957-75

a. Method. The sources of statistical data on the Palestinians in Kuwait are primarily the five censuses conducted since 1957. However, two main qualifications have to be kept in mind: these data provide information on the Palestinians and the Jordanians. The first category refers to Palestinians who still maintain their citizenship (Palestinians living in Lebanon, Syria, Gaza) while the second category refers to Palestinians and East Jordanians. To estimate the number of the Palestinians in this category, therefore, we applied the percentage of 95.[35]

The second qualification pertains to Palestinians with Kuwaiti citizenship, whose number is difficult to estimate from published statistics. Thus, unlike the cases of Lebanon, our estimates here do not include Palestinians with Kuwaiti citizenship.

b. Demographic Development. Kuwait is the most important example of Palestinian emigration to the oil states in the Arabian Gulf, since they started to come here first. But due to the importance of this phenomenon, we shall treat it in more detail later. For now we shall only present global rates of growth from 1957 to 1975.

This development is clearly shown in Table 1.3. The Palestinians multiplied more than 14 times in less than 19 years, where their absolute numbers increased from 13,000 in 1957 to 194,000 in 1975. The global annual growth rate declined steadily with time: from 24.1 per cent to 18.4 per cent to 12.8 per cent and to 6.5 per cent during the respective periods 1957-61, 1961-5, 1965-70 and 1970-5. On the other hand, the ratio of the Palestinians to the entire population of Kuwait went up from 6.5 per cent in 1957 to 19.5 per cent in 1975.

7. Palestinians in Selected Countries in the World, 1975

About 94 per cent of all Palestinians live in the areas discussed above; the other 6 per cent are concentrated mainly in the oil states within the

Arab world, but the dearth of published data prevents us from studying these areas. However, through the application of certain global growth rates on reliable population figures from 1970, we reached estimates on the size of the Palestinians resident in selected countries/regions in the world in 1975.

Table 1.4 provides the geographical distribution of the Palestinians in selected countries/regions in 1970 and 1975. It shows that more than one-half of the Palestinians continue to reside in historical Palestine (24.5 per cent in the West Bank, 14.1 per cent in Israel, 12.6 per cent in Gaza). The remainder are concentrated in the East Bank (20.8 per cent), Lebanon (9.3 per cent), Kuwait (6.3 per cent) and Syria (5.9 per cent). If we consider the Palestinian ratio to the total population of each of these countries, we find that the Palestinians constitute 43.1 per cent of the total population of historical Palestine, 46.4 per cent of the East Bank, 19.5 per cent of Kuwait, and 11.3 per cent of Lebanon.

With this brief overall picture of the demographic distribution of the Palestinian people, we shall look closely, in the remainder of this chapter, at major demographic characteristics of this people. We shall focus on fertility and mortality, and we shall give special attention to migration due to its political significance in shaping the history of this people. In fact if the usual explanation of fertility and mortality in the Third World (differentials in the educational level and life-style in general) is applied to the Palestinian case, the pattern of Palestinian migration cannot be wholly explained by these factors; it must be explained by the specific political circumstances (Israeli racism, 'Jordanisation' of the West Bank) under which the Palestinians live.

III. Demographic Characteristics

1. Distribution by Age and Sex

It must be pointed out from the outset that the age and sex composition for 1970, which is presented below in Table 1.5, is an approximate distribution, based on imprecise compositions in the first place. What concerns us here, however, are the basic dimensions of this composition, not the specific details. The age and sex composition for any population reflects, in the short and the long run, the factors of fertility, mortality and migration. Any change in the level of fertility of a population during a specific time period is reflected in certain age groups. Further, the impact of wars and migration, for example, is manifested clearly in the sex ratios of certain age groups. Here, because of the deficiency of the reports on which we have to rely, we shall not be able to show all the

Table 1.4: Distribution of Palestinians Resident in Selected Countries/
Regions, in 1970 and 1975 (in Thousands)

Year	1970	1975		
Country/Region		Volume	Percentage of Total Palestinians	Percentage of Population of Country of Residence
Israel	363.6	436.1	14.1	12.5
East Bank	591.8	644.2	20.8	46.4
West Bank	683.7	758.4	24.5	100.0
(Jordan)	(1,275.5)	(1,402.6)	(45.3)	(65.3)
Gaza	345.6	390.3	12.6	100.0
Palestine	1,392.9	1,584.8	51.2	34.1
Lebanon	247.0	288.0	9.3	11.3
Syria	155.7	183.0	5.9	2.5
Kuwait	140.3	194.0	6.3	19.5
Egypt	33.0	39.0[a]	1.3	
Saudi Arabia	31.0	59.0[b]	1.9	
Iraq	30.0	35.0[a]	1.1	
Rest of Arabian Gulf	15.0	28.0[b]	0.9	
Lybia	5.0	9.0[b]	0.3	
Total: Arab world	2,650.0	3,064.0	99.1	
United States	25.0	28.0[c]	0.9	
Grand Total	2,666.7	3,092.0	100.0	

a. We applied to these figures in 1970 a 3.2 per cent rate of increase.
b. Here we applied a rate of increase of 12.8 per cent. This was the rate of increase
   for Palestinians in Kuwait during 1965-70.
c. We applied to these figures in 1970 a 2.0 per cent rate of increase.
Note: In a recent study by J.S. Birks and C.A. Sinclair one can note that the
distribution of Jordanian/Palestinian workers in 1975 was as follows in the different
Gulf States: Bahrain 600, Iraq 5,000, Kuwait 47,700, Libya 14,200, Saudi Arabia
175,000, Qatar 6,000, United Arab Emirates 14,500, total 263,000.
  J.S. Birks and C.A. Sinclair, *International Migration in the Arab Region. Rapid
Growth, Changing Patterns and Broad Implications* (ECWA Seminar on Population
and Development in the ECWA Region, Nov. 1978, Amman, Jordan), p. 8.
Author's note: The figure for Saudi Arabia seems rather high.

Table 1.5:   Percentage Distribution of Palestinians by Age and Sex in
1970

| Age Groups | Percentage | | | Sex Ratio |
	Male	Female	Total	Male/Female
0-4	9.7	9.0	18.7	107.7
5-9	8.7	8.1	16.8	107.5
10-14	7.1	6.4	13.5	110.6
15-19	5.2	4.9	10.1	107.4
20-24	3.8	3.9	7.7	98.3
25-29	3.5	3.5	7.0	99.8
30-34	2.9	2.7	5.6	108.6
35-39	2.5	2.4	4.9	101.7
40-44	2.0	1.9	3.9	108.0
45-49	1.6	1.4	3.0	108.8
50-54	1.1	1.1	2.2	104.5
55-59	0.8	0.8	1.6	104.6
60-64	0.9	0.8	1.7	103.1
65-69	0.7	0.5	1.2	118.2
70+	1.1	1.0	2.1	112.3
Total	51.6	48.4	100.0	106.5

demographic changes which we are discussing, but shall attempt to present the basic features of this change.

Table 1.5 makes it amply clear that Palestinian society is a young one. Those aged 14 years and below constitute 49 per cent of this population, whereas those between 15 and 59 and 60 and over constitute 46 and 5 per cent respectively. This characteristic, however, can be found in most Third World countries due to a high fertility level.[36]

A review of the sex ratio reveals a deficiency in the registration of females in the age group of 15 years and below. This is found frequently in most Arab states due to some cultural values which favour males (age group 0-4), or which ignore females altogether at puberty (10-14). Sex ratios reveal, further, a lower percentage of males in the age group 20-39, which might be explained by the loss of males in war. A study of sex ratios among the Palestinians in Israel makes this explanation very clear. A loss in the percentage of males appears in the following age groups: 20-49 in 1956, 25-54 in 1961[37] and 35-64 in 1971. The systematic surfacing of this loss from one time period to the next attests to a real loss, rather than errors of data collection. This phenomenon can be explained by losses among Palestinian fighters during the period following the revolt of 'Izz al-Din al-Qassam from 1936 to 1948.

2. Fertility

a. Method. The two areas which lend themselves to the study of Palestinian fertility are the East Bank and Israel. We must be reminded, however, that the available statistics pertain to the non-Jews in Israel and to the entire population of the East Bank. For our purposes, we consider the fertility of those two populations as representative of fertility levels among the entire Palestinian population.

The source for fertility data for non-Jews in Israel is the civil registration. As for the East Bank, there is the census of 1961, plus two special sample surveys on fertility; one was conducted in 1972, and the other was a part of the World Fertility Survey conducted in 1976. The data presented in the civil registration in Israel also suffer from registration errors. But what is important here in terms of comparison is the level, rather than the specific figures.

b. Fertility Level. Table 1.6 below gives age-specific fertility rates[38] for the East Bank and Israel from 1965 to 1975. This table indicates, further, that the fertility level in both regions is almost equal – total fertility rate[39] in 1975 was 6.83 for Israel and 6.55 for the East Bank. The rise in this level in 1965 for Israel is explained in terms of registration errors, rather than a real decline in the fertility level of non-Jews at the end of the period.

If we examine the gross reproduction rate[40] for the non-Jews in Israel during 1955 to 1975, we find two different levels: a higher level (3.5-4) for Muslims and Druze and a lower level (2) for Christians. It is interesting to note that the rate for Christians is equivalent to that of Oriental Jews, especially during 1960-9, where the figures coincide completely. As for Ashkenazi Jews and Jews born inside Israel, their gross reproduction rate was 1.5.

The difference in fertility levels between Muslims and Christians may be explained partially in terms of the differences of the mean age at marriage. In 1973, for Muslim males it was 25.1 years and for Muslim females 20.4 years.

3. Mortality

a. Method. The statistical data on mortality among the Palestinians in Israel and Jordan are not in any better shape than those on

Table 1.6:   Age-Specific Birth Rates for Palestinian Women in the East Bank and Israel during 1965-76 (for 1,000 women)

Region Age Groups	East Bank 1976	1965 Total	Muslim	Israel 1975 Christian	Druze	Total
−19	56.8	111.7	104.8	37.3	64.6	91.7
20-24	231.6	359.8	345.5	198.3	298.2	318.3
25-29	292.8	406.2	383.3	199.5	396.2	349.2
30-34	275.7	370.2	348.4	139.2	316.9	307.3
35-39	226.9	255.8	242.8	76.7	210.5	202.7
40-44	140.2	131.0	96.1	17.3	76.4	75.8
45+	85.5	49.3	28.6	(2.1)	(6.3)	20.7
Total fertility rate[a]	6.55	6.42	7.75	3.35	6.85	6.83

a. These figures are for one woman, whereas the rest of the rates are on the basis of 1,000 women.

Sources: Israel: Israel, Central Bureau of Statistics, *Statistical Abstract of Israel 1976* (Jerusalem), p. 81.

East Bank: Shuja El-Asad and Atef Khalifa, *Family Structure in Relation to Fertility in Jordan* (1977), p. 68.

fertility. Whereas there are some specialised studies on fertility, we find nothing of the sort on mortality. The method we used to estimate the life table[41] for Palestinians in Israel was based on a comparison of the figures for same age groups in the 1961 and 1972 censuses. For Jordan, we applied the theory of quasi-stable population[42] on the age composition of females from the 1961 census.

b. Mortality Level. We can say that the level of mortality among the two Palestinian populations is similar, with a slight edge in favour of Palestinians in Israel. In Israel, life expectancy at birth[43] in 1961-71 reached about 55 years, as compared to only 47 years for the same period in Jordan.

As for infant mortality among non-Jews in Palestine prior to 1948, we find a slightly lower rate for the Christians. Muslims and Druze had a similar rate, but higher than that of the Christians. This pattern persisted during the period following the establishment of Israel.

Infant mortality rates of the Christians were systematically lower than those of the Moslems, and the relative difference increased over time (from 9 percent in 1924-1926 to 28 percent in 1940-1942)

... The difference between the two religious groups was even more conspicuous with regard to the mortality rate for the entire first five years of age (the Christians' rate was 2/3 that among the Moslems in 1927-1930 and 1/2 in 1940-1942).[44]

The explanation for these differences in the levels of fertility and mortality between Jews and non-Jews, and among the various Palestinian religious groups, lies in differences in the educational levels and in the rural-urban style of life. In 1961, about one-half the non-Jews of 14 years and older never attended school; this ratio declined to one-quarter in 1974. The ratio for the Jews, however, was 13 and 8 per cent respectively. Similarly, the ratio of those who continued their education beyond 13 years did not exceed 5 per cent among non-Jews in 1974, whereas it reached 16.6 per cent for the Jews.[45]

The Christians maintained a high enrolment ratio of 97 per cent in Arab schools for children 6-13 years of age from 1966-73. The ratio for the Muslims ranged from 79 to 89 per cent and for the Druze from 85 to 92 per cent.[46] The figures from the 1961 census indicate further that 87 per cent of males and 66 per cent of females among Christians had formal schooling, whereas the figures for Muslims and Druze were 61 and 14 per cent and 68 and 28 per cent respectively.

Another phenomenon which might help explain this difference is that the majority of the Jews live in urban areas, whereas the majority of non-Jews live in rural areas. Moreover, the Christians, among the non-Jews, maintain an urban style of life as contrasted with the Muslims and the Druze who are concentrated in rural areas.[47]

The important effect of the educational level on the levels of fertility and mortality has been made very clear. The results from the World Fertility Survey in Jordan amply support this relationship. The rate of live births for women between 35 and 49 years was 8.4 for illiterates, 6.4 for those with elementary and junior high school education, and 4.1 for those with high school education and higher.[48]

To sum up: the characteristics of fertility and mortality levels for the Palestinian people are very similar to those in most Arab countries. Compared with other levels, that of fertility is high and stable; the mortality level, even though relatively high, is declining with time.

4. Migration

In contrast to the levels of fertility and mortality, which follow a similar pattern to the rest of the Third World in general and the Arab world in particular, the pattern of migration reflects the peculiar political conditions under which the Palestinians live. Socio-economic motives simply do not explain compulsory Palestinian emigration in 1948 and 1967, nor do they explain Palestinian migration inside Israel and emigration from the West Bank since the early 1950s. The explanatory variable for this phenomenon is basically political, namely, the policy of Zionist settlement in Arab lands in Palestine and the 'Jordanisation' policy for the West Bank.

a. Pull and Push Regions. Briefly, we shall look at the regions of pull and push, with a special emphasis on the West Bank as a region of push and Kuwait as a region of pull. Again, caution is necessary: the rates introduced here are approximate, since they are not based on specialised sample studies on migration, for such studies do not exist. The rates, therefore, depend, at times, on the numbers of arrivals and departures (Jordan, Lebanon and Israel), and, at others, on a comparison between the figures of the existing and expected populations (West Bank, Gaza and Kuwait).

Table 1.7 gives approximate rates of annual migration for Jordan, West Bank, Gaza, Israel, Lebanon and Kuwait. It is clear that the major push areas were the West Bank and Gaza, especially since the 1967 War. The volume of refugees from these two regions in the wake of the war reached 178,000 from the West Bank, and 127,000 from the Gaza Strip. This table indicates, further, the existence of a very weak Palestinian emigration from Israel, if compared, for example, with emigration rates from Jordan.

Kuwait, on the other hand, represents the major pull region for the Palestinians. Annual rates of immigration to this country, between the early 1960s and 1975, never fell under 6,000 persons. Contrary to popular expectation, however, Lebanon was never a strong pull region for the Palestinians – the annual immigration rate for the period 1950-72 was only 1,500 persons. Moreover, the rate for the period 1965-72 was negative (−600), which meant that Lebanon, in fact, had become a push, rather than a pull region for the Palestinians.

b. The West Bank: a Push Region, pre-1967 War. In estimating the volume of emigration from the West Bank for this period, we used the 1952 population count as the base, and then we applied a certain rate of natural increase until 1961 and compared the results with population numbers obtained in the 1961 census. It appears from this process that about 148,000 people emigrated from the West Bank during this period. This extrapolation was based on data showing that the actual volume of

Table 1.7: Annual Rates of Palestinian Migration by Country/Region during 1950-75

	Country/Region	Annual Rate	Country/Region		Annual Rate
Jordan:[a]	1950-61	−6,600	Israel:[c]	1961-7	−400
	1962-7	−27,100		1968-75	−1,800
	1968-75	−28,900		1961-75	−1,100
	1950-75	−18,400	Lebanon:[d]	1950-64	2,000
West Bank:[b]	8/1952-11/1961	−16,000		1965-72	−600
	11/1961-6/1967	−24,000		1950-72	1,500
	1967 refugees	−178,000	Kuwait:[b]	1957-61	4,700
	1968-75	−8,900		1961-5	8,600
	1952-6/1967	−19,100		1965-70	10,800
	6/1967-1975	−30,200		1970-5	6,000
Gaza:[b]	1967 refugees	−127,000		1957-75	9,400
	6/1967-1975	−20,900			
	1968-75	−6,600			

a. These estimates include both Banks until June 1967. Only the East Bank is included after this date. These estimates were calculated on the basis of arrival and departure statistics.
b. This calculation was achieved by subtracting expected population at the end of a certain period from the existing population.
c. Based on arrival and departure statistics.
d. Based on arrival and departure statistics in addition to estimating the ratio of the Palestinians of the total Jordanian emigrants.

existing population increased from 742,289 to 801,356, whereas the expected volume should have reached about 950,000 people.

The application of this method for the period between the 1961 census and September 1967 led us to conclude that there were about 301,000 emigrants. Furthermore, we were able to estimate the volume of migrants to the East Bank at 25,000 and to areas outside it at 114,000 during the period 1961-May 1967.[49]

Post-1967 War. As was pointed out earlier, the volume of Palestinian refugees during the immediate period after the war was 162,000. If we add to that the 16,000 people who left between September and the end of 1967, we get an overall refugee volume, until the end of the year, of 178,000.[50] Table 1.7 makes it clear that the stream of emigration from the West Bank continued to flow from 1968 to 1975 at an annual rate of about 9,000 people.

How can we explain this pattern of emigration? We have argued already that political factors constitute the main explanatory variable for this phenomenon. Indeed, the economic and social situation in the West Bank during the early 1950s was much more favourable than that on the East Bank.

Despite its economic backwardness in comparison with other Palestinian regions, the West Bank was much more developed than the East Bank. Agriculture, at the time of annexation by the Hashemite regime, was more developed and stable than in the East Bank. The level of industrial development, albeit primitive with artisan character, was noticeably more advanced than its counterpart in the East Bank. Also, the level of skilled training and education for human productive force was more superior to that of the East Bank.[51]

Nevertheless, the constant fear of secession, which might have materialised sooner or later, prompted Jordanian authorities to concentrate investments in the East Bank. 'Thus, not a single industrial establishment could be found in the West Bank in the early sixties. Furthermore, a quick look at the guide of industrial establishments shows that only about 8 percent of these establishments are concentrated there.'[52]

The policy of 'Jordanisation' of the West Bank is the chief explanatory factor for Palestinian emigration during this period. The factors which explain the continued emigration flow during the period extending from the 1967 War to 1975 lie in the colonial and racist policy used by Israeli forces of occupation towards the Arab population.[53]

Even though Israel did not formally announce the land area which it took over or expropriated, it is certain that this area constitutes a large portion of the total area of the West Bank, the Gaza Strip, and the Golan. In the West Bank alone, Israel took over all the lands which were under the disposal of the Jordanian government, and whose area exceeded one million dunums (about 1/2 the area of the West Bank) . . . Furthermore, Israeli authorities confiscated 328,789 additional dunums of the land of the 'absentees' . . . and 10,402 homes of 'absentees' (most of whom were dispersed by the June war of 1967). Additional 21,000 dunums were expropriated in Jerusalem and its environs. These figures, of course, do not include entire areas, which the occupation authorities fenced off for 'military' reasons.[54]

Kuwait – a Pull Region. We have stated already that the number of Palestinians in Kuwait multiplied more than 14 times in less than 19 years: in absolute numbers from 13,000 in 1957 to 194,000 in 1975. The annual rate of immigration reached its peak during 1965-70, with 10,800. However, the rate declined to 6,000 during the following time period (1970-5).

An examination of the distribution of Palestinians in Kuwait[55] by age and sex shows that the global sex ratio declined from 311.5 per cent in 1957 to 111.8 per cent in 1975. The ratio of children under 10 years of age (in relation to all resident Palestinians) increased from 15.2 per cent at the beginning of this period to 42.6 per cent at the end. It can be concluded from these figures that Palestinian immigration to Kuwait has changed in quantity and quality. Initially it was temporary immigration of young males but later became semi-permanent immigration which included also women and children. The ratio of job-seeking immigrants declined from 46.3 per cent (in relation to all resident Palestinians) in 1965 to 23.2 per cent in 1975. Simultaneously, the ratio of immigrants who joined their families increased from 52.4 per cent in 1965 to 75.9 per cent in 1975.

The characteristics of Palestinian immigration to Kuwait would most probably apply to other Gulf states, except for the time difference. The situation in Saudi Arabia today, for example, is similar to that in Kuwait in 1965. But what are the future directions of Palestinian immigration to the Gulf, and is this immigration likely to continue? It is difficult to be precise since the migration process is tied equally to the pull and push regions. In the case of the Palestinian people, moreover, the political situation in the Middle East as a whole determines the outcome. However, we can say that the pace of Palestinian immigration to Kuwait will slow down within the next ten years, whereas it will continue increasing in other Gulf states.

Before we conclude our discussion on Palestinian migration, we need to say a few words about emigration from Israel. We have indicated earlier that the rate of emigration from Israel is much lower than that from Jordan. This difference can be explained by a variety of reasons. (1) The love of the land and the attachment to it. The Palestinian people have demonstrated, and continue to do so, their attachment to the land, and their determination to regain it, regardless of the sacrifices. (2) The series of racist laws, issued by Israeli authorities, which relate to the expropriation of Arab land, restriction of movement, etc. Israel has expropriated most of the property of the Palestinian 'absentees', and those who have been prevented from returning to their homeland since

1948. Also, vast areas of land owned by the Arabs who remained in Palestine were expropriated. In the light of this, Arab emigrants from Israel are not assured that they will be readmitted if they leave the country, nor that their lands will not be expropriated. (3) The Palestinians who live in camps in the Arab countries have never been in an enviable position. All of these reasons, we believe, contribute to an understanding of the low rate of Palestinian emigration from Israel in spite of the racist policy which is applied against them.

IV. Demographic Estimates

Is it possible to venture into demographic projections for the Palestinian people by age, sex and region? The problem is that realistic projections must include the emigration factor, and this, as we saw, is intimately connected to the political situation in the Arab world. Nevertheless, we shall attempt to offer some preliminary projections concerning the future population of the Palestinians.

Table 1.8 gives some estimates for the Palestinians in Israel (1967 boundaries), Jordan (both banks), Palestine (historical boundaries) and the world from 1975 to 2000. It is clear from this table that the Palestinians will constitute about 15.5 per cent (939,000) of the population of Israel in 1990 and that the numbers of the Palestinians in Jordan will range from 1,912,000 to 2,835,000 for the same date, depending on changes in the emigration factor. Assuming an annual overall rate of increase of 3.5 per cent for the Palestinians in all of Palestine, they will constitute in 1990 more than half of the population of Palestine (50.9 per cent), even if we consider the annual rate of Jewish immigration to Israel of 40,000. The total number of Palestinians will range between 6,492,000 and 8,189,000 by the end of this century.

Since its establishment, Israel has invested a great deal of effort in attracting Jewish immigration to ensure its security and 'safety' through a Jewish majority. Thus, from 1948 to 1974, about 1,299,000 Jews immigrated to Israel. This volume constituted about 58 per cent of the overall demographic increase, or, in other words, the factor of immigration was larger than the factor of natural increase. More than once, Israeli officials expressed their fear of Palestinian numbers. 'Mrs. Meir confessed (and not for the first time) how disturbed she gets during her sleep every time she thinks of the numbers of Arab babies who were born the night before. From her view point the Israeli borders should be widened.'[56] Israel Koenig, the commissioner of the Northern District (Galilee), worries about the Arab numerical increase in his district and suggests 'a series of measures whose goal is to limit, within the coming two years,

Table 1.8: Demographic Projections for the Palestinians in Jordan (Both Banks), Historical Palestine, and the World during 1970-2000 (in thousands)

Year	1970	1975[d]	1980	1985	1990	1995	2000
Region							
Jordan[a]							
Migration assumption 1	1,288.1	1,519.7	1,802.9	2,151.7	2,569.6		
Migration assumption 2	1,288.1	1,381.0	1,498.9	1,652.0	1,911.7		
Migration assumption 3	1,288.1	1,381.0	1,498.9	2,154.3	2,834.8		
r = 3.0%:[b]							
Palestinians in Palestine		1,615.0	1,872.0	2,170.0	2,516.0		3,381.0
Palestinians in the world		3,101.0	3,595.0	4,168.0	4,831.0		6,492.0
r = 3.5%							
Palestinians in Palestine		1,654.0	1,965.0	2,334.0	2,772.0		3,910.0
Palestinians in the world		3,177.0	3,773.0	4,482.0	5,323.0		7,509.0
r = 3.8%							
Palestinians in Palestine		1,679.0	2,023.0	2,437.0	2,937.0		4,265.0
Palestinians in the world		3,223.0	3,884.0	4,680.0	5,640.0		8,189.0
Israel[c]		530.9	642.0		939.5		

a. The calculation of these figures was based on the following assumptions:
 (1) decrease in relative fertility rates by 5 per cent every 5 years after 1975;
 (2) migration was calculated on the basis of the following assumptions:
 (i) absence of migration; (ii) continued emigration at an annual rate of 25,000;
 (iii) emigration annual rate 25,000 until 1980, and a return of the emigrants to Jordan after that date, at an annual rate of 5,000.
b. We applied the following equation:
$$P_n = Po(1 + r)^n$$
 where:
 P_n and P_o stand for the population at the beginning and the end of the period,
 r = rate of growth
 n = number of years
c. Including the population of East Jerusalem for Israel. See Israel, Central Bureau of Statistics, *Statistical Abstract of Israel 1972* (Jerusalem), p. 44.
d. These figures are different from those given in Table 1.4 due to the different estimations techniques.

the demographic factors which allow the Arabs to constitute a majority in Northern Israel'.[57] The question is: what will be the Israeli demographic policy towards the Arabs who, within a mere 12 years, will constitute more than one-half of the population, not only in one region but in all of Palestine? The ghost of Palestinian numbers will haunt the dreams of old and new Zionists, and further expansion by occupying new Arab lands will not benefit them, since from a numerical point of view at least this will lessen their proportion to the total population. The only solution which will dissipate this fear, and which will guarantee the legitimate national rights of the Palestinian Arab people, is the establishment of a democratic, secular state in all Palestine where Muslims, Christians, Druze and Jews can coexist.

Summary

We have reviewed in this chapter the basic features of demographic development of the Palestinian people from the beginning of the British Mandate until the present. We must re-emphasise the difficulties which confront the researcher in this area. First, there are large gaps in the basic data relating to the demographic, social and economic conditions of the Palestinians. Second, the problem of naturalisation of some Palestinians renders the distinction between those who continue to retain their Palestinian citizenship and those naturalised in the countries of residence very difficult. Third, the geographical dispersal requires an accurate knowledge of the conditions of the Palestinians in more than one country in the Arab East, at a time when serious deficiencies in the data pertaining to their own citizens exist. Certain international and regional organisations recently (especially since the October War of 1973) became aware of these statistical deficiencies and tried to remedy this situation by conducting the necessary researches in this sphere.[58] Consequently, the United Nations Commission for Western Asia issued two recommendations during its third session, May 1976, pertaining to the Palestinians: (1) the need to conduct a comprehensive census for the Palestinian people, and (2) the need to conduct a socio-economic study of them.[59] In addition, the participants at the combined meeting of the Arab League and the United Nations Fund for Population Activities (Cairo, May 1975) recommended the following:

United Nations Fund for Population Activities respond to the requests put by the Palestine Liberation Organization in connexion with the implementation of population projects, including the related studies and necessary services for the Palestinians within their occupied homeland and beyond.

We must not forget, however, that this increasing concern for study-ing the conditions under which the Palestinian people live and the variety of statistical studies are not a goal in themselves. Statistical studies must serve primarily the process of social and economic growth, which is an interrelated whole and which must aim in the final analysis at advancing the life of the individual and the people to the highest level.

The major goal of social and economic growth, which considers population objectives and policies an integral part of it, is the improve-ment of the standard of living and the quality of life. Man is still the most important element in the world. His knowledge and abilities for controlling himself and his environment will continue to grow. Thus, it is possible to render the future of humanity infinitely bright.[60]

However, the question may be asked: how is it possible to advance the individual Palestinian in the shadow of Zionist occupation to Palestine? Or, in the shadow of the discriminatory laws under which the Arabs in Israel live? Or, in the shadow of the denial of the right of this people to return to their homeland, and their right to struggle by all available means to regain their rights according to the United Nations Charter? Or, in denying this people the right to represent itself through the Pal-estine Liberation Organization without dependence on and containment on any side? The answers ought to be very clear: unless these and other barriers are removed from the path of progress of the Palestinian people, there will be no development and the recommendations will become words void of content.

Real growth cannot take place in the absence of national independence and liberation. Foreign and colonial dominance, foreign occupation, aggressive wars, racial discrimination, and neo-colonialism in all its forms remain until now among the major barriers on the road for total liberation and progress of the develop-ing countries and all concerned peoples.[61]

Notes

1. We used this figure for two reasons: (a) through a review of the distribution of Christians by sects in the 1931 census and the isolation of sects whose members are most likely not of Arab origin, e.g. Anglican, Protestant and some Roman

Catholics and Greek Catholics; (b) this figure was used also in M. Pinner, *How Many Arab Refugees?* (London, 1959), p. 29.

2. This definition does not include Palestinian Jews who lived in Palestine prior to the intensification of Zionist immigration in the early 1920s.

3. Palestine, Department of Statistics, Anglo-American Committee of Inquiry, *A Survey of Palestine* (Jerusalem, 1946), vol. I, p. 156.

4. Ibid., p. 152. These are average figures for 1931-44.

5. We must keep in mind that some Christians are of non-Arab origin.

6. Palestine, Department of Statistics, *Statistical Abstract of Palestine, 1944-1945*, English edn (Jerusalem, 1946), p. 36.

7. Ibid., p. 43.

8. As a result of Israel's policy of expropriation and annexation, the land area of the West Bank was reduced by about 2,146 sq. km. The land area of the Gaza Strip shrank by about 66 per cent (734 sq. km).

9. The United Nations mission of 1949 estimated the number of Palestinian refugees to be between 716,000 and 726,000. See UN, *Final Reports of the U.N. Survey Mission for the Middle East* (UN, AAC 256, New York, 1940), Pt. I, p. 22. Janet L. Abu-Lughod in an excellent article gives a higher figure ranging from 770,000 to 780,000. See J.L. Abu-Lughod, 'The Demographic Transformation of Palestine' in Abu-Lughod (ed.), *The Transformation of Palestine* (Northwestern University Press, Evanston, 1971).

10. Ibid., p. 33.

11. We arrived at this distribution by deducting the actual total after the creation of Israel from the expected distribution of the population by religion before dispersal.

12. Israeli authorities have spent a considerable effort in distinguishing between Muslims and Druze for the purpose of attracting the Druze to their side. In attempting to divide the Arab population, Israel insisted that this sect constitutes a 'nationality' (it is known that the identity cards of the Druze carry formally the word 'Druze' for the 'nationality' item). By and large, however, this attempt met with failure.

13. It is clear from the results of the 1961 census that 91 per cent of the Christians were born in Israel. On the other hand, if we add the Greek Catholics. the Greek Orthodox, and 83 per cent of the Roman Catholics who were surveyed in the 1972 census, we conclude that Christian Arabs constitute 96 per cent of all the Christians in Israel for that period.

14. As indicated earlier, these figures do not encompass the Palestinian population of East Jerusalem which Israel occupied in 1967.

15. See Israel, Central Bureau of Statistics, *Statistical Abstract of Israel 1975* (*SAI*) (Jerusalem, no. 26), p. 23.

16. The computation of these figures is based on data from the 1961 census.

17. Sabri Jiryes, *The Arabs in Israel*, French edn (Beirut, PLO Research Center), p. 254.

18. See *SAI 1956/7*, No. 8, p. 9 and *SAI 1975*, No. 26, p. 28.

19. See Israel, CBS, *Demographic Characteristics of the Population* (Jerusalem, Population and Housing Census, 1961), Pt. II, 1962, pp. 21-2.

20. See Israel Shahak, *Le Racisme de L'Etat d'Israel* (Paris, Editions Guy Authiers, 1975), pp. 153-68.

21. Jiryes, *The Arabs in Israel*.

22. Actually, the percentage for 1974 is slightly higher than the figure given due to the inclusion of the population of East Jerusalem.

23. Jiryes, *The Arabs in Israel*, 2nd edn (Institute for Palestine Studies, Beirut, 1973), p. 178.

24. See Table 1.3 below for the numerical increase of the Palestinians in

the West Bank and Gaza from 1952 to 1975.

25. If the global rate of growth continues as it was in 1973-5, the population of the West Bank will not exceed that which existed on the eve of the war until after 1980.

26. By Jordanians we mean only the population which traces its origins to Transjordan and not the entire population of Jordan with its 1948 borders.

27. We take this estimate of the population of Transjordan to be more accurate since it is based on the estimates of the British High Commissioner at the time.

28. The basic problem which confronted us here was to estimate the ratio of emigrants by Bank, and to estimate their ratio on the basis of whether or not they were Palestinians or Jordanians. Based on the 1961 census results which pertain to Jordanians abroad, we concluded:

    (a) The West Bank is the source of 80 per cent of net emigration, and the East Bank is the source of 20 per cent,

    (b) Until 1967, 94 per cent of the emigrants were Palestinians and 6 per cent Jordanians. Since 1967 the respective ratios became 96 and 4 per cent.

29. Rather, we can say that net migration during this period was negative, since it reached about −3,500.

30. No population census has been conducted in Lebanon since 1932. The only study on which one can rely for an estimate of the population of this country is an 'Active Population Survey' conducted by the Department of Central Statistics in 1970.

31. Lebanese statistics distinguish between Palestinians and Jordanians; the latter, however, include Jordanians and Palestinians living in Jordan. In order to account for the factor of migration, we applied the same ratios we used earlier in determining whether emigrants from Jordan were Jordanians or Palestinians (refer to note 28).

32. See UNRWA, *UNRWA's Area of Operation, 30 June 1977.*

33. We applied to the Palestinians who were counted in the 1960 census (or 112,571) the same rate of natural increase which we had calculated for Jordan from 1950 to 1960, and we have estimated the volume of Palestinian refugees who moved to Syria in 1948 at 85,000.

34. Syrian Arab Republic, Central Bureau of Statistics, *Statistical Abstract 1977*, vol. 30, p. 111.

35. We arrived at this figure by using the results of the 1961 Jordanian census pertaining to Jordanians in Kuwait.

36. The percentage distribution of those who are less than 15 years in 1975 in Syria, Iraq, Lebanon and East Bank were 40.3 per cent, 48.9 per cent, 41.6 per cent and 47.2 per cent respectively. See ECWA, *Demographic and Related Socio-Economic Data Sheets for Countries of the Economic Commission for Western Asia* (no. 2, Beirut, January 1978).

37. An examination of the sex ratio in the 1961 census of Jordan reveals a loss in males within the age group 15-54.

38. Age-specific birth rate: number of live births to women in a specific age group (e.g. 25-9) per 1,000 females in that group at mid-year.

39. Total fertility rate: sum of the age-specific birth rates (ASBR). It states the number of births 1,000 women would have if they experienced a five-set of ASBR throughout their reproductive span.

40. Gross Reproduction Rate (GRR): it measures the total number of daughters a group of women will have by the end of their childbearing period regardless of mortality.

41. A life table is, in essence, one form of combining mortality rates of a population at different ages into a single statistical model. It is principally used to measure the level of mortality.

42. A society is considered quasi-stable if it satisfies the following conditions: stable fertility level, slight declining mortality level, and an absence of migration.

43. Life expectancy at birth: expected number of years to be lived, on the average, in a definite group of births.

44. U.O. Schmelz, 'Infant and Early Childhood Mortality Among the Non-Jewish Population in Palestine and Israel' in *Late Foetal and Infant Deaths in Israel 1948-1972* (Jerusalem, CBS, Special Series no. 453, 1974), p. 57.

45. *SAI 1975*, p. 599.

46. *SAI 1975*, p. 620.

47. Refer to p. 22 of this chapter.

48. World Fertility Survey in Jordan.

49. We based our estimates of emigrants from the West Bank to the East Bank on: Jordan, Department of Statistics, *Population Census and Internal Migration for Amman, Jerusalem, Ruseifa, Irbid and Aqaba* (Amman, 1967).

50. Estimates of refugees in the wake of the June War of 1967 ranged between 188,000 (based on UNRWA Report for July 1966-June 1967) and 361,000 (based on the report of the High Commission for Aid, June 1968). Using the latter figure, we arrive at a West Bank population on the eve of the war of 1,011,000, or at an overall rate of increase from 1961-7 of 4.3 per cent. This is very hard to believe, since the rate of natural increase for this period never exceeded 3.2 per cent, let alone the factor of emigration (at an annual rate of 24,000 for this period).

51. Jamil Hilal, *The West Bank: Social and Economic Composition (1948-1974)* (PLO Research Center, January 1975), p. 51.

52. N. Aruri, 'Jordan: A Study in Political Development, 1921-1965', unpublished PhD dissertation, University of Massachusetts, 1967, p. 77.

53. Begin's latest stance on the 242 resolution as inapplicable to the West Bank reflects over and over again this colonial policy.

54. Hilal, *The West Bank*, pp. 26-261.

55. See the Kuwait censuses which distribute the Palestinians and Jordanians by age, sex and reasons for residing in the country.

56. Shahak, *Le Racisme de l'Etat d'Israel*, p. 172

57. *Le Monde*, 9 September 1976, p. 5.

58. In reality, this recent statistical concern resulted from the increasing political concern by the United Nations and its agencies in the Palestine question, following the mounting role of the Palestinian revolution and the results of the October War. We must recall here the recommendation of the General Assembly in its 29th session, 22 November 1974, in which it emphasised the legitimate rights of the Palestinian people, including the rights of self-determination, independence, national sovereignty and return to the homeland. The General Assembly recognised, further, the indispensable role of the Palestinian people in peace-making in the Middle East, and it requested the Secretary-General to be in continuous contact with the PLO on all matters pertaining to the Palestine question. We must also be reminded here of the General Assembly resolution 3379, during its 30th session, which condemned all forms of racial discrimination, and which considered Zionism a form of racial discrimination.

59. UN, Economic Commission for Western Asia, *Report on the Third Session, 10-15 May 1976* (ECOSOC, 61 ses., supp. no. 12, New York, 1976), pp. 27-9.

60. UN, International Conference on Populations, *Proceedings of the Conference in Bukharist* (August 1974), pp. 14-15.

61. Ibid., p. 15.

2 REFLECTIONS ON TWENTIETH-CENTURY PALESTINIAN CLASS STRUCTURE

Elia Zureik

This chapter provides a theoretical framework for dealing with the development of twentieth-century Palestinian class structure, taking into account the following interrelated factors: (1) the place of Palestine in the Ottoman Empire and the specific politico-economic features of the Oriental state which shaped Arab Palestine; (2) the extent to which Palestine was drawn into the world capitalist orbit since the middle of the nineteenth century; (3) the specificity of Palestinian class structure in the context of Zionist colonisation of the area; and (4) the effect of the 1948 Palestinian dispersion and the ensuing events of 1967 which further affected Palestinian social structure. The analysis is confined to the Palestinians living in historical Palestine.

I. Palestine in the Oriental-Capitalist Nexus

Writers about the Oriental state stress the presence of specific sociological features which differentiate the development of the Middle East when compared to other societies, in particular to the Western experience. First, there is the specificity of Middle Eastern feudalism; second, the dominant patrimonial nature of the Oriental state; and third, the uneven process of Middle Eastern urban development.[1]

It was Marx and Engels who drew attention to the peculiar features of Asiatic, as contrasted to Occidental, societies.[2] In the Asiatic context, it is argued, state monopoly, particularly over land, compounded with the general absence of private property in land (under the Ottoman rule, citizens could mainly use but not own, in a private sense, the land), hindered the development of social classes, and in a sense prevented the crystallisation of class conflict. Thus, stratification in those societies tended to be variegated; unlike Western societies, identification tended to be group-based along tribal, familial, sectarian and ethnic lines, where primordial attachment rather than class consciousness typified these societies.

The Oriental state is the embodiment of its absolute ruler, rather than that of any corporate groups in society, and it acts as the main appropriator of social resources. Moreover, the absence of autonomous feudal lords, as evident in the European experience, was another important by-product of the Oriental state. The locus of authority rests in a patrimonial form of political domination:

> Patrimonial authority is rooted in the household administration of the ruler; the intermingling of courtly life and governmental functions is its distinctive feature, and officials are recruited from the personal retainers or servants of the ruler. Where patrimonial domination is exerted over large territories, however, a broader basis of recruitment is necessary, and frequently a tendency towards decentralization of administration develops providing a basis for a variety of tensions and conflicts between ruler and local patrimonial officials or 'notables'.[3]

Two main conclusions can be derived from patrimonialism. First, the primacy of the political over the economic, which led some writers to observe, rather naively, that contrary to the Marxian principle, which defines politics as shaped mainly by economic arrangements in society, the converse is true in the Oriental state.[4] Second, due to the control of resources by the central authorities, 'there tended to develop within patrimonial societies narrow markets confined to small sectors of the society, the flow of resources between which was rather limited.'[5] This phenomenon assumed special importance in the case of urbanisation. The segmented nature of the Oriental city, its division into ethnically bound quarters, and the reluctance of the central government to grant authority to any corporate groups in society hampered the integration of Oriental society. The Oriental city was foremost, and continues to be, the seat of power devoid of the urban-industrial character which typifies Western cities. In due course, and after the disintegration of the Ottoman Empire, the Oriental city (particularly in Palestine) assumed a parasitic status *vis-à-vis* the countryside. It relied on the latter for sustenance and yet failed to reciprocate to the countryside any of the economic benefits accruing to the city. According to Turner, 'It was in [the European] city that urban piety, legal authority, occupational associations and political involvement developed; hence, the autonomous city had very important connections with the rise of European capitalism.'[6] The situation in the Oriental state was expressed succinctly by Anderson:

> The particular character of the urban economy and government in the Ottoman lands was always governed by the constraints of the Sultanate. Neither provincial workshops, nor a vast capital, nor periodic concern by individual rulers, could alter the basically inimical relationship of the Ottoman State to cities and industries. Islamic

political traditions possessed no conception of urban liberties. Towns had no corporate or municipal autonomy; indeed they had no legal existence at all.[7]

The above is not to be construed as meaning that the Islamic city was always underdeveloped or that social classes were absent. Middle Eastern cities flourished at a time when Europe was passing through its darkest periods of history. All one has to do is refer to Rodinson,[8] Ashtor[9] and Goitein's[10] works to realise that incipient or primitive forms of capitalism were a permanent feature of the Islamic state and that class antagonism, albeit of an ethnic and religious character, existed all along. Likewise, one should not stress the monolithic nature of the Islamic state and minimise the tolerance of ethnic and religious liberties throughout the history of the Islamic state, even under the Ottoman regime.

What concerns us in this discussion is not the absence or presence of capitalism, urbanisation or accountable political authority *per se*, but the specific features which these developments assumed in the context of the Islamic state, of which Palestine formed a part.

In the light of the above, it is possible to appreciate the peculiarities, and in a way weaknesses of Palestinian society at the turn of this century during the disintegration of the Ottoman Empire and the advent of imperialism and Zionism into Palestine.

The picture of Palestine at the turn of this century given by writers of differing ideological shades is in line with the above theoretical discussion. It is possible to summarise the situation in the late nineteenth and early twentieth century in Palestine along the following lines. (1) The non-functional integration of the village and the city kept the former underdeveloped and gave it an autarkic character which, while contributing to its self-sufficiency, increased its isolation and eventually contributed to its total dependency upon the city. (2) The 1850s Ottoman land reform, which intended to privatise land and secure tax revenues to support the declining Ottoman Empire, even though it was far from being a notable success, contributed in the long run to the emergence of a strata of city land-owners and the pauperisation of Palestinian peasantry. (3) Capital was siphoned into the hands of foreign and local landlords who did not attempt to invest their revenues either in agricultural or industrial developments of the country. (4) There was no significant stratum of Palestinian industrial proletariat which could act to transform Palestinian class structure. (5) Peasants were being displaced off the land and there was evidence of a continual increase in the size of the rural proletariat in the Levant region as early as the 1850s. (6) The countryside was dominated by land-owner-city-dwellers who, unlike European feudal lords, asserted their hegemony on the village without residing in the countryside. (7) The significant role played traditionally in the Islamic state by non-Muslim economic and intellectual elites limited the influence of indigenous elites.

Before one hastens to assign a single, causal and linear explanation to the development of Palestinian society, it is important to single out two divergent aspects of nineteenth-century Palestinian economic history. First, as Owens[11] claims, it is not clear that the Palestine of the late nineteenth century was on the verge of economic deterioration as depicted by other writers. He notes that the Tanzimat and the belated attempts by the Ottoman state to introduce order and civilian political administration in its provinces improved in a relative sense the economic prospects of Palestine. It also further encouraged settlements in the sparsely populated areas as well as expansion in agricultural areas. He notes, for example, that while there was an uneven pattern of development in Palestine, owing in part to the emerging link with the international market, the size of its trade showed noticeable increase. This trade relied heavily on citrus export, and although the volume of trade increased significantly in the first decade of this century, there had been a corresponding increase in imports. In certain periods the volume of imports by far exceeded that of exports which, as is shown later, became a permanent feature of twentieth-century Palestine. Second, there was also an increase in the number of Arab-owned small-scale industrial and handicraft establishments prior to World War One. But here too it experienced a noticeable decline in later years due in part to its inability to compete with Zionist penetration into Palestine. This was accompanied by industrial capital, technological know-how, and the backing of an exclusivist trade union movement, the Histadrut.

Second, the incorporation of nineteenth-century Syria, Lebanon and Palestine into the orbit of international capitalism was evident, according to Smilianskaya,[12] as early as the 1850s. The outcome of this dependency was most evident in the decline of certain agricultural activities and the restructuring of others, such as cotton-growing in Syria and Palestine and silk production in Lebanon. The European penetration had the following consequences: first, by introducing money economy it transformed village economies from subsistence to surplus ones, with urban landlords reaping most of the benefits; second, it contributed to the privatisation of land, and in Lebanon, to the strengthening of feudalism which lasted well into this century; third, to the increase of a visible strata of rural proletariat; fourth, to the dependence on foreign capital and the crystallisation, particularly in Lebanon and to a lesser extent in Palestine, of a strata of 'compradores', who linked up with foreign merchants and industrialists as brokers, usurers and money-lenders, and exploited the impoverished peasantry.

The peculiar process of rural proletarianisation, as is shown later, became a distinguishing feature of Palestinian social structure, and was further aggravated during the British Mandate and the Zionist colonisation of Palestine. It is worth while quoting Smilianskay's summary concerning the process of economic restructuring of the area:

> While feudal relations of production disintegrated, they survived in semifeudal forms. The stability of feudal and semifeudal forms of exploitation in the village was determined not merely by the nature of agrarian development but also by the absence of widespread capitalistic relations in industry. These factors were the outcome of the transformation of Syria, Lebanon and Palestine into semi colonies of the European bourgeoisie.[13]

With the above background, Yassin's opening comment in *The Struggle of the Palestine People Before 1948* becomes meaningful:

> At the end of the nineteenth century the national-industrial bourgeoisie of Syria (including Palestine) was trying to emerge and establish itself in the midst of serious opposition from Turkish rule and foreign capital. In actuality, its evolution was weak to the extent that it found it difficult to assume an important role in the administration and running of the economy of the country, subsequent to the Turkish coup of 1918 which saw the emergence of the Turkish bourgeoisie in its wake. The weakness of this Palestinian strata led it to form secret political societies which did not rely on the masses to the same extent they did on the higher classes and the English and French who acted in concert to divide between them the Ottoman Empire.[14]

Without belabouring the point, it is sufficient to say that although there had been more than just a trace of economic activity in late-nineteenth-century Palestine, its socio-economic structure exhibited features which were common to other patrimonial states at the time. Later, in the face of British imperialism and Zionism, these presented inherent weaknesses and urban distortions such as those prevalent in numerous Third World countries today.

Still, one must not exaggerate the weakness of the above system as Migdal[15] does. He sees the isolation of the village in Palestine and the concentration of political power in the hands of urban land-owners as a central factor in furthering the grip of the Palestinian bourgeoisie over the countryside as well as over the artisan and merchant strata in the city. While it is true that the strata of city land-owners blunted the emergence of a significant force of urban industrialists which would challenge its political hegemony, the politicisation of Palestinian peasantry was clearly apparent early this century and later as, for example, in its opposition to the British and Zionists, including the land-owning families themselves during the Arab revolt of 1936-9. As Porath[16] notes, the power position of the land-owning Palestinian families was significantly weakened in the eyes of the peasantry as a result of land sales to the Zionists. This collaboration in land sales, in addition to the relentless interfamilial Palestinian rivalry, acted as an important factor in weakening the unified struggle of the Palestinians against Zionism and British imperialism. Paradoxically, the weakness of Palestinian feudalism and the prevalence of the equalitarian *Musha'a* land tenure system in Palestine contributed in a significant degree to the relative freedom among the peasantry in its fight against Zionism and British imperialism. Thus, Tom Bowden, who identified the 1936-9 Palestinian Arab rebellion as a 'spontaneous' peasant revolt went on to discredit the notion that the peasantry was manipulated by urban elites:

> The Arab revolt was a peasant war of major proportions in duration, cost and casualties. For a time it ended Mandatory control in certain areas of Palestine and threatened it, and the *Yishuv*, everywhere. However, it was an unsystematic, unstable insurging prone to anarchic lapses. Above all, it was not the product of the Mufti's machination attempting, as some would have it, to establish a Caliphate with himself as the Caliph. The control which the Mufti exercised over the actual revolt and especially the guerrillas in the field was minimal.[17]

II. The Duality of Pre-1948 Palestine

The internal weakness of Palestinian social structure notwithstanding, European and Zionist penetration of the area created a new form of dependency built on a dual society, the Palestinian Arabs and Zionist colonists, with the former occupying a subordinate position in the power structure of the British Mandate period.

Because of the dual nature of Palestine during the Mandate, it is assumed by many writers that this duality between the Arabs and the Zionists embodied two autonomous, non-functional socio-economic entities.[18] This is clearly the position taken by most Zionist writers, who stress the autonomy of the two societies in order to highlight, on the one hand, the non-exploitive and non-colonising aspects of the Zionist venture in Palestine, and on the other, the historical backwardness of Arab Palestine.

As the Palestinian social structure before 1948 is explained elsewhere,[19] suffice it here to outline the main aspects of Palestinian society, focusing mainly on the arguments pertaining to separate developments and the features of the dual Palestinian-Zionist societies. While the Jewish population comprised around one-third of the population of Palestine in 1948, its legal ownership of the land did not exceed 7 to 8 per cent of the area of Palestine. Admittedly the regional concentration of the Zionists into all-Jewish enclaves gave them the added advantage of concentrating their efforts into the development of Jewish colonies; the political and economic structure of Mandatory Palestine had a great deal to do with the overall political structure in the country, which was determined to a very large extent by the British.

First to be noted is the economic framework of the country following World War One, particularly after the Balfour Declaration of 1917. As pointed out above, the social structure of Palestinian society at the turn of this century reflected neither the characteristics of a totally traditional nor of a modern society, neither a capitalistic nor a feudalistic one. It embodied a mixture of all of these elements, which, when considered in the context of the competing elements in the region, resulted in a dependent economic status for the Palestinian Arabs. This dependency had a dual component to it in terms of providing an unlimited reservoir of cheap, unskilled Arab labour, and in weakening the fledgling stratum of Palestinian industrial bourgeoisie.

Many factors contributed to the unlimited supply of unskilled Arab labour dependent for its livelihood on the Zionist and British governmental sectors. The land inheritance system and the traditional Arab social structure played important roles in this regard. However, of the external factors Zionism and the Histadrut were crucial. They championed the ideology of 'Hebrew Labour' and conducted their policies according to discriminatory criteria by advocating the exclusion of Arab workers from the Jewish economic sector and alienating them permanently from the land once it was defined as 'Jewish' land. Although the overt rationale of this policy was to 'normalise' Jewish class structure

in the Diaspora and ensure the economic well-being of the Zionist colonists, the by-product was its failure to implement successfully the
exclusivist ideology which, nevertheless, contributed to perpetuating a
disadvantaged position of the Arab workers and furthering their
dependent status on Jewish economy. Weinstock captured the impact
of this exclusivist policy:

> But for the Arab peasants, the *fellaheen*, the policy of exclusively
> Jewish labour had dramatic results. It meant not only that they were
> evicted from the land they tilled after the Arab landowner had sold
> it to the Zionist concerns, but also that they were prevented on
> principle from finding employment on the Jewish farms, or in
> industry. Likewise, the policy of Jewish produce (i.e. the boycot-
> ting of Arab produce) impeded the development of an Arab bour-
> geoisie and proletariat in Palestine. Thus Arab resentment of Zionist
> colonization could be channelled into neither bourgeois nationalism
> nor proletarian socialism, since the social classes that normally convey
> these policies remained embryonic owing to the Zionist segregation-
> alism which blocked their emergence.[20]

The asymmetrical interdependency between the two sectors is
evident in the exploitation of Arab workers as seen in the drastic wage
differentials between Arab and Jewish workers performing *similar* jobs
in the Zionist as well as the British sector. It is instructive to add further
evidence here in challenge of the upheld Zionist thesis that the Arab
and Jewish sectors developed separately with no functional connection
between them. Sussman,[21] in *Wage Differentials and Equality Within
the Histadrut*, notes that in 1930 out of 5,811 agricultural workers
employed in five large Zionist colonies, close to 53 per cent were Arab
workers. Again, considering the Jewish sector only, he finds that in
1936, after the policy of 'Hebrew work' had been put to the test for
more than a decade, 15 per cent of all workers in the Jewish sector
were Arabs. Of the workers in agriculture, 35 per cent were Arabs; in
construction, 12.4 per cent were Arabs; in industry, 8.7 per cent; 25
per cent in transportation and 6.7 in commercial services. Likewise,
between 1931 and 1939 Sussman finds consistently in various branches
of the economy drastic differences in wages in comparable sectors.
Sussman uses his data to shed doubt on the argument of separate
development and to further show that wage differentials existed *within*
the Jewish sector as well, contrary to Histadrut ideology. He argues that
the abundance of unskilled Arab labour contributed to a depressed wage

level in the unskilled (compared to the skilled) Jewish employment
sector.

Maintaining wage differentials in government and private sectors was
the result of successful pressure exerted by the Zionists in Palestine. It
is interesting to note that various arguments were advanced by the
Zionists in support of their claims, ranging from high unemployment
(which was more severe in the Arab sector) to the fact that they contributed more to the revenues of the Mandate on *per capita* basis (which
shows that the Jewish sector was more industrialised), to the invocation
of arguments reminiscent of South Africa's racist labour laws whereby
the Zionists argued that lower Arab wages could be justified on the
basis of different life-styles reflected in 'the peasant's cultural habits'.[22]
Carmi and Rosenfeld, while failing to see the functional asymmetry
connecting the Arab to the Jewish sector, summarised the situation in
Mandatory Palestine:

> We find, by comparing Arab wage statistics, that throughout the
> mandate period, wage rates in the new economic branches (govern-
> ment services, port refinery, citriculture, building, transport, etc.)
> approximated what was estimated to be the average yearly earning
> of the peasant . . . In any branch of industry in which he worked,
> even the most profitable, he did not receive the labour price in that
> branch, that is, according to his productivity, etc., but rather he
> received the equivalent of the subsistence returns of a peasant.[23]

Applying Marx's 'Asiatic' conception of social development to the
Middle East, Avineri[24] notes that the economic backwardness of the
Arab Middle East, like that of India and even China, is governed by the
indirect form of colonialism exercised by British imperialism in the area.
Thus for Avineri the failure of a revolutionary Arab ideology to develop
is an inevitable product of the historically feeble status of the Arab
bourgeoisie (a necessary ingredient for class antagonism) and the dominance of non-Muslim, non-indigenous elites as carriers of ideology
(both of which are dictated by an indirect European colonialism). This,
Avineri notes, is a feature which distinguishes Zionism from Arab
nationalism. The former, according to him, provided the necessary
indigenous ideology of modernisation which was absent from Arab
nationalism.

There is no doubt that in the light of what has been said here so far,
as well as by other conventional economic historians, the weakness of
Arab society is to be located in its peculiar social class development. It

is equally misleading, however, to transplant Marxism, as Avineri does, in order to advocate a revolutionary role for Zionism, not only for the Jews, but also for modernising the class structure of Arab society. Avineri sees in the Zionist venture a catalyst in bringing about the sort of change in the Middle East which, because of its peculiar features, British imperialism did not succeed in doing (as was anticipated by Marx), namely the dismantling of traditional social structure.

As Turner[25] points out, this type of analysis, which allocates to Zionism the role of a revolutionary form, is fraught with problems. Both British imperialism and Zionism played a direct role in 'stunting' the development of Arab society. Moreover, Israel's class structure, with the nature of the *Yishuv* during the British Mandate, does not resemble that of European-capitalist societies. Historically, the means of production in Zionist Palestine was not dominated by a property-owning bourgeoisie. As pointed out above, the nationalist and exclusivist character of the Zionist economy and ideology could not have brought about the changes advocated by Avineri. Hence, to Turner there is no parallel with Marx's model of capitalism or even with his discussion of British imperialism in India. The situation is closer to Britain's relationship with Ireland:

> For a number of reasons (in terms of colonization, depending on foreign capital and the peculiarities of the class structure) Israel is a society which is very different from Marx's theoretical model of capitalism; therefore the attempt to form an analogy between the Middle East and India or between indirect Chinese rule and Middle East imperialism is not only superficial, but misleading. Just as Marx noted a 'stunting effect' in Britain's relationship with Ireland so one might find a stunted development in the Middle East under the dual impact of British and Israeli colonization.[26]

Without elaborating on the complex nature of British policies in Palestine, it is sufficient to note two economic aspects which reflected the asymmetrical nature of Palestinian economy – first, the further drawing of Palestine into the international capitalist system, and second, the significant economic concessions made by the British to the Zionist colonists.

Patricia Garrett[27] argues that with the further transformation of Palestine into a money economy and as a result of tax and other revenues, the British have managed to compensate the expenditures they incurred during the Mandate. As an index of economy transformation,

Garrett shows the extent of the increase in money circulation in Palestine whereby it increased by 2.7 times between 1927 and 1944. Overall, the economic viability of Palestine to the British was reflected in the volume of foreign trade which multiplied by six times during the Mandate. However, she goes on to show that Palestine by the late 1940s became persistently an importing region.

Regarding the economic concessions made to the Zionists, Garrett mentions six major concessions made in 1939 and five in 1942. Only one concession, an importing food agency, was in the hands of Arabs. The rest, including the Palestine Electric Corporation, Palestine Salt Company, Palestine Potash and Sulphur Quarries, etc., were in exclusive Zionist hands. In communications, Jewish interests managed to obtain concessions from the British for setting up a modern transportation and road system which served the colonisation interests of the Zionists. George Mansur, a Palestinian union organiser, said:

> Certain roads, on the other hand, have been built on account of the [Jewish] National Home. The Jewish Agency refers to them as 'security' roads. These go from Haifa to Jaffa, from Tulkarem to Nathania, and from Affula to Nahlal in one direction and from Affula to Beisan in the other. The work on the latter was given to Jewish labourers at the cost to the treasury of £80,000, whereas an official engineer's estimate was £27,000 [presumably this is to meet higher wages which had to be paid to Jewish rather than Arab workers]. These roads were not built until Arab inhabitants, who might have profited from them, had been driven out of that part of the country and it had been completely Judaised.[28]

It is important to underscore the asymmetrical by-product of the dual nature of Arab-Jewish societies in pre-1948 Palestine. As noted earlier, differences in wages for performing similar work became a permanent feature of the economic landscape of Mandatory Palestine. This is even true during the so-called boom periods. Patricia Garrett remarks that while there had been a general rise in the proportion of goods received in wages in Palestine, an overall rise from 37 per cent in 1939 to 45 per cent in 1942, she goes on to say that

> Arab workers, however, received a decreasing share. Their wages dropped from 38 per cent of gross output in 1939 to 29 per cent in 1942. Jewish workers, on the other hand, received an increased share — 41 per cent in 1939 and 49 per cent in 1942. Likewise,

employees of the state concessions which were mainly in Zionist hands received a large share—25 per cent in 1939 and 37 per cent in 1942.[29]

Similarly, because of a direct correlation between Zionist colonisation of Palestine and Arab unrest (which culminated in the 1936-9 Arab rebellion), the British government found itself increasingly diverting a larger portion of its budget to financing its social control agencies, the police and the military.[30] This was one direct cause of the lowering of its contributions to the social and educational needs of the Arab sector, thus widening an already existing gap between Arab and Zionist institutions

By the eve of the 1948 Palestinian dispersion, Palestinian Arab society had failed to resolve any of the main contradictions which it had faced all along. Socially, it continued to belabour under a rural-urban dichotomy, manifesting deep cleavages which stood in the way of any meaningful social integration. The rural countryside continued to be underdeveloped, while the urban centres lacked any meaningful existence to contribute towards the development of the hinterland. Politically, Palestinian social life was dominated by a familialism which provided insurmountable difficulties in terms of articulating a unifying Palestinian ideology. The intellectual-cum-political elites of the period were more interested in Western ideals than they were in the aspirations of the masses. And as products of Western educational systems, they espoused a form of cultural nationalism which could not transcend in its comprehension its narrow social class interests, even though they espoused on numerous occasions anti-Western and anti-Zionist programmes. Economically, Palestinian society continued to exhibit traditional structures in the midst of what appeared to be nascent industrial activity. The economic ideology of the city land-owning elites was such that, while they stifled the emergence of a politically viable industrial bourgeoisie (hence a stratum of industrial proletariat), their own economic activity regarding the industrial development of Palestine was confined to mercantile pursuits of a non-productive nature.

III. Post-1948 Palestine

In contrast to pre-1948, the Palestinians in post-1948 experienced important changes in their social structure. First, of 900,000 Palestinians who comprised the majority of the population in what became Israel, more than 700,000 were dispersed in the 1948 War. Second, following the 1948 War, the bulk of the urban Palestinian sector found itself either as refugees in various parts of the Arab world or residents of towns and cities outside the 1948 borders of Israel and cut off from the remaining Palestinians in Israel. Third, accompanying this development there occurred a significant migration of middle-class Palestinians, who included among them the political leadership which existed prior to 1948.

Socially, politically and economically the reality which faced the Palestinians in post-1948 was quite different. In addition to being reduced to a minority they were brought under a system of Zionist domination which exhibited specific features of its own. Before summarising the effects of this system of domination upon the Arab minority, let us delineate its components.

First, it perpetuated an important aspect of the British system of control manifested through the adoption by the Zionists of the 1945 Defence (Emergency) Regulation Laws which were originally designed to cope with the 1936 Arab unrest in Mandatory Palestine. It is interesting to note that these very laws and measures were labelled as unconstitutional by the Hebrew Lawyers' Union when applied against Zionist violence in Mandatory Palestine. Detention without trial, house arrest and confiscation of land, not to mention the notorious Israeli military government which curtailed the civil and political rights of Israeli Arabs for eighteen years, are carried out in the name of state security through the invocation of the inherited British Emergency Regulations.

Second, between 1948 and the late 1950s, Israel introduced a series of additional laws[31] designed to further dispossess Arabs of their land in the name of the national interest. It is these laws, together with the national, exclusivist policy of the Jewish National Fund which account for the fact that whereas by 1948 the Zionists could not lay legal claim to more than 8-9 per cent of mandatory Palestine, now they have managed to label as 'Jewish land in perpetuity' more than 90 per cent of pre-1967 Palestine.

Third, Israel adopted a definition of citizenship based on religious and national grounds which, while not stating exclusion explicitly, made it impossible for Palestinian Arab refugees to reclaim possession of their land and deserted property or even settle there if they so desire. Jews, on the other hand, living anywhere in the world, are granted under the Nationality Law and Law of Return the automatic right of Israeli citizenship.

Fourth, through an ultra-nationalistic definition of key para-state Zionist institutions, such as the Jewish Agency and the Jewish National Fund, it was (and continues to be) possible to channel resources and funds to the development of the Jewish sector only. The use of a para-state agency for this purpose protected the Israeli government against charges of discrimination.[32]

Fifth, a powerful system of patronage and co-option was utilised by the Zionist apparatus of the state (including the Zionist party machines) in order to reward and punish the Arab citizens of the state. This implied that social mobility and career rewards were governed not by meritocracy and universalistic criteria but by loyalty to what appears to them to be alien Zionist institutions.

Considering the specific features of pre-1948 Palestinian society, the demographic changes which accompanied the 1948 dispersion, and the nature of the control system implemented by the Zionists, the repercussions for the Palestinian Arabs in Israel were quite serious. They exhibited foremost a system of domination which, unlike the system of duality and dependency which existed in pre-1948 Palestine, is characterised this time by internal colonialism, the consequences of which could be summarised in the following points: (1) the continuation of the proletarianisation process among Palestinian peasantry which had begun in pre-1948; (2) further land expropriation and marginalisation of the Arab sector; (3) the further stunting of the development of a significant stratum of Palestinian industrial bourgeoisie which would be capable of playing its respective role in the normalisation of Palestinian class structure; (4) the impossibility of forming political institutions which would reflect the national aspirations of the Palestinian minority along non-Zionist lines; (5) continued cultural domination of the Arab minority via the school system and mass media through state manipulation of Palestinian national and political symbols; and (6) the gradual politicisation of the Palestinians as reflected in various protest movements and an increase in identification with the Communist Party, *Rakah.*

Israel's occupation of the West Bank and Gaza has created a different system of relationship to the Palestinians. To all intents and purposes, the occupied territories are Zionism's 'Bantustan' regions. Utilisation of the West Bank for cheap labour in Israel, without granting any political or economic rights to the Arab workers, has reduced the territories to becoming an economic satellite of Israel. As it stands, the only noticeable economic activity in the West Bank and Gaza is evident in subcontracting on a small scale, primarily commodity production, mainly foodstuffs, and, of course, supply of Arab labour to the Israeli market in wages which are substantially below those paid to Israeli workers.[33]

Some Israeli social scientists have become sensitive to this South African or Rhodesian-like situation, which is increasingly making a mockery of the Zionist claim of 'normalisation' of Jewish social structure. Thus, according to one Israeli social scientist, Israel is becoming a 'nation of bosses'.[34] Other Israeli and Western social scientists describe the economic relationships between the occupied territories and Israel in terms of traditional, neo-classical economics where politics is portrayed as separate from economic development. Thus, it is stressed that the benefits accruing to the occupied territories in terms of raising the GNP outweigh any other disadvantages. There is no doubt if such a comparison were to be carried out, using routine economic indicators and without taking the long-term political and national implications into account, the blacks in South Africa and even in Rhodesia would also come out better off than most blacks in neighbouring African countries. The trouble with this analysis is that it divorces politics from economics, and does not see, or is not willing to acknowledge, that the political consequences of colonialism in the name of GNP growth are neither a preferred moral nor national goal.

Even if one analyses the short-term effects of Israeli economic policies *vis-à-vis* the occupied territories, the picture points to a stagnant, dependent economy. The much-vaunted rise in GNP, which is due in great measure to exploited Arab labour in Israel and to the influx of Palestinian earnings in the Arab world, is offset by the lack of any industrial development and investments, severe retardation of the once thriving tourist and commercial sectors, no noticeable improvement in the Arab agricultural sector to enable it to compete with Jewish agriculture, and substantial emigration of Palestinian males seeking employment in other parts of the Arab world.

The status of the Palestinian Arabs in the West Bank under Jordanian rule is not all that different in its dependent status *vis-à-vis* Jordan. Like Israel's, Jordan's policy was to discourage any indigenous economic development within the West Bank and any genuine form of political participation.

One could say that there is one notable exception in the guiding principles of each regime. The Jordanian rule was on the whole quasi-patrimonial, designed to sustain the authority of the royal household, while Israel's goals are not designed to serve the interests of one ruler *per se*, but to further the 'national' goals as they are defined by Zionist ideology.

Notes

1. See Perry Anderson, *Lineages of the Absolutist State* (New Left Books, London, 1974), pp. 361-94.

2. For a view which challenges the presence of the so-called 'Asiatic mode of production' see Barry Hindess and Paul Q. Hirst, *Pre-Capitalist Modes of Production* (Routledge and Kegan Paul, London, 1977), pp. 178-207.

3. Anthony Giddens, *Capitalism and Modern Social Analysis* (Cambridge University Press, London, 1971), p. 127.

4. See James A. Bill, 'Class Analysis and the Dialectics of Modernization in the Middle East', *International Journal of Middle East Studies*, vol. 3 (1972), pp. 41-434; S.N. Eisenstadt, 'Convergence and Divergence of Modern and Modernizing Societies', *International Journal of Middle East Studies*, vol. 8 (1972), pp. 1-27; see pp. 12-13.

5. Eisenstadt, 'Convergence and Divergence', p. 16.

6. Bryan Turner, *Weber and Islam* (Routledge and Kegan Paul, London, 1974), p. 98.

7. Ibid., pp. 472-3.

8. Maxime Rodinson, *Islam and Capitalism* (Pantheon Books, New York, 1973).

9. Eliyahu Ashtor, *Social and Economic History of the Near East in the Middle Ages* (University of California Press, Berkeley, 1976).

10. S.D. Goitein, *Studies in Islamic History and Institutions* (E.J. Brill, Leiden, 1966), pp. 217-41.

11. Roger Owen, 'Economic History of 19th Century Palestine: Some Points and Some Problems', prepared for the Tenth Annual Convention of the American Arab University Graduates, October, 1977.

12. I.M. Smilianskaya, 'From Subsistence to Market Economy, 1850's' in Charles Issawi (ed.), *The Economic History of the Middle East* (University of Chicago Press, Chicago, 1966), pp. 222-47.

13. Ibid., p. 239.

14. Abd El-Kadder Yassin, *The Struggle of the Palestine People Before 1948* (Palestine Liberation Organization Research Center, Beirut, 1975), p. 9.

15. Joel Migdal, 'Urbanization and Political Change: "The Impact of Foreign Rule"', *Comparative Studies in Society and History*, vol. 19, no. 3 (1977), pp. 328-49.

16. Yehoshua Porath, 'The Land Problem in Mandatory Palestine', *The Jerusalem Quarterly*, no. 1 (1976), pp. 18-27.

17. Tom Bowden, 'The Politics of the Arab Rebellion in Palestine: 1936-1939', *Middle Eastern Studies*, vol. II, no. 2 (1975), p. 168.

18. For a critical assessment of this assumption, see Talal Asad, 'Anthropological Texts and Ideological Problems', *Economy and Society*, vol. 4 (1975).

19. See my *The Palestinians in Israel: A Study in Internal Colonialism* (Routledge and Kegan Paul, London, 1979), Chapter 3.

20. Nathan Weinstock, 'Introduction' in Abram Leon, *The Jewish Question* (Pathfinder Press, New York, 1970), p. 55.

21. Zvi Sussman, *Wage Differentials and Equality Within the Histadrut* (Massada Press, Israel, 1974), Chapter 3 (Hebrew).

22. Shulamit Carmi and Henry Rosenfeld, 'The Origins of the Process of Proletarianization and Urbanization of Arab Peasants in Palestine', *Annals of the New York Academy of Science*, vol. 220 (1974), p. 479.

23. Ibid., p. 478.

24. Shlomo Avineri, 'Modernization and Arab Society: Some Reflections' in

Irving Howe and Carl Gresham (eds.), *Israel, the Arabs and the Middle East* (Bantam Books, New York, 1972).

25. Bryan Turner, 'Avineri's View of Marx's Theory of Colonialism: Israel', *Science and Society*, vol. XL, no. 4 (1976-7), pp. 385-409.

26. Ibid., p. 406.

27. Patricia Garrett, 'Orphans of Empires: A Case Study of the Palestinian Refugees', unpublished MA thesis, University of Wisconsin, Madison, 1970.

28. George Mansur, *The Arab Worker in the Palestine Mandate* (The Commercial Press, Jerusalem, 1936), p. 25.

29. Garrett, 'Orphans of Empires', pp. 74-5.

30. See Asad, 'Anthropological Texts', p. 265.

31. See Michael Adams, 'Israel's Treatment of the Arabs in the Occupied Territories', *Journal of Palestine Studies*, vol. VI, no. 2 (1977), pp. 19-40.

32. See the excellent analysis of the post-1967 activities of the Jewish National Fund in Uri Davis and Walter Lehn, 'And the Fund Still Lives', *Journal of Palestine Studies*, vol. VII, no. 4 (1978), pp. 3-31.

33. Jamil Hilal, 'Class Transformation in the West Bank', *Journal of Palestine Studies*, vol. VI, no. 2 (1977), pp. 167-75.

34. Cited by A. Samed, 'Entering the Proletariat', *Journal of Palestine Studies*, vol. VI, no. 1 (1976), p. 160.

3 THE QUIESCENT PALESTINIANS: THE SYSTEM OF CONTROL OVER ARABS IN ISRAEL

Ian Lustick

What has been most striking about that portion of the Palestinian Arab community that has lived in Israel since 1948 has been its political quiescence. This is in contrast to the Palestinians who have lived in Jordan and Lebanon, where their presence has resulted in problems of crisis proportions, and in contrast to the inhabitants of the West Bank and the Gaza Strip, who have helped make the disposition of those areas an international problem of first-rank importance and *the* major issue in contemporary Israeli politics. Without ignoring important manifestations of discontent, such as *El-Ard* (a small group of Arab nationalists that operated semi-legally in Israel from 1959-65) and the Land Day demonstrations of March 1976, one can safely say that the now half-million-strong Arab minority in Israel has constituted virtually no threat to the smooth operation of the Israeli political system. In fact, the absence of independent Arab political parties or newspapers, of an Arab civil rights movement, or of sustained clandestine activities, and the generally low salience of the internal Arab problem in Israeli politics seem to contradict a strong international trend towards the forceful and troublesome expression of communal demands. For in scores of 'national' political arenas, from the United Kingdom, Spain and Canada to Malaysia, Iraq and Cyprus, the demands of minority groups have figured as major if not decisive challenges to the integrity and stability of political systems.

Associated with this phenomenon has been a fascination by social scientists with the dynamics of ethnic differentiation and a search for means by which rival communal groups can relate to one another without conflict, chaos and the disintegration of large political units. Out of an abhorrence for violence and oppression, interested academics have devoted considerable attention to group compromise as a method to achieve stability in 'deeply divided societies'.[1] The purpose of this chapter, however, is to demonstrate how an alternative approach—one that focuses on effective group *control* over rival group(s)—can explain political stability in Israel, a society deeply divided between a Jewish majority and an Arab minority severely discontented with the conditions of its existence.[2]

The 1948 War between Israel and the Arab states resulted in the exodus of approximately 85 per cent of the Arab population of the territory which became the state of Israel. But the Arabs who stayed behind, in addition to those who infiltrated back across the border or who were admitted into Israel under the reunion of families plan, have constituted a minority of 12-15 per cent of Israel's population. Thus, although nothing near the 49 per cent Arab minority envisioned under the terms of the United Nations partition plan,[3] the non-Jewish population has been substantial ever since the birth of the state.

Although a subordinate position for Arabs in a Jewish-Zionist state can be inferred from Zionist ideology, such was not an explicit part of Zionist thought or Zionist planning. Accordingly, the political programmes of Israeli leaders in the early years of statehood did not include an analysis of, or a solution for, *habaayah haAravit* (the Arab problem). Rather, policies towards the Arab minority emerged as by-products of the new regime's efforts to cope with the difficult problems of sudden statehood. In connection with its major objectives the leadership of the new state wanted to prevent the Arab minority from serving as a fifth column or abetting large-scale infiltration. It also wanted to acquire from Israeli Arabs a large percentage of their land holdings and to take advantage of Arab resources (homes, shops and farm land) to absorb new immigrants. It further was anxious to exploit Arab labour for the rapid development of the Jewish-controlled Israeli economy, to aggregate political support among Israeli Arabs for partisan advantage, and to prevent the Arab minority from becoming a burden in the arena of international politics.

The regime did not want, nor did it strive to achieve, the integration or absorption of the Arab population into the Jewish community. Nor did it entertain seriously the possibility of wholesale expulsion, though various schemes of population transfer were discussed. Rather it set out to maintain the social segregation of Arabs and Jews, to extract certain important resources from the Arab population, and to regulate and direct the behaviour of the Arab minority to serve the interests of the Jewish majority. Israeli policy towards the Arab minority thus came to be determined in effect by one overriding objective – to *control* the Arab community in Israel rather than to eliminate, integrate, absorb or develop it.

I. The Control of Israeli Arabs

1. *Three Levels of Analysis*

The evacuation of all large Arab cities during the 1948 War and the dis-

appearance of the commercial, political and intellectual elites which
they contained are facts of enormous significance in explaining the
susceptibility of the remaining Arab community to manipulation by
outside forces. (Consider Table 3.1, where (approximate) non-Jewish
population figures are given for the major Arab cities in Israel-Palestine.)

Table 3.1:   Arab Urban Populations in Israel-Palestine: 1948

City	Before the War	After the War
Jerusalem	75,000	3,500
Jaffa	70,000	3,600
Haifa	71,000	2,900
Lydda-Ramle	34,920	2,000
Nazareth	15,540	16,800
Acre	15,000	3,500
Tiberias	5,310	—
Safed	9,530	—

Also important in explaining the susceptibility of the Arab minority to
Jewish control are aspects of Arab social structure and culture, including
reliance on the traditional 'go-between' (*wāsta*) and strong personal com-
mitments to hierarchically organised village-based clans. These were
circumstances easily exploited for purposes of control by Jewish authority
structures able to link themselves to patriarchal leaders. The economic
underdevelopment and infrastructural backwardness of Arab Palestine
before 1948 contributed significantly to the inability of Arab entrepreneurs to compete with Jewish enterprises after 1948.[4] This set of
conditions constrained Arabs to rely on Jewish sources of employment
for their livelihood and severely hampered the emergence of autonomous
centres of Arab economic power which, had they materialised, could
have served as a base for sustained political action. In addition, within
the Arab community, traditional rivalries between bedouin and villagers,
between Muslims, Christians and Druze, between rival clans within villages, and between rival villages within certain regions all served as barriers to united Arab political action.

   To focus on such circumstantial 'givens' as explanatory variables, be
they economic, social, cultural or ecological, is to operate on what may
be termed a 'structural' level of analysis. 'Structural' here is meant only
to suggest the relative constancy of these factors. They may change, but
they will do so only very gradually or as a result of some cataclysmic

event (the 1948 War, *vis-à-vis* the Arabs of Palestine, is an example of such an event). The general idea is that these phenomena are in some sense 'prior' to the prevailing pattern of group-to-group relations. They are the sort of phenomena that can rarely be created or radically changed by manipulative policies, though such policies may often be designed to reinforce, exploit or mute their social, economic or political implications.[5]

A second level of analysis may be labelled 'institutional'. It involves a focus on the *unintended consequences of the normal operation of dominant political and economic organisations.* In the Israeli case, what is of interest on this level of analysis are the constraints placed on the Arab minority and the opportunities to achieve control by Jews over Arabs that result from the normal operation of Israel's major institutions. The ideology of the super-ordinate group (in this case, Zionism) comes into focus on this level: (1) as a doctrine which can be used to legitimise political demands only by those able to draw upon it; and (2) because it may find concrete expression in the standard operating procedures of institutions organised according to its tenets.

The development of a whole panoply of Zionist institutions dedicated to the mass immigration and absorption of Diaspora Jews and to the consolidation of a sovereign Jewish state in Palestine was of decisive importance for the emergence of the state of Israel. Moreover, the Zionist movement and the institutions it produced, including political parties, kibbutz movements, the Histadrut (General Federation of Workers of the Land of Israel), the Jewish Agency, the Jewish National Fund and the World Zionist Organization, have dominated the life of the Jewish state since its establishment. Both the ideology and the institutions of Zionism developed apart from any important considerations relating to their impact on non-Jewish Israelis. Yet the standard operating procedures of Zionist institutions have had systematic consequences for the Arab minority — denying Arab citizens effective access to the primary routes of social, economic and political mobility in Israeli society, depriving Arabs of opportunities for political alliances with dissident Jewish groups, and providing the Jewish regime with organisational mechanisms for the differential development of the Jewish and Arab sectors.

For example, since 1948 the Jewish Agency (*Sochnut*) which disburses funds collected for Israel from Jewish communities abroad, has channelled over $4 billion into the development of the Jewish sector. Arabs do not have access to these funds (which include subsidies for farmers, shopkeepers and businessmen, free installation of electrical and water systems in new settlements, the paving of roads, etc.) since the Jewish Agency,

as a Zionist institution, is mandated to address itself only to Jewish
Israelis. The Jewish National Fund (*Keren Kayemeth Le'Yisrael*), the
land acquisition and development arm of the World Zionist Organ-
ization, owns nearly 50 per cent of Israel's surface area (excluding the
Negev desert wasteland), including virtually all prime agricultural land.[6]
As a matter of standard operating procedure the JNF, as a Zionist organ-
isation, leases its land at negligible rates for 49-year leases, but to Jewish
Israelis only.

Neither the Jewish Agency nor the Jewish National Fund fashion
policies designed to hinder economic development in the Arab sector
or to force Arabs into economic dependence on the Jewish population.
Of interest on this *institutional* level of analysis, however, is that the
standard operating procedures of these (and other) major Israeli institutions, clearly reflecting the tenets of Zionist ideology, do indeed have
the consequence of depriving Arabs of effective access to capital resources, of protecting Jewish farmers and businessmen from Arab competition, and of institutionalising Arab economic dependence on Jewish-
owned sources of employment.

These 'structural' and 'institutional' factors could not, however,
account for the sustained manipulation of the Arab minority to serve
the interests of the Jewish majority. Rather, these circumstances constitute the raw material from which mechanisms of control can be
fashioned. Without policies designed and implemented to exploit these
conditions, Arab land, for example, could not be transferred to Jewish
control, Arab votes could not be secured for the major Zionist parties,
public expressions of Arab support for the Jewish state, useful in the
international arena, would not be forthcoming, small Arab dissident
groups could not be prevented from proliferating, nor could potentially
significant social, economic and political trends within Arab villages be
monitored. On the *programmatic* level of analysis, attention is focused
on such calculated policies of control, whether involving super-ordinate
group regulation of the behaviour of subordinate group members, sur-
veillance, resource extraction or the reinforcement and exploitation of
convenient structural and institutional circumstances.

Though hardly noticed outside the Arab sector, the Jewish regime,
represented primarily by the Labor Party (1948-76), has co-ordinated a
wide variety of policies towards the Arab minority. These policies were
developed and implemented by the military government (*memshal
tzvai*), by the Arab departments of various Ministries, the Histadrut
and the Labor Party, and by the office of the Adviser to the Prime Minister on Arab Affairs. They were tailored specifically, if not explicitly,

in accordance with the general objective of achieving and maintaining control over the Arab population.

From 1948 until the early 1960s, the military government enforced an elaborate array of travel restrictions. In order to leave their villages, most Arabs required travel permits specifying routes, destination, time of arrival and time of return.[7] The expropriations committee of the Finance Ministry, the Agriculture Ministry and the Interior Ministry have worked in close co-operation with the Jewish National Fund, the Custodian of Absentee Property and the Development Authority to expropriate and transfer Arab lands to Jewish control.[8] The military government itself was intimately involved in this effort. One method of land expropriation and transfer began with the military government declaring a particular tract of Arab land a 'closed area'. As a result of such a declaration, Arab farmers were barred from cultivating or even entering the area. After three years of 'abandonment' the Agriculture Ministry would issue certificates classifying the fields as 'uncultivated'. This opened the way for the Ministry to expropriate the lands in question under the terms of the 'Cultivation of Waste Lands Ordinance' (passed by the Knesset in October 1948). Once expropriated by the government, the military authorities removed the 'closed area' classification, the land would be made available to the Jewish National Fund, and thereby added to the general land reserve for Jewish settlement.[9]

Non-governmental agencies, aside from the Jewish Agency and the Jewish National Fund, have worked closely with the official state organs in the implementation of control policies in the Arab sector. The office of the Adviser to the Prime Minister on Arab Affairs operates a widespread network of informers in Arab towns and villages. The Adviser's office circulates up-to-date information concerning specific events and personalities to various administrative and political organs inside and outside the government.[10] Particularly important have been the Arab departments of the Histadrut and of the ruling political parties. By developing links with patriarchal leaders in every Arab village, by playing upon clan and religious rivalries, and by judiciously distributing and withholding favours, Jewish politics have bolstered traditional forces within Arab society, reinforced familial fragmentation in Arab communities, and secured enormous influence over day-to-day life in Arab areas.[11]

Also of interest on the programmatic level of analysis are the substantial efforts that have been devoted to preserving divisions and rivalries among Muslims, Druze and various Christian sects. Muslims, for example, are effectively barred from service in the armed forces (and thus from veteran status). Christians can volunteer for service. Druze are conscripted and serve in special units. Additional policies for the achievement and maintenance of control include the establishment of puppet parliamentary factions of Arab notables,[12] discrimination against Arab local councils regarding grants and loans for development,[13] the withholding of building permits and the demolition of illegally constructed houses as a means of pressure to sell land or accept compensation for expropriated land,[14] the blacklisting of educated Arab dissidents,[15] and the selective use of such coercive measures as arrests and deportations.[16]

The deliberate differentiation of three levels of analysis – structural, institutional and programmatic – is useful in a number of important ways and suggests itself as appropriate for the kind of sorting operation necessary in any study of control in deeply divided societies. Interaction between implemented policies (programmatic level) and institutional or structural conditions may be based on calculation *or* coincidence, but the maintenance of sharp distinctions between the kinds of factors involved, on different analytical levels, makes it less likely that hypotheses of comprehensive conspiracy involving the creation or 'arrangement' of structural and institutional circumstances will be embraced. In the Israeli case, the structural and institutional levels of analysis permit the exploitation of anthropological, economic, political and sociological studies of Israeli society which bear no direct relation to the problem of accounting for the effectiveness of Jewish control over Arabs. Studies, for example, comparing the increased vigour of Arab village *hamulas*, or clans, in Israel compared to their declining political role before 1948,[17] or research documenting trends in intra-hamula marriages, take on added significance when considered in conjunction with Jewish attempts to reward and support traditionalist elements in the Arab sector.[18] Analysis of major Israeli institutions as expressive of Zionist ideology and as loyal and effective instruments of the Zionist movement can be seen as directly relevant to an understanding of the economic and political vulnerability of those Israelis who, as Arabs, have no access to the resources which such institutions command.[19]

This multi-level approach also makes it possible to follow the advice of Manning Nash, an early student of political control in deeply divided societies. Based on his study of Guatemala's 'multiple society' in the mid-1950s, he counselled scholars to analyse, systematically and in detail, 'how the multiple society operates, the mechanisms of political control, and the social and cultural circumstances which are amenable to, or inimical to, the perpetuation and continuity of such a political structure'.[20] Indeed, as continued analysis of the Israeli case will show, the multi-level

approach presented here sensitises one not only to structural and institutional conditions which may conduce towards effective control but
also to those which militate against it by providing opportunities for
resistance or by constraining the direct employment of superordinate
group resources for purposes of inter-group control.

Still, for purposes of comparative research a multi-level analysis of
control is in itself insufficient. Lists of 'typical' structural, institutional
and programmatic 'mechanisms' of control are useful, but not much
more useful in comparing the achievement   and maintenance of control
in different societies than the lists of 'typical' control techniques provided by the plural society school.[21] The concepts of 'control' or 'domination' are too abstract to guide effectively the analysis of 'amenable'
or 'inimical' circumstances. Nor can they be used to differentiate among
policies which may be designed to achieve control in different ways by
exploiting different kinds of circumstances or only in combination with
one another. These problems can only be solved by subdividing the concept of control in a manner appropriate for the particular case at hand.

2. Three Components of Control

In Israel it is worth while to think of control over Arabs as *a system
made up of three components and the network of reinforcing relationships which obtains among patterns which can be traced within each
component on three levels of analysis.* Each component fulfills somewhat different functions, so that although separately no one component
results in control, operating in conjunction the three components form
a system which does. Figure 3.1 may serve as a helpful mnemonic.

Figure 3.1: The System of Control

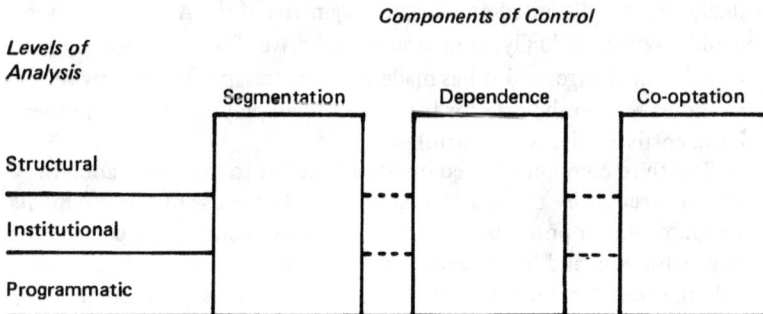

The three components are 'segmentation', 'dependence' and 'co-optation'. 'Segmentation' refers to the isolation of the Arab minority from the Jewish population and the Arab minority's internal fragment-ation. Understood as a component of a system, the 'function' of seg-mentation has been to deprive Arabs in Israel of facilities for united political action – whether involving alliances among Arabs on a country-wide basis or between groups of Arabs and politically significant groups of Jews. But segmentation does not imply the atomisation of the Arab population and thus it cannot ensure that relatively isolated groups of Arabs – Muslims, Bedouin tribes, large clans, churches or villages – will not act in sustained ways to sponsor political activities which the Jewish regime would find unpleasant. Nor can segmentation itself enable the regime to extract certain highly valued resources from the minority population, such as land, cheap and dependable labour and electoral support. Neither can segmentation provide the regime with a surveillance capacity over the Israeli Arab population with which to monitor develop-ments in the Arab sector and to notice if and how policies need to be adapted to changing circumstances at any given time and place. It is only in combination with the 'dependence' and 'co-optation' components that overall control over the Arab minority can be achieved.

'Dependence' refers to the reliance of Arabs on the Jewish majority for important economic and political resources. In terms of the 'function' which it has fulfilled as a component in the system of control it has meant, most importantly, that Arab Israelis have lacked autonomous bases of economic power – bases of power which could have been used to support dissident political parties or movements. It has also meant that Arabs have generally been extremely vulnerable to *non-coercive* forms of pressure and reprisal. Overall, 'dependence' has made it less likely that the disunited and isolated segments of the Arab population could, even individually, launch sustained drives for social, economic or political change, and it has made it less necessary than otherwise would have been the case for the regime to employ coercive and other more costly methods of control.

The third component – 'co-optation' – refers to the penetration of the Arab sector by the Jewish majority and to the use of side payments to Arab elites or potential elites for the achievement of this penetration.[22] 'Segmentation' and 'dependence', even in combination, could not pro-vide the Jewish authorities with effective access to Arab resources. Neither could these two components have provided a comprehensive sur-veillance capability – that continuing flow of information which has made it possible, at relatively low cost, to identify dissidents, to locate centres of authority within individual Arab villages or clans, and to monitor emotional, social and political trends within the Arab sector as a whole. To accomplish these tasks the Arab sector had to be penetrated. The 'function' of the co-optation component has been to serve as a non-coercive means of gaining access to members of the Arab minority, as a vehicle for their effective manipulation, and as a transmission belt for the extraction of Arab resources.

Keeping in mind the three levels of analysis described earlier, a discussion of these three components of control cannot be limited to consideration of how specific policies of the Jewish regime were designed to fragment the Arab minority, to isolate it from the Jewish majority, to make Arabs dependent on Jews, or to co-opt potential leaders of the Arab community. On the structural level those cultural habits, primordial identities, historical patterns of ecological and economic development, etc., which have contributed to making the Arab minority *susceptible* to control based on such techniques, have been of crucial importance. It is necessary as well to appreciate how the normal operation of Israel's major institutions has contributed to the isolation of the Arab minority, to its internal fragmentation, to its dependence on the Jewish majority, and to the co-optation of Arab elites. By describing the segmentation of the Arab minority, its dependence on the Jewish majority, and the co-optation of its potential leadership, the *effectiveness* of the system of control can be demonstrated. By describing the appropriate ways in which policies were designed and adapted to harness, exploit and reinforce convenient institutional and structural conditions and by discussing the mutually reinforcing relationships which exist among the components, the *low cost* of effective control is explained.

II. Control as a System

From an analytic standpoint the systemic character of control in Israel derives not only from mutually reinforcing relationships within each component among structural, institutional and programmatic factors but also from the synergistic relations that exist among the three components themselves. As has been emphasised, the three components of control, although they perform analytically discrete functions, do not operate independent of one another. The overall effectiveness of Israel's control of her Arab population and the low costs at which this control has been maintained have been due in large measure to the mutually reinforcing relations among them. For example, the institutional segmentation of Jews and Arabs has resulted in the channelling of nearly all national development funds into the economic development of the

Jewish sector. This has reinforced the structural underdevelopment of the Arab sector and increased Arab economic dependence on the Jewish community. In addition, the geographical and residential isolation of Arabs in Israel means that Arab workers are laid off first in a recession and rehired last after a business upturn. This is so because Arabs, in general, commute to work in Jewish cities while labour exchanges in those cities are required to give preference to local workers. The fragmentation of the Arab population, another aspect of the segmentation component, has also contributed to the economic dependence of the Arab sector. Since the Arab community possesses no country-wide financial institutions, the liquid capital which Arabs have accumulated is primarily deposited in Jewish-owned banks and used, ultimately, for investment projects in the Jewish sector.

Furthermore, the dependence of educated Israeli Arabs on Jewish-controlled white-collar jobs has made their co-optation relatively easy and inexpensive. If a substantial number of such positions were available in Arab-controlled institutions or companies, then, at the very least, the rewards offered to co-operative high school and university graduates would have to be greater, not only financially but socially and politically as well. The absence of autonomous centres of economic power in the Arab sector, combined with the physical and linguistic segregation of Arabs and Jews, has provided the regime with thousands of teaching positions in Arab villages which are ideal for purposes of co-opting young educated Arabs. For teachers in Arab primary, intermediate and secondary schools continue to reside in their villages and continue to live under the influence of clan elders and inter- and intra-clan politics. Extremely vulnerable to the retribution of politically victorious but hostile clans, they come to depend on the Ministry of Education and Culture, as well as on their own clans, to protect them and their salaries, promotions and benefits. Kept under close surveillance by school administrators and government informers, they know that the exhibition of 'extremist tendencies' will likely result in their dismissal.

But there are many ways, besides the concentration of educated Arabs in the teaching profession, in which 'dependence' reinforces 'co-optation'. The economic dependence of Arabs on Jewish agriculture and industry has encouraged Arab workers to remain loyal to their traditional kinship groups and to those patriarchal leaders most conveniently co-opted by the regime. At the same time, the desire of all Arab villagers for the introduction of various municipal services and other amenities found in Jewish localities has encouraged local leaders to look to the government for assistance in achieving these goals. The dependence of local leaders on connections with the Jewish authorities has been reinforced by the loss (mainly through expropriation) of agricultural land—i.e. that which traditionally constituted the economic foundation of the power and prestige of local Arab elites. Bereft of private economic security, and knowing that they are soon likely to be replaced by the representatives of rival clans, local council chairmen and deputy chairmen have typically exerted themselves while in office to establish connections in the Histadrut, the Labor Party, the office of the Adviser on Arab Affairs and various Ministries, so that when they leave office sinecures of some kind will be available for themselves and/ or for their sons.

Segmentation also reinforces co-optation. The fragmentation of Arab villages into fiercely competitive hamulas forces the leaders of each hamula to protect themselves from the ascendancy of their opponents by seeking support from the government.[23] Furthermore, the relative isolation of Israeli Arabs from the Jewish-Zionist political arena and the predominance (until 1977) of the Labor Party in almost all spheres pertaining to the life of the Arab minority has meant that, in general, competition among Jewish parties for the loyalty of Arab elites has not been particularly intense. In this context the rewards offered to Arab notables by the Labor Party to induce co-operation have remained minimal.[24]

Finally, co-optation itself has contributed to the continued dependence of the Arab minority on the Jewish sector as well as to the internal fragmentation of the Arab population. Having sought out and supported 'traditionalist' elements in Arab villages, the Jewish authorities have, in effect, helped to give power to those in the Arab community who are often least desirous of rapid social and economic development (including the introduction of co-operatives, the establishment of local industries, the consolidation of scattered parcels of agricultural land, the abolition of the bride price, etc.). Furthermore, regardless of how desirous of socio-economic change hamula leaders in particular villages may be, they are, as a group, in terms of their literacy rate, their understanding of the principles of modern management and accounting, and their command of other clerical and technical skills, particularly ill-equipped to perform the required tasks. The incompetence of traditional elites is one important reason why some government monies, officially budgeted for use by Arab villages, are sometimes left untouched at the end of the fiscal year. Many local Arab leaders have simply not mastered the techniques of applying for all the various loans available to them. Jewish officials are, indeed, quick to blame the incompetence of local Arab leaders, their traditionalist mores and their petty family quarrels for the slow pace of economic development in the Arab sector. What bears emphasis here is that it is precisely the policy of co-opting traditionalist elites which has been primarily responsible for the dominance of hamula leaders over local Arab politics.

The co-optation of rival local hamula leaders reinforces the fragmentation of the Arab population as well as its economic dependence. For their co-optation has given the regime valuable leverage in playing one clan off another and in creating, if and when it wishes, an atmosphere of intense suspicion and mistrust among rival kinship groups or local religious communities.

Multiple examples of how segmentation, dependence and co-optation can be seen to have reinforced one another on all three levels of analysis could be provided. The point, however, should not be clear. Deprived of facilities for united political action (segmentation), Israeli Arabs have found it difficult to protect their economic interests and to develop autonomous centres of economic power. Economically dependent, then, on the Jewish sector, Arab elites and potential elites have been relatively easy to co-opt. The access to the Arab population which co-optation has provided has, in turn, helped the regime to maintain the fragmentation of the Arab sector and exploit its economic dependence. The stability of the system of control over Israeli Arabs, as measured by uniformity of the regime's policy over time, the continued absence of mass-based Arab nationalist groups or political parties, and the insubstantial intrusion which the Arab minority problem has made on the Israeli political scene, has been due, then, not only to the multi-level patterns of segmentation, dependence and co-optation which I have discussed, but also to the synergistic relationships which have obtained among them.

III. Challenges to the System of Control

Having accounted for the effectiveness of the system of control as well as its low cost, questions nevertheless remain regarding the possibility that control over Arabs is weakening or that it will weaken substantially in the future. Indeed, there can be no doubt that the election of a Communist mayor of Nazareth in December 1975, the general strike called by the Communist Party on Land Day (30 March 1976) and the local riots and killings that ensued, the growing Arab vote for Rakah in recent Knesset and Histadrut elections, and the tensions generated on Israeli campuses by the presence of Arab students' organisations reflect a need for the regime to adapt its techniques to new circumstances if it is to maintain that level of control over the Arab minority to which it has become accustomed.

However, space does not permit a systematic evaluation of the performance of the system of control, the possibilities of breakdown or adaptive transformation, or the opportunities for effective resistance open to Arabs. Yet a conceptual scheme which discouraged a focus on such issues would certainly be less than satisfactory.

As an analytic construct, the system of control is not meant to comprehend all of Israeli social and political reality, most of which is substantially irrelevent to the control of Israeli Arabs. Yet there are aspects of that reality which have militated against co-optation, segmentation or dependence. These are structural or institutional circumstances which interfere with or contradict the dominant patterns and can be thought of as 'aberrations'.[25] As noted, weaknesses in the system of control have in recent years been signalled by relatively sustained and visible examples of Arab dissent, by the increased though still very limited use of coercion, by increased unfavourable international publicity concerning the treatment of Arabs in Israel, and by an increase in the amount of attention directed towards the minority problem in the media and by high-level decision-makers. These trends can be traced directly to specific 'aberrations'.

For example, the isolation of the Arab minority, one aspect of segmentation, has been far from total. On every working day tens of thousands of Arab villagers who commute to work in Jewish metropolitan areas are exposed to the opportunities, life-styles and attitudes prevailing in the Jewish sector. Inevitably, this has contributed to a breakdown in traditional mores and patterns of belief which have served as structural supports for co-optation and segmentation.

The link between Israeli Arabs and the Soviet Union, an alternative source of education, political status and economic rewards, which Rakah has constituted, represents an institutional aberration in regard to both segmentation and dependence. For example, for young Arabs who wish to break out of their dependence on the regime, Rakah has been able to offer scholarships to study medicine, engineering or journalism at universities in the Soviet Union and in Eastern Europe. Hundreds of Israeli Arabs, many of them the sons and daughters of the party faithful, have taken advantage of these opportunities.[26] Arab access (through Rakah) to resources independent of the Jewish sector is tolerated by the Jewish authorities primarily because of their unwillingness to sever Israel's remaining links with the Soviet Union and its large Jewish community. The growth of the Communist Party as a powerful proxy voice for Israeli Arabs and as a repository for protest Arab votes has been the result.

Another important institutional aberration is the existence of a 'civic realm', where *Israelis*, Arabs as well as Jews, share certain rights and privileges *qua* Israeli citizens. Regardless of how attenuated and how lacking in symbolic accoutrements, the existence of this 'civic realm' has meant universal adult suffrage in the Arab sector and the extension of modern educational norms into Arab villages. In educational terms this break in the pattern of the institutional isolation of Arabs has meant mandatory primary schooling for Arab boys and girls and the graduation of thousands of Israeli Arabs from high schools and colleges. The presence of intellectually articulate young men in villages, the limited introduction of coeducation in Arab school systems, and the generally high literacy rates in both Hebrew and Arabic among the Arabs of Israel have contributed to the gradual disintegration of the traditional social structure.

As power and influence in the Arab community continue to shift from patriarchal figures and sectarian leaders to larger numbers of younger educated men, co-optation as a strategy for gaining effective access to the Arab population becomes more expensive. For as power within the Arab community is diffused, the number of individuals whose co-operation the regime needs to induce in order to maintain the same level of control increases. Moreover, the types of rewards valued by educated elites—white-collar jobs, modern conveniences and status and influence in Israeli society at large—are more difficult to provide than the types of favours with which traditional elites have typically been satisfied.

As has been suggested, the Jewish authorities have exploited and reinforced prevailing patterns of religious fragmentation and rivalry among Israeli Arabs. But with higher levels of education and lengthy exposure to secularist attitudes such parochial attachments have faded substantially. The pattern of fragmentation that has characterised the Arab minority since 1948 has also been weakened by the gradual 'Palestinianisation' of Israeli Arabs. The emergence of 'Palestinian' as a strong overarching identity can be traced directly to the impact of Israel's ten-year occupation of the West Bank and Gaza Strip, and the consequent exposure of Israeli Arabs to a strongly nationalistic mass of Palestinian Arabs with whom they could easily empathise.

IV. Conclusion

Jewish officials with responsibility for the affairs of the Arab sector are now attempting to adapt policies to meet these 'challenges' to the system of control, i.e. the slow but steady erosion of traditional beliefs and patterns of social interaction, the crystallisation and growth of Rakah as a framework for the expression of Arab discontent and opposition to government policies, and the development among Israeli Arabs – Christians, Muslims and Druze – of a strong sense of themselves as Palestinians. Effective adaptation of the system of control, its break-down or its abandonment are all possible. All that is implied by the analysis presented here, however, is that as structural circumstances conducive to the techniques that have been used in the past change, the costs associated with operating a system of control based on those techniques will rise. But there is, in fact, every reason to believe that the regime will be ready, willing and able to pay those costs.[27]

For a basic transformation in Jewish-Arab relations in Israel would require a fundamental change in the very nature of the country – from a Zionist state endowed with a peculiarly Jewish historical mission to an ethnically neutral Middle Eastern state whose institutions were designed to serve the interests and aspirations of its citizens. The firm commit-ment of Jewish Israelis and their political leadership to the former con-ception of Israel was well illustrated by the unequivocal rejection of a proposal made in 1976 by a group of Arab mayors with close ties to the government. They urged that Israel think of itself, not as a Jewish state, but as a bi-national state within which Jewish and Arab communities would coexist on a basis of equality under the law, non-discriminatory access to the resources commanded by public institutions and cultural autonomy. An editorial in *Haaretz*, Israel's most prestigious newspaper, was typical of Jewish reaction.

> The structure that Israel has adopted and will not part with has to allow the Arab citizens wide possibilities so that they can go on living as Arabs in the state of the Jews . . . But as a basis for represent-ation we cannot accept anything else but the Arab individual [in con-trast to national group representation – author].
> We understand that this is not optimal from a national point of view. But the Arabs have to understand that this is the maximum they can expect as a minority . . . We do not ask from them any more than communist Rumania is asking from the Hungarian minority living there.[28]

Then Prime Minister Yitzhak Rabin utterly rejected the mayors' proposals, including the assumption that Arabs be assigned the status of a national group, by declaring once again that 'Israel is a Jewish-Zionist state in which a minority of Arabs live with religious and cultural distinctions.'[29]

If Israel has the means and the will to maintain control over the Arab population, still the costs of that control *are* likely to rise and the demands made upon the Israeli political system by the presence of an Arab minority are likely to increase. Recent population projections put the Arab population of Israel (excluding the occupied territories) at 23 per cent by 1990.[30] In addition the emergence of some sort of independent Palestinian entity on the West Bank and the Gaza Strip is, contrary to the beliefs of many leftist Israelis, likely to exacerbate rather than relieve tension between Jews and Arabs inside Israel.

It can be imagined, for example, that in five to ten years hundreds and thousands of middle-aged Arab schoolteachers in Israel would be considerably more discontented with their lot if, across the fields from their villages, there was a state where friends and relatives could aspire not only to skilled technical positions, directorships in banks, factories and commercial institutions, editorial positions with prominent newspapers, senior civil service posts, etc., but also to the highest military and political offices in the land. A recent poll showed that 60 per cent of Israeli Arabs would prefer Israel's borders to those established by the United Nations partition plan.[31] Keeping in mind that central Galilee, Wadi Ara and other areas stated to have become part of the Palestinian Arab state in 1947 are still overwhelmingly Arab, it is quite reasonable to expect that unsatisfied Israeli Arab demands for national self-expression would be translated into demands for local plebiscites on the question of secession. Such efforts would most probably elicit strong political and material support from the Palestinian state itself.

Regardless of whether the Communist Party, a breakaway faction of that party, or a new non-Communist Arab nationalist group spearheads such a drive, if a sustained mass-based Arab struggle for self-determination emerged, that would signal the failure of the system of control.[32]Unless the regime at that point were prepared to reconsider its basic objectives regarding the Arab minority, then radical and politically expensive measures, such as the reimposition of military government, the dispersion of Arabs from areas in Israel where they form a large majority, and selective deportations might well be undertaken. Thus the continued military occupation of the West Bank and the Gaza Strip, with or without the active co-operation of Jordan, plays an important role in preserving stable, low-cost and effective control over Arabs inside Israel.

Notes

1. This term is used by Eric Nordlinger in *Conflict Regulation in Deeply Divided Societies* (Harvard University Center for International Affairs, Occasional Paper no. 29), January 1972. For examples of and comments on the 'consociational' or 'accommodationist' approach see Arend Lijphart, *The Politics of Accommodation* (University of California Press, Berkeley, 1968); Kenneth McRae (ed.), *Consociational Democracy* (McClelland and Stewart, Ottawa, 1974); Donald Rothschild, 'Ethnicity and Conflict Resolution', *World Politics*, vol. XXII, no. 4 (July 1970); Hans Daalder, 'The Consociational Democracy Theme', *World Politics*, vol. XXVI, no. 4 (July 1974); and Brian Barry, 'Review Article: Political Accommodation and Consociational Democracy', *British Journal of Political Science*, vol. 5, Part 4 (October 1975).

2. Aside from Heribert Adam's *Modernising Racial Domination* (University of California Press, Berkeley, 1971), the 'control' or 'domination' approach to the explanation of political stability in segmented societies has attracted relatively little attention. For a critique of this literature see my paper '"Control" and the Explanation of Stability in Deeply Divided Societies: Reflections on Jewish-Arab Relations in Israel', delivered at the American Political Science Association convention in Washington, DC, 1 September 1977.

3. United Nations Special Committee on Palestine (UNSCOP), Report to the General Assembly, vol. I, p. 54. This percentage is based on the projected establishment of Jerusalem as a *'corpus separatum'*, and does not include an estimate of anticipated Jewish immigration.

4. For comparative analysis of Arab and Jewish economic development in Palestine before 1948 see P.J. Loftus, *National Income of Palestine, 1944* (Palestine, Government Printer, 1946), no. 5 of 1946.

5. For examples of candid statements by Israeli officials regarding the purpose of Israel's policies in the Arab sector see Yigal Allon, *A Curtain of Sand* (Hebrew) (Hakibbutz Hameuchad, Tel Aviv, 1959), pp. 328 and 331, and Shimon Peres, *Jerusalem Post*, 21 January 1962. See also a confidential memo prepared by the Interior Ministry's District Commissioner for the Galilee (where the bulk of Israeli Arabs live), Israel Koenig, 'Koenig Memorandum', *SWASIA* (weekly news digest), vol. III, no. 41 (15 October 1976).

6. Joseph Weitz, 'Land Ownership', in *Immigration and Settlement* (Keter Publishing House, Jerusalem, 1973), pp. 106-8; and Efraim Orni, *Agrarian Reform and Social Progress in Israel* (Ahva Cooperative Press, Jerusalem, 1972), pp. 32-3.

7. Concerning the operation of the military government from 1948 to 1966, see Sabri Jiryis, *The Arabs in Israel* (Monthly Review Press, New York, 1976), pp. 9-71. For a valuable report on interviews with officers of the military government see H. Baruch, 'Facing the 180,000: How the Military Government Rules', reprinted from *Davar*, in *Ner*, vol. X, nos. 3-4 (December 1958-January 1959).

8. Concerning the joint efforts of the Jewish National Fund, the Government of Israel, the Custodian of Absentee Property, and the Development Authority to transfer Arab land to Jewish ownership see Abraham Granott, *Agrarian Reform and the Record of Israel* (Eyre and Spottiswoode, London, 1956), pp. 102-6. See also Joseph Weitz, 'Land Ownership' in *Immigration and Settlement* (Keter Publishing House, Jerusalem, 1973), pp. 103-8; and Yitzhak Oded, 'Land Losses among

Israel's Arab Villagers', *New Outlook*, vol. VII, no. 7 (September 1964).

9. For an example of how this technique has been employed, see the description of the case of *Mahmoud Yunis v. Ministry of Finance*, as set forth in the *Jerusalem Post*, 16 March 1954. See also Yaacov Aviel, 'The Uprooted and the Abandoned', *Haaretz*, 7 January 1955; Yosef Alghazi, *Zoo Haderech*, 3 September 1975; and *Ner*, vol. XII, nos. 11-12 (July-August 1962), p. xxvi. The demonstrations held in the winter and spring of 1976, including the general strike declared by the Communist Party on 30 March, were triggered by fears that the closure, by the Army, of 'Area Nine' would lead eventually to the expropriation of Arab agricultural lands within it. See articles translated from the Hebrew press on this issue in *Israleft Bi-weekly News Service*, nos. 78, 79 and 81.

10. Personal interview with Shmuel Porath, Director of the Information Centre – Arab Branch, Prime Minister's Office, Jerusalem, 28 March 1974. In this connection, see S. Ginat in *Yamim ve Laylot, Maariv* supplement, 21 May 1976, p. 27.

11. For two in-depth accounts of the influence wielded by government and non-government agencies over the day-to-day affairs of Arab villages in Israel, see Subhi Abu-Ghosh, 'The Politics of an Arab Village in Israel', unpublished PhD dissertation, Political Science Department, Princeton University, 1965; and Abner Cohen, *Arab Border Villages in Israel: A Study of Continuity and Change in Social Organization* (Manchester University Press, Manchester, 1965).

12. Concerning the 'affiliated Arab lists' see Jacob Landau, *The Arabs in Israel* (Oxford University Press, London, 1969), especially pp. 38, 166, 195-8, and 243-5.

13. Concerning the contents of a government-sponsored but never released report regarding discrimination in this area, see *Zoo Haderech*, 13 September 1975.

14. See *Haaretz*, 26 February 1976, 14 February 1976, and especially *Zoo Haderech*, 13 September 1975.

15. See, for example, Eli Rekhess, *A Survey of Israeli-Arab Graduates from Institutions of Higher Learning in Israel (1961-1971)*, Shiloah Center (American Jewish Committee, Jerusalem, 1974), p. 31.

16. Fouzi El-Asmar, in *To Be an Arab in Israel* (Frances Pinter, London, 1975), gives details concerning his experiences as an administrative detainee.

In the last two years the use of strong police actions in Arab villages (Sakhnin, Arrabe, Baka-el-Gharbiyeh and Majd-el-Krum) as well as arrests of selected participants at Arab weddings for singing subversive songs have increased.

17. Cohen, *Arab Border Villages in Israel*, pp. 8-18 and 104-18; and Abu-Ghosh, 'The Politics of an Arab Village in Israel', pp. 85-90.

18. See Henry Rosenfeld, 'The Contradictions between Property, Kinship and Power, as Reflected in the Marriage System of an Arab Village' in J.G. Peristiany (ed.), *Contributions to Mediterranean Sociology* (Acts of the Mediterranean Sociological Conference, Athens, July 1963).

19. See, for example, Granott, *Agrarian Reform and the Record of Israel* (a study of the Jewish National Fund by one of its directors).

20. Quoted by M.G. Smith in 'Some Developments in the Analytic Framework of Pluralism' in Leo Kuper and M.G. Smith (eds.), *Pluralism in Africa* (University of California Press, Berkeley, 1971), p. 418.

21. For comments on the work of M.G. Smith and others in this regard see Ira Katznelson, 'Comparative Studies of Race and Ethnicity', *Comparative Politics*, vol. V, no. 1 (October 1972).

22. This use of the concept of 'co-optation' is very different from that made popular by Philip Selznick in *TVA and the Grass Roots* (Harper and Row, New York, 1966). For Selznick, 'co-optation' involves the absorption of new elements into decision-making processes as a method of stabilising an organisation. My

notion of 'co-optation' as a technique of manipulation based on 'side payments' or 'bribes' is closer to what Selznick refers to as 'formal co-optation' (p. 261).

23. At least up until the Likud victory in spring 1977, a typical Arab village election consisted of a fierce contest among anywhere from two to eight hamula lists, all supported by the Labor Party, one or two lists supported by the National Religious Party, a weak list of young 'reformists', and a Communist Party list. For highly interesting and detailed accounts of such elections see 'Elections for Eight Local Authorities in the Arab Sector in the Years 1971, 1972', Ministry of Interior, Arab Department, June 1972 (Hebrew).

24. The victory of Likud in the 1977 Knesset elections and continued Labor Party control of the Histadrut have created a new and interesting situation for enterprising Arab elites. In spite of Likud's hard-line approach to the Arab minority issue and in spite of the immediate swing of many co-opted Arabs into the Likud camp, opportunities may now exist for some local Arab elites to play the Labor Party and the Likud against one another. In the past the Labor Party and Likud have come to 'gentlemen's agreements' in response to such tactics.

25. A 'programmatic aberration' would be a policy which was inefficiently designed to exploit available structural and institutional conditions. Policy adaptation would be in order. For Yigal Allon's argument in favour of the abolition of the military government in the late 1950s on the basis that there were available more 'efficient' (*yaeel*) methods of control available see Allon, *Curtain of Sand*, p. 325ff.

26. Personal interviews with David Zechariah, Tel Aviv, 29 January 1974 (at that time director of the Arab Department of the Labor Party); with Ibrahim Bayadsi, Baka al-Gharbiyeh, 20 April 1974 (Communist Party representative in that village); and with Suleiman Mohammed Salim, Deir Hana, 1 March 1974. See Aliza Auerbach, 'Ibni the Doctor', *Jerusalem Post Weekly*, 20 January 1976; *Zoo Haderech*, 22 April 1976, p. 5; and Yair Kutler's interview with Rakah MK Tawfiq Tubi, reprinted in *SWASIA* (weekly news digest), 21 May 1976, p. 7.

27. For a detailed analysis of different proposals, generated within the Jewish establishment, for the adaptation of the system of control, see my contribution concerning Israeli Arabs in the anthology on ethnic politics: Ann Cottrell and Jeffrey Ross (eds.), *The Mobilization of Collective Identity: Comparative Perspectives* (University Press of America, Washington, DC, 1978).

28. *Haaretz*, 8 June 1976.

29. *Maariv*, 7 June 1976.

30. *Middle East International*, January 1977, no. 67, p. 24.

31. *Middle East International*, no. 76, October 1977, p. 22.

32. For an attempt by one Palestinian to provide a theoretical and ideological basis for such a struggle see Khalil Nakhleh, 'On "The Cure for Nazareth": A Reply,' *New Outlook*, vol. XIX, no. 2, (February-March 1976), pp. 62-3, and, by the same author, 'Cultural Determinants of Palestinian Collective Identity: The Case of the Arabs in Israel', *New Outlook*, vol. XVIII, no. 7 (October-November 1975), pp. 31-40.

For an argument against the establishment of a Palestinian state precisely because such a struggle by Israeli Arabs might be triggered see Moshe Moaz, 'The "Moderation" of the PLO and Israeli Policies', *Maariv*, 12 December 1975. Moaz is the Director of the Afro-Asian Studies Center at the Hebrew University in Jerusalem.

4 THE PALESTINIANS IN THE WEST BANK AND GAZA: THE SOCIOLOGY OF DEPENDENCY*

Salim Tamari

The first decade of Israeli dominance in the West Bank and the Gaza Strip may prove to be crucial in shaping patterns of change in the character of the two regions for many years to come. So far, however, both the political dispute over the future of the territories and the nature of the potential settlement of that dispute, highlighted by the Egyptian-Israeli negotiations in the beginning of 1978, have been the main focus of discussion about the areas. Less well known have been changes which were brought about by the regions' *de facto* integration into the Israeli social structure—a process which seems to have transformed not only the basic pattern of Palestinian social organisation and the consciousness of the subject population but that of Israeli society as well.

The relationship of the Israeli state to its 1967 colonial acquisitions raises many challenges to the current state of development theory. The relatively small size of the regions occupied, and their geographic proximity to the controlling power, compel us to re-examine in a new light the relevance of such concepts as neo-colonial domination (metropole-satellite relationship and peasant proletarianisation). Furthermore, the hegemony of Labor Zionism in Israel until the sixties must now be re-assessed in the context of a new reversed relationship between Jewish industries and Arab labour in Gaza and the West Bank.

I. The Demographic-Territorial Dilemma in Israeli Policies

Israeli policies towards the 'administered territories', as they are referred to in official statements, have been from the beginning of the occupation the subject of controversy between contending factions within Labor Zionism, and—with the coming of the Likud into power—between those who favour a territorial settlement and those who oppose it. It seems, however, that regardless of the political settlement that might be arrived at, the government was determined to hasten the process of

*This is a shortened and modified version of a paper presented at the tenth annual conference of the Association of Arab-American University Graduates in Detroit on 21 October 1977. I wish to thank Teodor Shanin, Kenneth Brown, Judy Blanc and Elfi Nunn for their critical comments on the earlier draft.

merging the Palestinian communities within the boundaries of pre-1967 Israel. If territorial concessions have to be made, then there will be an existing single socio-economic entity which is becoming increasingly difficult to divide. This conception is confirmed in a 1970 Ministry of the Interior publication, titled *Guidelines for Regional and Physical Planning.* In it the plan suggested for the West Bank emphasised

> the settlement of the unpopulated Jordan valley and Dead Sea area and making it arable, the expansion of agriculture wherever possible, the utilization of available water resources, the clearance of slums and refugee camps, the development of the economic rural functions of the bigger villages, . . . the development of the periphery of Samaria and Judea so that it may become integrated with the rest of the country.[1]

Politically these objectives were translated into a policy of 'creeping annexation' guided by the thinking of Moshe Dayan and his supporters under the Rabin government. This policy was based on a three-pronged approach: (1) the transfer of administrative power and social services to local Palestinian institutions (municipal and village councils, and the various bureaus of the Jordanian administration in the West Bank), so that Israeli rule can be 'felt but not seen'; (2) the absorption of the surplus labour force into Israeli employment and the gradual elimination of refugee camps with the aid of the local authorities; (3) the mainten- ance of the 'open bridges' policy with Jordan to facilitate the exchange of goods and population contacts between the occupied territories — and implicitly Israel — and the Arab world.[2]

The main opposition to this policy of integration came in the early seventies from the 'doves' within the Labor Party, and from Mapam. Both found a spokesman for their fears of 'demographic encirclement' in Pinhas Sapir, the then Minister of Finance, and ultimately expressed this fear concretely in the Allon Plan, which proposed a territorial div- ision of the West Bank between Jordan and Israel. Sapir argued, quite effectively for a period, that the presence of over a million Palestinians within the boundaries of Israel would dilute the Jewish character of the state, and — given the substantially higher birth rate in the Arab family — would eventually threaten the ability of its institutions to govern effectively. However, both the desire to keep the occupied territories and the needs of Israeli capitalism for Arab labour decided the issue in favour of the integrationists. The argument of the opposition was taken into account by Dayan's suggestion that the areas be incorporated into

Israel without the extension of Israeli rule over them. After the 1973
October War this proposal came to be known as the functional division
(as opposed to the territorial division) of the territories, by means of
which Israel would maintain sovereignty over the two regions, ostensibly
for security reasons, while Jordan would regain its administrative role
of the pre-war period. The employment of Palestinian workers in Israel
and the extension of the areas' market for Israeli commodities to the
rest of the Arab world were seen, in Israeli eyes, as the cementing bond
of an eventual settlement.

Begin's 26-point plan concerning the future of the West Bank and
Gaza, which was submitted in January 1978 to the Israeli Knesset,
attests to the final recognition of the notion of functional division, and
to the incorporation of Dayan's proposals into official policy (see
especially items 17, 22 and 24 regulating the relationship of Gazans
and West Bankers to the Jordanian regime).[3]

Simultaneously, an extensive settlement policy was being implemented to forestall the consequences of Israel's having to withdraw
from the occupied territories in the eventuality of a settlement. Under
the Labor government the declared purpose of these Jewish settlements
was defensive; that was the explanation given for the concentration of
colonies along the Golan Heights, the Jordan Valley, the Rafah approaches, and even in the Latrun area. The exceptions to this policy were to be
found in Jerusalem, where Judaisation was openly admitted, and in a
few formerly Jewish settlements (such as Kfar Etzion, and Kiryat Arba'
near Hebron) in which the government submitted to religious-nationalist
sentiments. By 1977, approximately 80 Jewish settlements (26 in the
Golan, 22 in Gaza and Sinai, and 32 in the West Bank—excluding the
suburban settlements around Arab Jerusalem) were already established.[4]

When the Likudists came to power in May 1977, the issue of settlements was primary in their programme. The Allon Plan (which envisaged
a territorial settlement with Jordan by which most of the West Bank,
minus a strategic belt along the Ghor, would return to Jordan) was
scrapped,[5] and the Sharon Plan was adopted. The latter was a comprehensive scheme of re-zoning the occupied territories for civilian Jewish settlement. It aimed at the encirclement of the Arab population in
the West Bank by civilian-military settlements along its four boundaries,
but especially along the Jordan Valley. In its second phase the plan
envisaged the segmentation of centres of Arab demographic concentration
in the West Bank with a gridlike network of interlinked Jewish colonies
(see Chart 3).[6]

The core of the plan is based on the establishment of five large urban

Chart 3: Sharon Plan: Phase Two

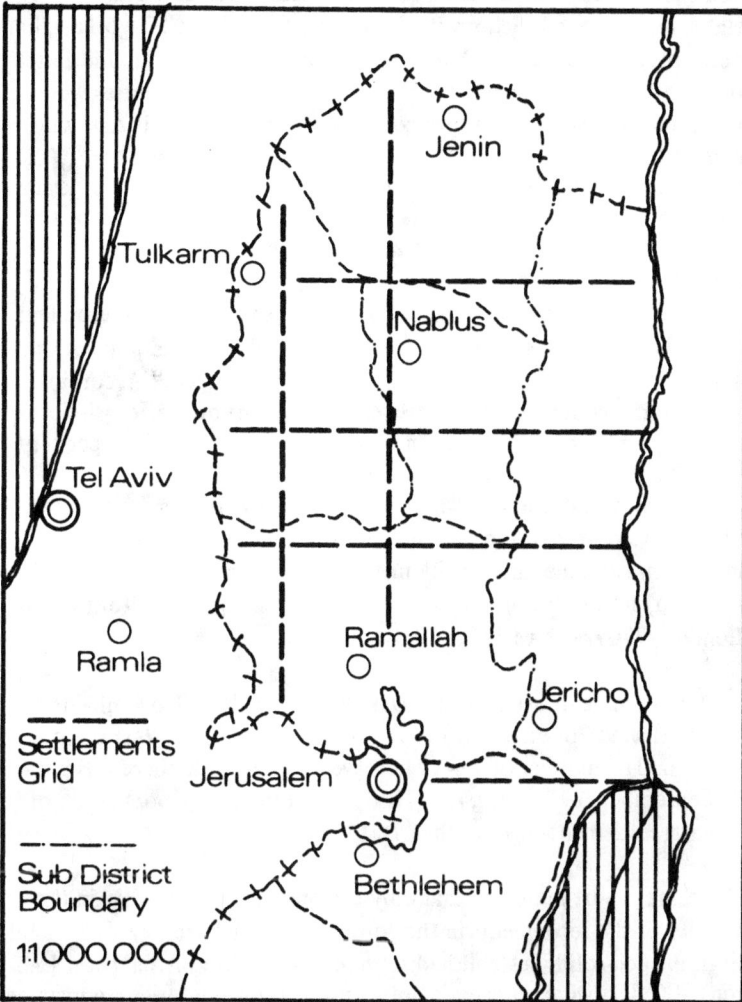

Source: *Shu'un Filastinyya*, 71 (October 1977), p. 229 (adapted).

centres in the West Bank (near the present areas of at-Taybeh, Mashah,
Beit Sira, Givan and Teqoa) by 1980. The several industrial plants which
had been already established under the Rabin government in Ma'ale,
Ha' Adumin, near Jericho, with each employing about 50 workers, had
been integrated with the Sharon plan to diversify the economic activity
of the settlements.[7] In most cases, however, the urban centres were
intended to serve as dormitory communities for Jewish citizens who will
commute daily to their work in the Israeli sector.[8]

The Sharon plan envisages 2,000,000 settlers in the West Bank alone,
with a proposed 150,000 settlers designated for the five urban centres
named above. Behind the hectic zeal for 'redeeming the land' lies the
decline in the proportion of the Jewish population in several areas of
settlement priority, most notable in the Galilee and greater Jerusalem.
In Galilee, Jews constitute today 52 per cent of the total population,
and in some sub-districts Arab majorities have emerged.[9] According to
a Ministerial committee for Jerusalem, the weight of the Jewish population in the city declined from 74 per cent in 1968 to 72.6 per cent
in 1975.[10]

The chief obstacle to Jewish colonisation efforts, besides the scarcity
of water resources of the Judean Hills, remains the problem of inducing
immigrants and members of Zionist settler movements (such as Gush
Emunim) to move to new settlements in the occupied territories. The
London *Observer* revealed recently that

> in the ten years after the Six Day War, the Labour Government
> established 76 settlements in the Golan Heights, the West Bank and
> Sinai. The number of Jews who have gone to settle there was put (in
> September, 1977) at 6,400. This means the average population of
> each settlement is fewer than 100.[11]

The same report indicated that only the presence of the army in the
vicinity of the settlements in the Jordan Valley has secured their viability.
Even in such solidly established settlements as Kiryat Arba' (near Hebron) 400 flats were reported empty, and 'the new factories are manned
by Arab workers'.[12] More recently, when Ariel Sharon, now Minister
of Agriculture, was urging for the construction of new settlements in
the wake of Sadat's visit to Israel, Gush Emunim were compelled to
admit — in a rare moment of public disclosure — that 'if the Government
wanted new settlements in the West Bank, the Government would have
to find the people to populate them!'[13]

The issue of colonial settlement in the occupied territories has been, so far, the most explosive aspect of the Palestinian-Israeli conflict, both from the perspective of territorial Zionism and in its association with the imagery of Palestinian dispossession. However, as a prelude to our discussion of economic dependency in the occupied areas, Jewish settlements have had a marginal impact on structural change for two reasons. First, with the exception of Kiryat Arba' and the Rafah settlements, these colonies have not been involved in the exploitation of Arab labour; their emphasis on the employment of Jews exclusively represents a belated attempt at reviving the notion of Hebrew labour, which—for all practical purposes—has now been abandoned in Israel. Second, because the settlements, as we have seen, are facing a serious crisis of viability, in terms of physical survival. Only if a sudden stimulant emerges among the Jewish population to move into those settlements, coupled with massive government investments and incentives for immigration, is this crisis likely to be overcome. Thus, if we are looking for the mechanism of current Israeli control over the territories, we should look elsewhere.

II. The Framework of Dependency: Arab Workers and Israeli Commodities

The most salient feature of the structural integration of the occupied territories into the Israeli economy has been on the one hand, the employment of almost half of the total Palestinian work-force (about 80,000 workers) in Israel, and on the other, the emergence of the two Palestinian regions as the main market for the 'export' of its commodities (after the United States).

The outcome of this economic integration has been interpreted differently, depending on the theoretical perspective utilised. One Israeli writer refers to the 'tremendous progress' made by the Palestinians under Israeli tutelage, especially in the agricultural sector. 'The West Bank', notes this economist,

> has been unique among developing areas in that rapid agricultural progress has not been accompanied by the emergence of a surplus rural population—in spite of lagging urban development—but by the eradication of unemployment (due to mass work opportunities offered by the Israeli economy).[14]

Using a more cautious tone, Arie Bregman, from the Bank of Israel, lists some of the major consequences of 'the creation of a common market between two economies complementary as regards their factors

of production and their structure'. Those include: an 11 per cent rise
in real consumption *per capita* (for the initial period of 1968-73), 20
per cent gross private savings (of disposable income as compared with
less than 10 per cent before 1968), 6 per cent annual increase in employment leading to a negligible rate of unemployment by 1973 (compared
with approximately 13 per cent unemployment under the Jordanian
administration), and an annual increase of daily wages by about 15 per
cent. However, despite the substantial savings and the increase in
labour productivity, there was no noticeable increase in capital stock,
investments or changes in the institutional infrastructure of the economy in the occupied territories.[15]

Bregman's optimism about the stimulating impact effected by the
Israeli economy was qualified in a follow-up study which took into
account the results of the 1975 recession in Israel.[16] GNP growth now
stood at the rate of 8 per cent increase annually (for 1974-5) compared
with 17 per cent for the 1969-73 period. Special emphasis was now
placed on the cyclical and unirrigated nature of West Bank agriculture
to explain the substantial decline in 1975 output, and the related 7 per
cent decline in industrial production.[17]

This, generally positive, assessment of the impact of Israeli occupation
on the Palestinian economy is not confined to the accounts of Israeli
economists and social scientists such as Ater, Bregman, Zarhi and Weigert.
In her study of the 'viability' of the West Bank as an economic entity,
Vivian Bull, an American economist, describes patterns of growth similar
to those claimed by Bregman, although her political conclusions would
probably differ from his.[18] The author is particularly impressed with
achievements in the agricultural field, where she sees Israel's role as

> emphasizing productivity increases, creating non-agricultural job
> opportunities, using the underemployed or unemployed rural labor
> force in local projects, encouraging capital investment where the
> marginal productivity of capital is greatest, and emphasizing the
> returns which can be generated from crops rather than being con-
> cerned with institutional arrangements.[19]

Moreover, similar achievements, albeit on a lesser scale, are noted in
the industrial sector,[20] the technical infrastructure (roads, communication, extension of the electrical grid, etc.),[21] and in the training of
the labour force.[22] The main economic obstacle to the continuation
of this positive development is seen in the limitations of the 'available
market for both agricultural and industrial commodities' produced

locally.[23] Another British economist, writing two years later, shares Bull's estimates of improvements in the standard of living, but not in the other sectors of the economy.[24]

The divergent conceptual categories used by dependency theorists, however, produce a radically different view of economic changes in the occupied territories. Jamil Hilal, for instance, in a comprehensive survey of the West Bank under Jordanian and Israeli rule, found that the chief dislocating impact of Israel on the territories was its regressive effect on industrial and agricultural productivity, and the active promotion of the service sector at the expense of those vital sectors of the economy.[25] Israeli official data are used to indicate a decline in the contribution of the agricultural sector (from 34.9 to 28.4 per cent for the 1968-72 period), and the manufacturing sector (from 7.9 to 6.2 per cent) to the two regions' GNP.[26]

Unequal exchange in terms of trade, direct exploitation of Palestinian cheap labour, and the dislocation and subordination of the Palestinian pre-capitalist economy to the needs of the advanced Israeli economy are the mechanisms by which surplus is transferred from the occupied territories to Israeli capitalism. Unequal exchange is demonstrated in that 'while the West Bank and Gaza exported to Israel agricultural products and labour-intensive agricultural products, they imported from Israel capital-intensive industrial products.'[27] Although 90 per cent of their total imports came from Israel, the two regions exported only 2 per cent of their products to Israel. Hilal calculated a trade surplus of 2,155 million Israeli pounds (I£) (around US $513m) in favour of Israel during the first seven years of occupation alone.[28]

The transfer of surplus through direct exploitation is seen as working on two levels: the benefits accruing from the employment of cheap Palestinian labour, and returns from direct investments in the territories, especially from subcontracting firms dealing in textiles and construction material (tiles, stone-cutting, etc.). One area of obvious manipulation involves deductions for social service taxes from the income of West Bank and Gaza workers in Israel, without the provision of these services (except for workers residing in the greater Jerusalem area which is officially under Israeli jurisdiction). But more important is the wage differential between Palestinian and Israeli workers — only part of which is accounted for by differences in training and productivity. In 1975 the average monthly wage for Israeli employees was I£2,466, compared to I£1,085 for Palestinian[29] employees. A critical Israeli report found that the utilisation of cheaper labour in the territories yielded a net benefit of I£615m in 1974 alone.[30] Figures on returns from Israeli investments in the territories are not readily available, but Van Arkadie mentions clothing firms (which are largely controlled by Israeli capital) as having one of the highest growth rates in industry (30 per cent annually).[31]

The major dislocating impact of economic annexation has been inflicted on the indigenous organisation of production, both in its precapitalist forms (peasant society and urban craft) and in the nascent capitalist sector (containment of manufacturing). As a result of the internal migration of small farmers seeking employment in wage labour, we observe an increase in the total area of neglected farmland (from 238,000 dunums in 1968-9 to 354,000 in 1969-70).[32] In many instances the Israeli government established customs regulations to prevent the entry of perishable food items (dates and fish from Gaza, grapes from Hebron, for example) to the Israeli market,[33] without establishing similar tariffs to protect West Bank and Gaza farmers from the considerably more powerful competition of Israeli crops.

Along the same lines, stagnation in the industrial sector has been measured by the declining rate of employment in indigenous manufacturing (from 10,800 employees in 1969 to 9,350 in 1973)[34] without any noticeable increase in productivity or investments in capital goods.[35] However, there is a dispute as to whether this stagnation is also true of the agricultural sector; Israeli official statistics provide data for crop production in money terms, very rarely in terms of actual output.[36] When Hilal talks of stagnation in agriculture, he refers to the decline of total agricultural employment and its stationary share in the GNP.[37] However, unlike the manufacturing sector, these indices are not very meaningful for a sector that is plagued by seasonal fluctuations. Altogether it seems that the major weakness of these discussions on Palestinian agriculture has been the failure to analyse adequately the internal dynamics and processes of the agrarian system and to investigate the differential impact of Israeli technology and marketing procedure on the various strata of Palestinian farmers.

The proletarianisation of Palestinian peasants and refugees, although measurable in terms of the extent of wage labour proliferation, has been one of the least understood aspects of social change under Israeli occupation. Rosenfeld, one of the very few Israelis who has done a systematic study of this process, found that one of the essential features of pre-1948 proletarianisation among Palestinian peasants was that it was accomplished without any significant urbanisation, so that the peasant-worker remained — and, in terms of wages and general attitudes— was treated as a casual labourer 'who had a pipeline to a village storehouse'; that is, he had one foot in subsistence farming.[38] Nor, he asserts, did the increased entry of the peasant into the wage-labour market have any adverse effect on agricultural productivity, due to the presence of non-productive surplus labour in rural society.[39] Zureik, dealing with the post-state period, maintains that this transformation is the most significant single change brought about by the impact of the Israeli economy. Palestinian peasantry are seen as having undergone 'marginal proletarianization' with two socio-economic consequences: the uprootedness of Palestinians from traditional village life by the necessity of having to seek employment in Jewish urban centres, and the transformation of the Arab village into a stagnant non-productive unit.[40]

So far, this process of proletarianisation is only in its beginning. As we shall see, it is lacking in the possibilities of trade-union organisation to enhance the peasant-turned-worker's bargaining position (*v.* his Jewish co-workers, and Arab and Jewish employers), and limited in terms of upward occupational mobility. Furthermore, proletarianisation has been determined by the imponderables of external demands for temporary labour, accentuating the instability of the Palestinian peasant as a member of a *farming* community, while negating his self-conception as a worker.[41] One important result has been to provide Israeli industries with cheap labour-power in times of industrial expansion. This boosted the competitive potential of Israeli capitalism in the European and American markets, without threatening the employment opportunities of Jewish workers since Palestinians occupied low and unskilled positions deemed undesirable by Jewish workers. This stable situation prevailed as long as expansionist trends in the Israeli economy, triggered by the 1967 War, continued. Simultaneously, Arab industries stagnated; they were unable to compete, or to pay wages equivalent to those paid by Jewish employers, low as they were. Their only chance of survival was in technological improvement and the introduction of labour-substituting machinery, but given their low capital stock and the prevailing insecurity, this chance was more than remote.

III. A New Stage in Israeli Colonialism?

It has often been suggested in the literature of the Arab-Israeli conflict that the process of Jewish colonisation in Palestine, in its broad thrust and objectives, had a fixed character, namely that the Jewish impacts on Palestinian society can be reduced to the question of displacement of peasants from their land, and their transformation into a sub-proletariat. This process of displacement has been regarded as a central point differentiating Israeli colonialism from the colonialism of European

countries of the old world, which have sought by various means to
exploit the resources and populations of the subject territories rather
than to destroy them. Thus Nathan Weinstock characterises Jewish
settlement prior to the 1948 War in the following manner:

> Zionist colonization, while unquestionably exerting a favorable effect
> on the standards of cultivation and health in the country, built a new
> society in which Hebrew capitalists exploited a Hebrew proletariat
> by implementing specific segregationist principles – at the expense of
> the Palestinians. This aspect of Zionist ideology precluded it from
> fulfilling the historically progressive function of colonialism – the
> generalization of the capitalist mode of production. Nor were the
> victims of the Zionist enterprise able to lead a consequent struggle
> for self-determination, since the underlying principles of Jewish col-
> onization led to the distortion of the Palestinian social structure and
> the obstruction of the development of the Palestinian bourgeoisie
> and the working class.[42]

The danger with this kind of analysis (though perhaps Weinstock himself may have managed to avoid it) is that it over-rates Israeli exception-
alism. That is, it extends what may have been true of one epoch of Jewish settlement in Palestine to succeeding periods. The analysis, further,
treats Palestinians as the constant *objects* of a process in which they
were mere instruments of a cruel fate. When they react, they do so either
in a heroic manner (resistance), or as helpless victims (refugees). There
is very little that Palestinians seem to engage themselves in besides these
two dramatic modes. Finally, the analysis ignores limits that are objectively inherent in the Zionist enterprise. These limits are related to the
discrepancy between the early ideals of the (Labor) Zionist movement
and its capacity to accommodate a radically transformed Jewish society
which has increasingly come to resemble the social structure of advanced
capitalist societies.

Thus the unique 'displacing' feature of Jewish colonisation in Palestine before the establishment of the state of Israel, which continued
in good measure during the fifties and sixties (e.g. land confiscation and
the prevention of already dispossessed refugees from returning to their
land), has taken a dramatic turn three decades later. Today the settlement policy of the Likud occurs in a radically different context, though
the intentions may have remained the same. Following the 1967 War
and physical incorporation of the remaining part of Palestine with half
of its total population within the boundaries of the Israeli state, object-

ive needs to expand the economy led to the abandonment of the ideology of Hebrew labour, both in theory and practice. In this process, both the Palestinian 'colonial' and the Israeli dominant class structures were transformed.

In the West Bank and Gaza the coming of Israeli rule was superimposed over a complex social structure which was shaped as much by the heritage of the Jordanian (and Egyptian) administrations (1948-67) as it was by the influx of dispossessed peasants and urban refugees during the war. While the prevailing view of stagnation and regional discrimination under those regimes is basically correct, it nevertheless disguises a substantial amount of differentiation and mobility that was taking place during the same period. The main factors which accounted for this mobility—especially in the case of the West Bank—were the state sector (the army, the civil service and the school system) and the high rate of out-migration; the latter contributing significantly to changes in rural class patterns as a result of stipends sent from abroad and investments in construction and machinery by returning migrants.[43]

Given the increased demand for a variety of trained personnel in the oil-producing Arab states, and the relative decline in land possession as a source of wealth, these two channels of occupational mobility (the state sector and the educational system) enhanced the position of the professional, and—to the less fortunate masses of its caricature: the clerk. In contrast to the situation of Palestinians who remained in Israel, where a vigorous capitalist economy had turned the majority of the labour force into potential wage-workers, there was a widespread attitude of contempt towards manual labour in the West Bank and Gaza. This attitude was partly a consequence of the overall stagnation in the economy, characterised by the marginality of the manufacturing sector and the absence of any major trends towards rationalisation or capitalism in agriculture. But it was also a cultural expression of the mannerisms of the old Palestinian elite diffused to the wider public. Only the presence of masses of refugees in the main urban centres (60 per cent of the total in Gaza, 20 per cent in the West Bank) produced a significant shift in the class structure from the one prevailing before 1948.

In contrast, Israeli society—up to the sixties—provided a model of rapid economic growth and modernisation based on the *importation* of European skilled immigrants, the mechanisation of agriculture, the development of industries generated with the help of foreign capital and the exclusion—or near exclusion—of the indigenous (Palestinian) population from this process. With the 1967 occupation—or to be more precise, with the integration of the Arab labour force within Israel in the early sixties—a new pattern of growth replaced the previous one. A new tendency now began to absorb Palestinian productive apparatus in a manner which seems functionally fixed for both the dominant and dominated society.

This process had the further consequence of stimulating upward occupational mobility for certain sections of the Jewish labour force[44] and the release of another substantial segment of the population for military mobilisation. The increased integration and fixity in the pattern of interaction between the two societies seem to have resisted both the recession of 1975 in the Israeli economy and the counter-demand for labour brought about by the construction and industrial boom in neighbouring Jordan. This is confirmed in a recent study by the Bank of Israel:

> In 1975, 83 percent of the [occupied] areas' total trade (export and import) was with Israel, compared with 73 percent in 1972 and 66 percent in 1968, when this common market came into being. The uptrend was sustained alongside a notable expansion of exports via the Jordan bridges from both the West Bank and Gaza (citrus) to Jordan, other Arab countries, and recently Iran.[45]

This trend was further reinforced by a more stable pattern of employment. Thus 75 per cent of the Palestinian labour force was reported as being employed for more than two years in Israel, and one-third for more than four years.[46] Altogether, however, this period is too short for a reliable projection of future trends.

So far the functional integration of the two ethnic national societies suggests a picture that is not dissimilar to the relationship between a metropolitan economy and its colonial satellite. We have emphasised changes in the Palestinian economy (labour organisation and the commodity market) which are oriented towards dependency on and supplement to the needs of Israeli capital. Our observations of structural transformations *internal* to Palestinian society are restricted by the amount of empirical data available. They are even more restricted due to the rapidly changing pattern of association with Israel, where political factors play a significant, if not decisive, role. However, it is possible to point out three factors which define and delimit the extent of potential structural change within the occupied territories. These are: (1) the limited capacity of the agrarian system to absorb labour; (2) the presence of a substantial unproductive (refugee) population in the urban centres; and (3) the absence of an infrastructure within the occupied territories which prevents the accommodation of the surplus labour generated by the traditional agricultural system and the refugee population. These elements combined explain the massive response by Palestinian workers to Israeli demand, coupled with the sudden restrictions on their movement to the Arab states.

The limited absorptive capacity of the land is related to the seasonal character of agriculture (especially the prevalence of olive crops), and to the fragmentation of land, to the point of inefficient plot size, as a result of the inheritance system. It is also related to ecological conditions of the terrain which, apart from citriculture in the Gaza district and the Jordan Valley, and certain areas of grain farming in the northern districts, have not been conducive to mechanisation or capitalisation in agriculture. Similar constraints have been observed among the Arab population of Israel (in the Galilee),[47] but we should keep in mind also factors of divergence between the two Palestinian communities. Among those factors are: (1) the role of emigration as a source of income and class differentiation of West Bankers and, to a lesser extent, Gazans; (2) the possibility of seeking short-term employment, partnerships and commercial contacts in neighbouring Arab states – not available to Israeli Arabs; and (3) divergence in the class composition due to the presence of a higher proportion of professionals and semi-professionals (as well as urban refugees) among West Banker/Gazans than among Israeli Arabs. Among the latter, the predominance of wage labour in general and of the working class in particular is more pronounced, both quantitatively and in organisational ability. In the final analysis, however, there are important contrasts in the internal social structure *between* the West Bank and Gaza, in addition to homogenising tendencies resulting from the increased integration with the Israeli economy. The longer Israeli occupation continues, the stronger we should expect these tendencies towards homogenisation to become.

The crucial factors as far as the structural transformation of the occupied regions is concerned, therefore, are the continued dependency of *one-half* of all wage earners in the population on employment in Israel, bringing home with them a sizeable proportion of the regions' income (about 30 per cent of the GNP), *and* the inability of local enterprises to create alternative employment opportunities for them.

Nevertheless, in both the West Bank and Gaza a significant amount of wealth was accumulated during the years of occupation from subcontracting, labour contracting, trade with Jordan and other business activities.[48] Investment, however, has been most noticeable in non-productive activities (see Table 4.1).

Table 4.1:   Gross Investment in the West Bank and Gaza, 1968-75
(I£ millions at 1974 prices)

	1968-9	1973	1974	1975
Public sector investments	75	116	123	159
Private sector investments of	85	395	484	510
which: construction	53	280	354	392
transport vehicles	32	115	130	121
Total gross investments (after changes in inventory)	173	455	733	588

Source: Israel Central Bureau of Statistics/Bregman Table II-5, p. 20 (partial).
The Bank of Israel provides separate figures for Gaza and the West Bank,
which are collapsed here. No change of inventory is given for Gaza
between 1973 and 1975.

Thus construction has accounted for about 70 per cent of all private
investment throughout the period 1968-75; the purchase of commercial
vehicles (for the transport of workers?) adds up to a substantial share
of the remaining investment. A negligible amount was invested in manufacturing. Furthermore, there are indications that hoarding is widespread, especially among peasants.[49] Not all the blame for this imbalance
in the allocation of wealth can be attributed to the heritage of the regional discriminatory policies under Jordanian rule. A major cause is the
immense competition the Palestinian investor would have to face from
Israeli production and actual administrative restrictions which prevent
the entry of certain West Bank and Gaza products to Israel, especially
in agriculture. The following excerpt from an Israeli report is indicative:

> The dates grown in Dir el Baleh in the Gaza Strip and in El Arish in
> Sinai . . . which support hundreds of families as basic income are
> perishable goods not suited for storage. At the height of the harvest
> of about 2000 tons a year, the growers receive a low price of 20 to
> 30 agorot a kilogram (retail dates average about 50 times that much
> in the Tel Aviv market). In contrast, there is a large population in
> Israel which loves the fruit but cannot buy it because of high price,
> a result of preventing selling Gaza and Sinai dates.[50]

Tariff barriers, competition and political uncertainty thus contribute
decisively to the curtailment of local investment activity. We should
not underestimate, however, the inability of the Palestinian bourgeoisie
in the West Bank to absorb a significant number of Arab workers in
local enterprises. This failure is rooted in its historical character as a

landlord-mercantile class which, when defeated as a dominant stratum in pre-1948 Palestine, turned to real estate speculation (in Lebanon, Jordan and the West Bank) and to professional occupations and safe careers in public institutions for its sons. Among a small number of more enterprising individuals, members of a newly established stratum of professionals and returning emigrants, we see a tendency to invest in light industries (pharmaceuticals, plastics and textiles). Furthermore, some of the traditional industries which flourished in the thirties and forties continue to operate under the patronage of their original founders (e.g. soap in Nablus, wood engraving in Bethlehem and glass in Hebron).

New employment opportunities became available in the occupied territories in a few exceptional situations after the 1973 October War, but it is unjustifiable to regard these opportunities as counter-trends because of the limited period in which they have appeared. After the 1975 recession, for example, there was an absolute decline in the number of workers from the two regions employed in Israel. In Gaza, seasonal agricultural workers (employed mostly in citrus picking and packing) were replaced by Israeli workers (and possibly by volunteer workers from Europe), and a portion of them managed to find employment at home.[51] Similarly, construction workers from the West Bank, made redundant in Israel, were partly absorbed by the increase in local construction, but mainly by the building boom in Trans-Jordan.

There have been some attempts by the military government to encourage Israeli investments in the occupied territories through credit incentives and the provision of other facilities to Israeli entrepreneurs.[52] Credit has also been made available to some Palestinian capitalists and subcontracting partnerships. One major industrial complex in Erez (near Gaza), exclusively funded by Israeli capital, has in fact been operating for a few years.[53] Another complex at Ma'aleh Adumim, near Jericho, was opened in 1977, but it seems to be designed for the employment of Jewish workers from settlements in the Judean hills.

In general, Jewish businessmen were reluctant to invest in the occupied territories, with the exception of joint (Arab-Jewish) subcontracting investments in textiles and building material which have shown considerable growth in the period following the October War. Subcontracting would seem to offer an alternative outlet for capitalist expansion in view of the shortcomings of local enterprises and since it has the open encouragement of the military government. However, there are inherent limitations in this type of investment due to its heavy dependency on women's labour. Van Arkadie summed up the problem of joint investments:

> The subcontracting system is entirely based on the availability of
> cheap labor. The growth of the system will require an increasing
> mobilization of female labor, since the alternative employment
> opportunities make it unlikely that there will be a ready supply of
> low-wage male industrial labor. It can be argued that subcontracting-
> related employment provides jobs for the workers who are unlikely
> to find incomes elsewhere. It can also be argued, however, that it
> only survives as long as wages are low, and that, because it involves
> only labor-intensive steps in the industrial process originating and
> being completed in Israel, its contributions to the industrial develop-
> ment of the territories will be minimal.[54]

Another main obstacle for industrial expansion is the underdeveloped
state of the infrastructure of the economy, that is, a network of transportation and communication linking the various subdistricts of the
occupied territories, a banking and monetary system to facilitate investment and capital accumulation, and a training programme for creating
a skilled labour force—in effect, an indigenous state apparatus whose
rationale is the balanced growth of the economy. To this respect, the
Israeli military government in the two regions seems to be interested in
creating programmes which have catered so far (understandably) to
the needs and deficiencies of Israeli industries. Thus vocational training
centres have offered short-term courses with the aim of improving the
performance of unskilled workers in specific jobs and services.[55]

IV. Stabilisation of the New Structure

To the extent that structural change did occur in the occupied territories,
it was the result of the rupture in the basic links connecting the system
with Jordan (and Egypt) and the subsequent re-integration of the system
in the industrial network of Israeli society. The Palestinian labour force
was incorporated into the lower sectors of the Israeli labour force such
that both underemployment in agriculture and the disguised and non-
productive employment in the urban sectors were eliminated. This integration fluctuated in response to market forces in the Israeli economy
itself—but always within the context of political-demographic constraints
—as well as to 'pull' factors from the Jordanian economy. By 1975,
however, the distribution of workers over the various economic sectors,
with minor exceptions (such as seasonal agricultural workers from
Gaza), had acquired a stable character (see Table 4.2).

Table 4.2: Distribution of Palestinian Workers (West Bank and Gaza) in Israel by Economic Branch, 1972-5 (percentages)

	The West Bank			The Gaza Strip		
	1972	1974	1975	1972	1974	1975
Agriculture	12	11	11	45	33	19
Industry	19	19	19	15	15	18
Construction	57	56	55	36	47	53
Others	12	14	15	4	5	10
Total	100	100	100	100	100	100

Source: Arie Bregman, *The Economy of the Administered Areas, 1974-1975* (Jerusalem, 1976), Table III-5, p. 32.

The stability of the employment structure in Israel suggested by Table 4.2, which withstood both the increased demand for labour in Jordan as well as a minor boom in construction in the occupied territories, should be contrasted to the relative instability of the occupation distribution and wage differentials within the territories themselves. This instability is related to the dominance of the non-productive sector (construction and services) and to the cyclical attributes of non-irrigated agriculture.

These figures should be compared with employment data for labour *within* the two regions (as opposed to workers who commute daily to Israel). Here, the figures for 1975 are typical for the whole previous period (with the exception of 1968 – an adjustment year) as evidenced from the data in Table 4.3.

Table 4.3: Employment of Palestinians in the West Bank and Gaza by Economic Branch (1968-75) (per cent)

Year	Total	Agriculture	Industry	Construction	Public Services	Trade Transport and Services
1968	100	35	14	10	14	27
1972	100	33	14	7	18	28
1973	100	31	15	7	18	29
1974	100	34	14	6	18	28
1975	100	32	14	7	18	29

Source: Bregman, *Economy of the Administered Territories*, taken from Table III-3, p. 28.

Only when we consider changes in the employment structure for both regions together (Israel and the occupied territories) are we likely to detect new patterns emerging during the period considered (1967-75). The most noticeable of these patterns is a decline in agricultural employment (from 34 to 26 per cent of total employed),[56] together with an increase in the proportion of construction workers (from 11 to 22 per cent), and a surprising drop in the category of trade and services, suggesting perhaps a tendency towards the elimination of small peddlers and artisans.[57] More probably, it reflects changes in the structure of Arab employment in Israel.

Moreover, if one attempts to establish any trends using the year 1968 as a starting-point, the evidence is likely to be inconclusive, considering that this was a year of post-war adjustment; this quite apart from the general caution one should adopt when dealing with collected data in 'enemy territory'. Yet, if we accept these statistics as a basis for establishing medium-range projections, and provided that there are no dramatic changes in the political picture, then it seems inevitable that 'the dominant tendency for the territories [is] to become a dormitory economy' for Israel.[58]

This conclusion is further highlighted by certain geographic aspects of commuting to work in Israel from the West Bank and Gaza. Any Palestinian village or town is at most between one hour to ninety minutes in travelling time from the nearest Jewish workplace (without taking into account, of course, availability of transportation). This fact, together with the casual character of employment, ensures that the process of land alienation is not likely to take a drastic turn for the worse since peasant-workers can always take time off in the harvest season to tend their farms.[59] A contributing factor in the opposite direction, although so far not a decisive one, is that the increase in food prices (and hence the profitability of selling crops) has been lower than the overall increase in the prices of general commodities, so that as the pattern of consumption of the rural population draws closer to that of urbanites, one would expect increased defections from the ranks of small farmers to employment in full-time wage labour. Negligence of small farms, already visible, and increased leasing to less capable peasants are inevitable consequences. An investigation of the effects of wage-labour attraction on different age categories, and on the sexual division of labour in the rural household would further illuminate this issue. In the Galilee, for example, greater involvement in wage labour was observed among the 18-34 age groups, while agricultural work inside the village was left to the 14-17 age categories, and to men over 55.[60]

Moreover, in the West Bank there is today a noticeable increase in the participation of women in tasks traditionally assigned to men (e.g. threshing and ploughing).

V. Consequences of Economic Integration

How stable and fixed is the edifice of economic integration that was imposed by Israel on the occupied territories? And, given a favourable political atmosphere, how reversible are these networks of dependency?

The thrust of Israeli policy towards the territories as discussed above—to the extent that a conscious policy was formulated—has centred around the gradual integration of the two regions into Israeli economic life through the creation of an employment market for Palestinian workers, the opening up of the territories as a major market for Israeli commodities, and the elimination of refugee camps through a process of resettlement and 'rehabilitation'. This scheme is being implemented in the framework of granting administrative autonomy to the territories, without the extension of Israeli civic rights to the subject population and while keeping them under strict military control.

Despite the strong resistance of Palestinians in the West Bank and Gaza to the Israeli presence, this policy has been largely successful. Indeed, one might be deceived by appearances if one seeks to reject this success of annexationism in the failure of relations of 'coexistence' between Arabs and Jews. Such indications abound and occasionally reveal surprising aspects about the character of Israeli control. On the tenth anniversary of the annexation of Jerusalem, for example, a symposium was held in the city in which relations between Arabs and Jews were reviewed:

> Jews and Arabs are divided all along the line, and even in mixed and border districts, neighborly relations have not come into existence. At work too, the tendency is to separate between Arabs and Jews. Contacts created at work despite this tendency do not continue because of different social frameworks.

> the number of Jewish-Arab partnerships was greater 7-8 years ago than now. In general . . . there exists a feeling that Jewish-Arab relations in Jerusalem are temporary, that there is no knowing what tomorrow will bring. Even stories of 'cooperation' in the underworld between Jews and Arabs have little basis.[61]

These sentiments, which can be felt and seen throughout the occupied territories (and probably with greater intensity among Arabs who have been living in Israel since 1948) tend to mystify rather than illuminate the issue at hand. To place the above illustration in context, perhaps it should be compared with the observations of Sai'd the Ill-Fated, the Galilean anti-hero of Emile Habibi's epic of the Palestinians. Sai'd, while recalling his difficulties in relating to the alien culture which engulfed the Arabs of Haifa after 1948, discovers to his amazement that the artisans of Nablus in 1967 have learned Hebrew faster than the Israeli tourists can buy their wares![62]

Changes in the fabric of daily life associated with wage-labour employment away from one's habitat – and related patterns of consumption and social interaction – should not be confused with feelings of injustice, antagonism and exploitation that have permeated the particular Israeli imposition of those changes. To be sure, wage-labour proliferation, class and occupational mobility, and urbanisation could have occurred under more 'just' conditions, that is conditions not involving land confiscation from the peasantry and without the current degree of political repression. But the consequences may then be just as irreversible: the land can be restored to the people, so to speak, but the peasants cannot be restored to the land – for we no longer have a peasant society.

One way of examining the question of reversibility is to evaluate the functional importance of the Arab labour force for Israel itself. It has been suggested by several economists that wage-labour remunerations of Arab workers have been more important to the occupied territories than the contributions of Arab labour to the Israeli economy. Van Arkadie, for instance, cited total Palestinian participation (for the West Bank *and* Gaza) as constituting only 6 per cent of total employment in the Israeli labour force, and 12 per cent of all manual workers.[63] In return, he argues, Arab workers earn an amount equivalent to one-third the gross national product in the two occupied regions, but have no meaningful source of alternative employment.

This argument cannot be reduced to a question of reciprocal benefits and liabilities, however, even if we assess the relationship in strictly economic terms. Remunerations from employment must be considered alongside the increased importance of the occupied territories as a main outlet for Israeli commodities. But in addition, Arab labour in Israel must be viewed in the context of its *critical function in key sectors of the economy* where neither replacement by Jewish workers nor mechanisation (optimum allocation of resources have been reached) is possible. Examples of this rigidity in the structure of employment can be found in the building trades and the service sector. In both cases it will be difficult to coerce Jewish workers to 'recede back' into jobs from which they have 'escaped' without incurring a high degree of strain within the labour unions and perhaps accentuating ethnic (Oriental-Ashkenazi) tensions.

In the agricultural sector there are more flexible possibilities for manoeuvre due to the presence of a potential pool of volunteer labour and the persistence of ideological (Zionist) predisposition towards agricultural work in the collective and co-operative settlements. This analysis, at any rate, is extremely conjectural, and should be examined against shifts in Jewish employment patterns as more Palestinians withdraw from work in Israel.

A comparison of the position of migrant workers in Western Europe with that of Palestinian workers in Israel might yield useful theoretical insight to our analysis. The case of Israel, nevertheless, is especially problematic because of the colonial relationship it maintains with the subject population and because Palestinian workers are commuters rather than (temporary) residents.

The framework adopted by Castles and Kosack for five major European recipients of migrant workers is quite relevant here.[64] Their conclusions may be summarised in the following points. (1) There, as well as in Israel, immigrant labour has become structurally necessary for the economy of the host (capitalist) country; undesirable jobs deserted by indigenous labour are filled by 'guest' workers who are increasingly becoming a subordinate section of the original working class. (2) Division of labour in production (between skilled and unskilled labour) is duplicated in the social sphere, where a split in the class consciousness of the indigenous workers occurs, blurring their solidarity with migrant workers. (3) The presence of migrant labour allows for actual (occupational) and subjective (status) mobility of the dominant section of the working class. A political consequence of this process is the negation of a dichotomous view of class conflict, to one that favours self-conception in terms of individual mobility.[65]

The ethnic heterogeneity of Israeli Jewish society, reinforced by successive waves of migration from diverse cultural backgrounds, has always been a determinant factor in shaping the class structure of Israel. The weak development of class consciousness among Jews should thus be attributed primarily to this ethnic diversity, rather than to Arab-Jewish labour relationship.[66] In this respect, the hypothesis suggested above by Castles and Kosack concerning the 'class blurring' impact of nationally diverse migrant workers should be modified in the Israeli case. Moreover, trade union consciousness (as opposed to class consciousness) is

particularly strong, and purely economic demands made by Jewish workers seem to be extended to protect the interests of those Israeli Arab
workers who are solidly organised and have stable employment. This
situation obviously applies only to a section of the Arab working class.
In the mid-sixties only one-third of the Arab employees were members
of the Histadrut,[67] and although that proportion has steadily increased
since then, there are still substantial numbers of the Palestinian labour
force working under non-contractual terms. In the occupied territories,
of course, the percentage of organised labour is much lower, probably
less than 5 per cent.[68] Here the impact of Israeli occupation has been
retrogressive; both the political repression of trade union organising
attempts and the predominance of casual labour among Palestinian
workers have eroded even the minute gains which workers' unions have
achieved under the Jordanian administration.

But erosion of control over the conditions of work by Palestinians
need not mean an automatic decline in their bargaining power. Wage
differentials between Israeli and Arab workers are more likely to *decrease* due to efforts aimed at counteracting the depressive effects of
cheap Arab labour on Jewish wage scales. Most probably such a protec-
tionist wage policy, if pursued by the Histadrut, will come into conflict
with the attempts of Israeli private capital, now given a freer hand by
the Likud government, to make the most of the seemingly unlimited
supply of unskilled Palestinian labour. Another, more encompassing,
source of conflict within Israel will be the continued disenfranchise-
ment of the Palestinians. So far, this issue has not been a bone of con-
tention either by the Israelis or the Palestinians, since the latter do not
see themselves as potential subjects of the Israeli state within which
they have to fight for their democratic rights. But as pressures arise for
maintaining Jewish hegemony in the political sphere, against the increasing role of Palestinians in its economy, the Israeli state will have to
acquire an infinitely more repressive character.

V. Conclusion

The peace plan proposed by Menahim Begin in January 1978 for the
future of the West Bank and Gaza (the 26-point programme) confirms
the final intention of Israel to maintain its sovereignty over the
occupied territories. This intention is no doubt reinforced by the present
balance of forces in the Middle East (and the world) which favours
Israel's intransigence on the question of withdrawal. Since this position
is unlikely to be challenged in the near future—certainly not by the
military means of the neighbouring Arab states—it seems appropriate,

even necessary, for the Palestinian movement to adopt a transitional programme of survival and adaptation for the one million Palestinians who will have to bear the brunt of the continued occupation.

Meanwhile, the quest for Palestinian national self-determination acquires a more complex dimension when the future of the occupied territories is viewed in the context of socio-economic developments in the West Bank and Gaza during the first decade of Israeli rule (1967-77). To retain its credibility the Palestinian movement would have to translate its demands for nationhood from a political slogan into a pro-grammatic policy. Such a policy would have to take into account the structural transformations that have affected the fabric of Palestinian society in the last eleven years. Those include: changes in the agrarian system; the erosion of traditional authority in several districts following the 1976 municipal elections; and the basic reorientation of the economy to serve the new needs of Israeli capitalism.

In the foregoing analysis we have chosen to stress one aspect of the complex results of Israel domination at the expense of others. The re-pressive apparatus of the Israeli military regime and its various activities in the occupied territories (deportations, imprisonment, transfer of pop-ulation, detention centres, demolition of houses, etc.) have been fully documented elsewhere.[69] Here we emphasised instead emergent patterns of employment among Palestinian peasants and refugees in Israel and the extension of the internal Israeli commodity market to the occupied regions. Those factors are seen as being more crucial at the moment for the future of Gaza and the West Bank than the issues of Jewish settle-ments and land confiscation. The assumption behind our analysis has been that the impact of the physical features of occupation (e.g. col-onies) can be much more easily overcome than the complex network of economic interdependence.

Given certain conditions, such as substantial investment in the public sector by an independent Palestinian state and the creation of a viable infrastructure for the economy, it is still possible to reverse the trend towards integration between Israel and the occupied territories in terms of labour and commodities. But important changes in the rural sector, such as demographic pressures on land, plot fragmentation, as well as massive proliferation of wage labour and related conditions of life-style, will ensure that this reversal will not take place — *if at all* — under the same conditions which prevailed during Jordanian rule.

Paradoxically, the conditions experienced by Palestinians living under occupation have generated an unprecedented movement for national independence precisely at a time when their daily activities are more embeded into the lives of their conquerors than ever before. How the Palestinian national movement will resolve this dilemma remains to be seen.

Notes

1. Quoted by J. Perara, 'West Bank: Up for Grabs', *The Middle East* (London), no. 36 (October 1977).

2. See *Israel Economist*, 'Two Approaches to the Administered Territories' (Tel Aviv) (August 1972 and January 1973).

3. 'Israel's Plan for the West Bank and Gaza', *The Guardian Weekly*, 8 January 1978.

4. For the economic foundations of these settlements see Ann Lesch, 'A Survey of Israeli Settlements', *MERIP Reports*, no. 60 (September 1977). For an analysis of their political significance see M. Fershafsky, *'al-mukhattat al-isra'ili lil-istila' ala ad-diffa wa-ghazza wal-julan'*, *al-Manar* (London), 14 January 1978.

5. 'The Allon Plan is dead – on the map, in the thinking and in the political conception of Israel, Prime Minister Begin has said when speaking about . . . what is expected in planning settlements beyond the green line.' Quoted from 'Likud Plan for Settlements in the West Bank' (Jerusalem Radio, 2 July 1977), *MERIP Reports*, no. 59 (August 1977), p. 23.

6. Ibid.

7. 'New West Bank Factories' (excerpts from Jerusalem Radio, 22 March 1977), *Merip Reports*, ibid., p. 22.

8. See comment by Y. Cohen, a leading architect of the Sharon Plan, in 'Likud Plan for Settlements'.

9. 'Minister Sharon Warns About the Arab "Gentile" Population and Calls for Saving the Galilee', *al-Ittihad* (Haifa), 12 September 1977.

10. Y. Litani, 'Cabinet Hears Statistics on Jewish Settlements', *Haaretz*, 12 May 1976.

11. Eric Silver, 'Cool Reception for General with a Dream', *Observer* (London), 11 September 1977.

12. Ibid.

13. H.D.S. Greenway, 'Israelis Ratify Expansion on Bank', *Guardian* (London), 11 January 1978.

14. Moshe Ater, 'Autonomous West Bank is Poor Economics', *Jerusalem Post*, 30 October 1975. See also 'Green Revolution in Judea and Samaria', *Israel Economist*, October-November 1975, where similar claims are made.

15. Arie Bregman, *Economic Growth in the Administered Areas 1968-1973* (Bank of Israel Research Department, Jerusalem, 1975), p. 6.

16. Arie Bregman, *The Economy of the Administered Territories, 1974-1975* (Jerusalem, 1976).

17. Ibid., pp. 7-15. 'Related decline' because olive oil and traditional soap manufacturing (in Nablus) are considered industrial commodities.

18. Vivian Bull, *The West Bank, Is It Viable?* (Lexington, 1975). For the author's political conclusions see pp. 143-53.

19. Ibid., p. 81. It is interesting that Bull, despite disclaimers (e.g. p. 44), shows more credibility in Israeli official statistics than Bregman, whose institution– presumably – was partly responsible for the collection of those data. See particularly Bregman's remarks on the reliability of official statistics on the occupied territories

in the Supplement to his *Economic Growth*, pp. 101-5.

20. Bull, *The West Bank*, pp. 96-103.

21. Ibid., p. 105.

22. Ibid., pp. 120-4.

23. Ibid., p. 144.

24. Brian Van Arkadie, *Benefits and Burdens: A Report on the West Bank and the Gaza Strip Economies Since 1967* (New York, 1977), pp. 68-9.

25. Jamil Hilal, *The West Bank: the Socio-Economic Structure, 1948-1974*, in Arabic (Beirut, 1975), p. 267.

26. Ibid., p. 252.

27. Jamil Hilal, 'Class Transformation in the West Bank and Gaza', *MERIP Reports*, no. 53 (December 1976), p. 10.

28. Ibid. See also *The West Bank*, pp. 207-10.

29. 'Palestinian' here refers to workers from the occupied territories, while 'Israeli' includes Arabs who are citizens of the state.

30. 'Israeli Colonialism in 1975', *Israel and Palestine* (December 1976). This report, however, is not reliable in terms of interpretation.

31. Van Arkadie, *Benefits and Burdens*, p. 124.

32. Hilal, *The West Bank*, p. 246.

33. Dan Tzidkoni, 'Colonial Policy in the Territories', *New Outlook* (Tel Aviv) (July-August 1975), p. 41.

34. Jamil Hilal, *The Palestinians of the West Bank and The Gaza Strip* (Beirut, 1976), p. 23.

35. This judgement is confirmed by Bregman, *The Economy of the Administered Territories*, p. 63.

36. For crop production figures see Gideon Weigert, *Ploughing New Fields: The Story of West Bank Farmers, 1970-1975*. The reader should handle these figures with caution as the booklet is selective and publicity-oriented.

37. Hilal, *The Palestinians*, p. 26.

38. Sh. Carmi and Henry Rosenfeld, 'The Origins of the Process of Proletarianization and Urbanization of Arab Peasants in Palestine', *Annals of the New York Academy of Sciences*, vol. 220, art. 6 (March 1974), p. 480.

39. Ibid. For a critique of Rosenfeld's thesis see Khalil Nakhleh, 'Palestinians in Israel: An Assessment of the Sociological and Anthropological Literature', *Journal of Palestine Studies*, vol. 6, no. 4 (Summer 1977), pp. 46-7 and 51.

40. Elia Zureik, 'Transformation of Class Structure Among the Arabs in Israel: From Peasantry to Proletariat', *Journal of Palestine Studies*, vol. 6, no. 1 (1976), pp. 56 and 58. Zureik's main emphasis here is on the status of Palestinians in Israel.

41. See A. Israeli, 'The Employment Revolution Among the Non-Jewish Minorities of Israel', *Hamizrah Hehadash*, vol. 26, nos. 3-4 (1976), pp. 232-9.

42. Nathan Weinstock, 'The Impact of Zionist Colonization on Palestinian Arab Society Before 1948', *Journal of Palestinian Studies*, vol. 2, no. 2 (1973), p. 63.

43. Cf. Abdullah Lutfiyya, *Baytin, A Jordanian Village* (The Hague, 1966), pp. 105-6; see also the section on migration in Walid Rabie *et al.*, *Turmus' ayya, A Study in Palestinian and Folk Heritage* (Beirut, 1973), pp. 195-8.

44. For a discussion of the position of the Arab worker in the Jewish labour market before 1967, see Yoram Ben Porath, *The Arab Labor Force in Israel* (Jerusalem, 1966), pp. 47-72.

45. Bregman, *The Economy of the Administered Territories*, p. 11.

46. Ibid.

47. Carmi and Rosenfeld, 'Origins of the Process of Proletarianization and Urbanization', p. 471; A. Cohen, *Arab Border-Villages in Israel* (Manchester, 1965), p. 34.

48. The Bank of Israel estimated the gross private savings for the year 1974 and 1975 in the West Bank to have been 543 and 446 million lirot respectively (in current prices), and in Gaza 264 and 277 million lirot. See Bregman, *The Economy of the Administered Territories*, Table II-4, p. 20.

49. One indicator of hoarding is the decline in the amount of deposits in banks (from 29 per cent of GNP during Jordanian rule to 4 per cent of GNP under Israeli rule), despite substantial increase in disposable income. Some of this wealth, however, was almost certainly deposited in Amman banks. Part of the increase in income was spent in consumer durables. It is questionable, moreover, whether we can consider the purchase of gold, for instance, by and for women as a form of hoarding.

50. Tzidkoni, 'Colonial Policy in the Territories', pp. 41-2.

51. Bregman, *The Economy of the Administered Territories*, p. 32. For trends in construction employment, see Table IV-5, p. 45.

52. The discussion here is centred around investment in the Arab sector and not around Jewish settlements inside the occupied territories. Substantial investment has been made in these colonies, but Arab employment in 'colonial' industries has been negligible, although not in the construction of these settlements.

53. For a discussion see Bregman, *Economic Growth*, pp. 62-7. On the weakness of local Palestinian enterprises, see Adel Samara, 'The Local Bourgeoisie and Work in Israel' in his *The Economy of the Occupied Territories: Underdevelopment Reinforces Annexation*, in Arabic (Jerusalem, 1975), pp. 28-32.

54. Van Arkadie, *Benefits and Burdens*, pp. 124-5.

55. See Bull, *The West Bank*, pp. 123-4.

56. Compare these data with similar patterns of Arab employment in Israel in Israeli, 'The Employment Revolution'.

57. Figures from Bregman, *Economic Growth*, p. 28.

58. Van Arkadie, *Benefits and Burdens*, p. 74.

59. Barring, of course, large-scale confiscation of land by the government.

60. Israeli, 'The Employment Revolution', p. 239.

61. Those are excerpts from a paper presented by Prof. A. Weingrod (of Beersheba University) at the Hebrew University symposium. Summaries can be found in *New Outlook*, vol. 20, no. 4 (June-July 1977), pp. 66-7.

62. Emile Habibi, *Strange Episodes in the Disappearance of Sa'ad Abu an-Nahs* (Haifa, 1974), p. 64; in Arabic—English translation forthcoming.

63. Van Arkadie, *Benefits and Burdens*, p. 61.

64. S. Castles and G. Kosack, *Immigrant Workers and Class Structure in Western Europe* (London, 1973), pp. 6-8.

65. An Israeli economist, Zarhi, rejects the comparability of Israel with Western Europe in this regard. His argument, however, seems to be politically motivated and is aimed at an economic rationalisation for the dovish (anti-annexationist) wing of the Israeli establishment. See Sh. Zarhi, 'The Occupied Territories— Economic Liability', *New Outlook* (January-February 1977), pp. 23-4.

66. See M. Machover and A. Orr, 'The Class Nature of Israeli Society' in A. Bober, *The Other Israel* (New York, 1972), pp. 91-3.

67. Walter Preuss, *The Labour Movements in Israel* (Jerusalem, 1965), p. 234.

68. A survey of the labour force conducted in the city of Ramallah in 1973 revealed that less than 10 per cent of the workers paid dues to the union, or identified with it at all. See S. Tamari, 'Notes on the Composition of the Labor Force in the West Bank' (in Arabic), *al-Quds* (Jerusalem), 4 December 1973. It should be noted that Ramallah, together with Nablus and Bethlehem, are the centres of an active labour union organisation.

69. An updated monthly chronicle of these activities in the West Bank and Gaza appears regularly in *Shu'un Filastiniyya* (Beirut) in the section edited by A.

Muharib. For an inside report of Israeli repression see F. Langer, *With My Own Eyes* (London, 1975), and *These Are My Brothers: Israel and the Occupied Territories* (London, forthcoming). For an analysis of the significance of Jewish settlements, see A. Lesch, 'Israeli Settlements in the Occupied Territories', *Journal of Palestine Studies*, vol. 7, no. 1 (1977), pp. 26-47.

5 PALESTINIAN COMMUNITIES AND ARAB HOST COUNTRIES

Naseer H. Aruri and Samih Farsoun

I. Introduction

This paper analyses the Palestinians as a 'minority' in the Arab host countries. These countries are the states to which Palestinian Arabs fled collectively or emigrated individually subsequent to the destruction of Palestine as a society in 1948 and in the wake of successive Arab-Israeli wars, especially that of June 1967. The chapter will analyse the conditions of Palestinian life and activities in the host countries, as 'minorities', and the attitudes and policies of the host states and people, as 'majorities', towards the Palestinians resident there and the Palestine national liberation movement in the region.

The study of the Palestinians in exile as 'minorities', fragmented and dispersed in the Arab host countries, is challenging. It is interesting both theoretically and methodologically, but it is difficult to conduct. Although the Palestinians in the Arab host countries can be conceptualised as a 'minority group' in terms of an abstract theoretical definition, they are not a 'minority' in terms of the usual attributes utilised to classify 'minorities' in Western social science. Theoretically, a minority group is defined by the society (nation-state) of which it is a part. It is a collectivity of people seen and treated as different by the rest of that society and its established institutions, and which perceives itself as being different. In this sense Palestinians are a 'minority' in Arab host countries. Collectively and individually, they are treated differently from the citizens of the host countries. Typically, they are circumscribed socially, economically and politically. But also, the Palestinians see themselves as different and seek freedom of action within their own communities. They also seek support from the people and institutions of the host countries for a liberation struggle that is not solely their own but which has implications for the host countries, both singly and collectively.

The Palestinians in the Arab host countries, however, are not a 'minority' in terms of the typical attributes or combination of these attributes utilised by Western social science. They are not an ethnic minority defined on the basis of differences in cultural heritage, values, norms, etiquette and food. Nor are they a minority based on religious

112

or sectarian differences in theology, organisation and life-style. Nor are they a linguistic or racial minority.[1] The Palestinians are culturally, linguistically, racially and religiously similar to the Arabs of the host countries. They do exhibit secondary subcultural variations, but the principal factor responsible for treating them differently in the colonially inherited Arab host states is their political history and their current political status.

Hence, political issues dominate the status and relations of Palestinians, both collectively and individually, with the host country's formal authorities and people. Thus, the Palestinian status in host countries revolves around the power relations. For 'minority status' is in essence defined in terms of power.[2] Irrespective of size, a collectivity is a 'minority group' in so far as another segment of the society dominates that group politically, economically and socially. Again, irrespective of size, the dominant segment is the 'majority' as it has the organised power to initiate policies to dominate, exploit and control the 'minority'. Such policies can be formal and legal as in South African apartheid, or informal and semi-legal as in Israel's treatment of the (Israeli Arabs) Palestinians, and the Palestinians under occupation in the West Bank and Gaza.[3] In short, the Palestinians in the Arab host countries are a 'minority' in so far as they are typically subordinated to the 'majority' and do not have the ability or power to freely make their own collective decisions, have less wealth, less prestige, and much more restricted life chances than the Arab 'majority'.

1. Origin of Minorities

Historically, minorities originate as a consequence of population movement or transfer. When a group with one or more of the above cited attributes moves or is forced to move into the society of another, minorities are created. According to van den Berghe and others, the most common causes of population transfer are invasion, expansion, forced movement of labouring classes, and the voluntary movement of dissatisfied individuals and groups. Palestinian population movement from Palestine, however, took place as a result of both forced expulsion by Zionists-Israelis and the fleeing of people in war situations—refugees who were never permitted to return by the conquering authorities, the Israelis.[4]

Population movements which resulted in various minorities in the modern world are a consequence of the dynamic and expansion of European capitalism in its two principal phases—colonialism and imperialism. The most devastating and bloodiest of European conquests had been settler colonialism, under which many of the natives were killed and the remainder reduced to exploited and dominated 'minorities'. European settler colonialism was most efficient and overwhelming in the New World, the Americas, Australia and New Zealand. In the Old World, South Africa, Rhodesia, Algeria and Palestine have been subjected to settler colonialism.

In Algeria, the French in a near-genocidal war in the 1830s conquered the native Arabs and pushed them off the fertile coastal land into the desert. French settlers then established a state which usurped Algeria's resources and exploited its labour. The struggle of the native Arabs finally succeeded in 1960 after a savage war of national liberation which drove off the French colonists and established an independent Algeria.

In the eastern Mediterranean, the creation of Israel upon the ashes of Palestine is the latest instance of European settler colonialism. This colonial venture is peculiar because it comes in a historical era, the twentieth century, in which all forms of classical imperialism are in retreat. It is also peculiar by its religious ethnic thrust, Jewish Europeans joined later by Oriental Jews. Since 1947, the Zionists and later the Israelis have conquered and forced out most of the indigenous Arab Palestinian population from what was Palestine. Israel usurped the land and set up military, political and economic domination over the Palestinian Arabs who remained – the minority. The Palestinian Arabs who were forced out became 'minorities' as well in the Arab host countries. During and since the June 1967 War, Israel has established a more crushing domination over one and a half million other Palestinian Arabs in the West Bank and Gaza and driven out as refugees hundreds of thousands of others. Also since 1967, Israel proceeded to colonise these two remaining sections of Palestine,[5] treating the population in the classic colonial manner of a dominated 'minority'.

In short, the origin of the Palestinian population dispersal and the creation of Palestinian 'minorities' inside their traditional homeland and outside it does follow some of the general outlines proposed by van den Berghe for the creation of minorities in the modern world.

2. Majority/Minority Group Relations: Policy and Response

Inter-group, as well as interpersonal relations, are set by the policy which the 'majority' as a collectivity adopts towards the 'minority' as a collectivity and by the response the 'minority' makes also as a collectivity. The 'majority' policy typically expresses itself in governmental or formal institutional policy. But it may also be an unofficial, publically unverbalised collective attitude and action. Indeed the public rhetoric may say one thing but actual behaviour – both institutional and private – is something else. For

example, the government of the Union of South Africa, controlled by
white Europeans, has an *explicitly* legalised policy towards the blacks
called 'apartheid', which is in essence a separate and unequal system of
subjugation. While in the United States, especially in the South, the
whites as a majority pursue collectively towards the blacks an informal
but observable policy of non-assimilation and subjugation despite formal
governmental laws to the contrary.[6]

Majority group policy and minority group response is a dialectical
relationship, the dynamic of which is determined by the material conditions under which the two live. Such conditions are internal to the
society but also external to it, regionally and globally. Furthermore,
the relationship is not a simple dialectic. It should be clear that although
one particular policy and one specific response may be dominant at any
one instance, *other policies* may be pursued by specific segments of the
majority group. Similarly, the response of the minority as a collectivity
is not singular at any one time. There may be one or more types of
response pursued by varied segments of the minority collectivity. Class-
based differences and perhaps other cleavages are the roots of such
variation. Majority group policies for dealing with minority groups include
genocide, population transfer (forced or peaceful), separatism (sym-
biotic independence), subjugation and exploitation, and assimilation
(allowed or forced). The responses of the minority group include armed
resistance, secessionism, separatism, assimilation (integration) or achieving self-determination in the full sense. For the two groups, a pattern of
mutual accommodation on one or more dimensions of the relationship
could also develop. What determines the policy and response are the
material conditions that exist locally, regionally and globally. For example,
settler colonists intent on usurping the land of the native may adopt
genocide as a policy in order to guarantee access to or control of the
land. In earlier centuries genocide was possible, but now it is less tolerable
internationally. Currently, forced expulsion is a more likely policy than
genocide. In either case, for the native, armed resistance is a typical
response. Indeed, armed struggle may be the only strategy for the dis-
inherited natives to regain or liberate their land. We have seen this
develop in Algeria, Rhodesia-Zimbabwe and Palestine. In short, the
minority/majority group relations are a complex dialectic, the specifics
of which can be understood only in their concrete historical context.

3. Methodological Problems of Studying the Palestinians

The analysis of the forced Palestinian dispersal and its consequences, i.e.
the Palestinians as minorities, is difficult because published and document-

ed data—statistical and otherwise—are at best incomplete and unreliable, and at worst deliberately distorted or unavailable. Furthermore, the available data are not appropriate for comparative analysis as the quantity, quality and variety of these data on the Palestinians in the various Arab states and Israel are collected, categorised, analysed and censored quite arbitrarily. They are also subjected to political manipulation by varied and often conflicting authorities. Thus, some of the analysis must by necessity be based on 'educated guesses' and 'educated impressions', as it were.

The analysis of the Palestinians in 'diaspora' is complicated because of the multi-faceted aspects of the Palestinian question, its intermeshing with the Arab national question and intra-Arab politics, and because of its populist/revolutionary thrust as well as its involvement with the class question. In addition, the rapid, frequent and sometimes multiple socio-demographic transformations of Palestinian communities since 1948 further complicate these relationships. Massive Palestinian population movements, both forced and voluntary, took place during and in the aftermath of wars in and around Palestine: the 1948, 1956, 1967 and 1973 Israeli-Arab wars, and the 'uncivil' wars of 1970 in Jordan and of 1975-6 in Lebanon. Additionally, economic dislocations and population pressure brought about massive emigration of Palestinians from Palestine and neighbouring countries to the Arabian peninsula, the Gulf, and overseas. In short, an accurate and relatively complete analysis of the Palestinian 'dispersal' and its political consequences in the Arab world entails almost a comprehensive account of the social-political history of the Arab *Mashreq* since at least World War Two. But, since this task cannot be accomplished within the limits of this paper, the present analysis will be more restricted to certain principal aspects which characterise the Palestinians in Arab host countries. These are: (1) size of the community; (2) conditions of residence; (3) economic role; (4) occupational structure (by necessity a gross breakdown); and (5) political role and consequences.

The Palestinians played a most critical and pivotal role in the political life of the Arab *Mashreq* and of the individual states in which they resided. Palestinians and the cause of Palestine helped politicise other Arab masses. The large-scale entry of the Arab masses into the political life of the Arab world coincides roughly with the Palestinian struggle. Furthermore, Palestinians originated and became the earliest participants in the two principal pan-Arab political movements of the post-World War Two period: the Arab Ba'ath Socialist Party and the Arab nationalist movement. The goal of both these movements has been the liberation

of the Arab world, including Palestine, from both Western domination
and Zionism. In addition, Palestinians became principal leaders and activists in the pan-Arab Nasserist movement outside Egypt.

On another level, Palestinians were most active in creating and participating in students', teachers', women's, and workers' unions and syn-
dicates in nearly all the host countries. These organisations took on
political colouring in addition to their economic and organisational
functions. Furthermore, the Palestinians were first in the streets in support of progressive political and social demonstrations and strikes. In
short, because of their tragedy, Palestinians became and continue to be
a highly political people.

Since 1948, the Palestinians in diaspora have struggled for their cause
in terms of the ideology of Pan-Arabism and of Arab unity. They believe
that their cause cannot be won except through pan-Arab effort and
through a pan-Arab party, the spearhead of which is their own political
organisation, the PLO. Thus, Palestinians rarely joined or supported
'provincialist' or sectarian movements or parties such as the Phalangists
or the Najjadeh in Lebanon. They resisted 'sessionist' (from the Arab
nation) tendencies such as Lebanese nationalism, Egyptian nationalism,
or Syrian nationalism.

Hence, recognising this general political thrust of Palestinians is
crucial for understanding the behaviour and relationships of Palestinian
communities to the host governments and people. Let us turn to analys-
ing the situation of the Palestinians in selected Arab countries.

II. East Jordan

The Palestinian community in East Jordan numbers over a million people,
approximately 60 per cent of the total Jordanian population. The Jordanian government granted these Palestinians rights of citizenship. And as
Trans-Jordan annexed the West Bank on 25 April 1950, Palestinians on
both sides of the Jordan River entered into all aspects of life in that
country.[7] Indeed, the economic development of Jordan proceeded
upon the effort of the Palestinians living there. Palestinian entrepreneurs
invested in agriculture, industry, trade and finance. For example, the
Palestinian-owned Arab Bank is the largest native bank in the Arab
world. With the right to own property, a Palestinian bourgeoisie flourished
in Jordan. Indeed, the consequences of this capitalist development created
a Jordanian middle class, the overwhelming proportion of which was
formed by the Palestinian community. Having been permitted to become
host country citizens they entered into all the official establishments of
the state – from government public school teachers to generals in the

Jordanian army and prime ministers. It is probably safe to say that the majority of the Jordanian civil servants have been Palestinians.

Jordan also has the largest Palestinian refugee population (over 500,000 people), most of whom became wage workers in agricultural projects, in services and in the embryonic industrial sector. It is estimated that nearly 70 per cent of Palestinians in East Jordan are working-class, poorly paid and living in very difficult and unsanitary refugee camps and shanty towns. In short, the Palestinians became fully integrated in the Jordan nation-state and reflected the typical structure of Third World underdeveloped society.

Although they were the numerical, economic and technical force of the country, the Palestinians (except for the few who were loyal to the King) were ruled over by the Jordanian minority and the bedouin army. From the beginning of royal rule in the wake of the annexation of the West Bank, Palestinian activists led, organised and joined pan-Arab political movements including the Ba'ath Party, the Arab Nationalist Movement, the Nasserist tendency, and even the Jordanian Communist Party. These political movements opposed the royal regime for its lack of nationalism, anti-imperialism and active anti-Zionism. In view of the unique situation of Palestinians in Jordan, a comprehensive survey of relations with the host country will be offered in this section, so as to delineate the salient features of this relationship and to trace its development up to the present day (1978).

1. The Two Communities

Although the Palestinians commanded numerical superiority in the newly established kingdom of Jordan, this did not guarantee them immediate political power. The social and political history of Jordan from its very inception has been dominated by contests between the politically influential and privileged minority and the urbanised and educated majority. The latter became subject to the state, but not psychologically members of the people.

The Palestinian convention that sealed the unification of the administrative and legal structure of East and West Jordan in 1949 was not held by representatives of the two communities but by an ambitious king who received the notables of his new Palestinian subjects and accepted their formal allegiance. His annexation of Palestinian territory and his subsequent efforts to come to terms with Israel made him, in the view of the Palestinians, an accomplice in the liquidation of Palestine. He was assassinated by a Palestinian in 1951. From the outset, the intense opposition of the Palestinians to any negotiations on their behalf relating

to matters of fundamental national rights indicated that national development in Jordan would be no simple matter.

Communalism was seen by most Palestinians as a temporary device
providing them with a territorial base from which to pursue their political objectives—namely, establishing sovereignty and reasserting their
separate identity. Control of the state machinery by the Palestinians
was, therefore, crucial to fulfilling their objectives. On the other hand,
the Hashemite establishment appealed to communalism in attempting
to consolidate an East Bank power structure combining the tribes, the
large property-owners, the army and the civilian bureaucracy. The difference in the perceptions of the two communities of their respective
roles made the consolidation of communalism a most difficult task.
Moreover, the two communities were too fragmented from the socio-
economic standpoint to achieve a political consensus.

The Palestinians were primarily city and village dwellers engaged in
agricultural and commercial occupations. The Trans-Jordanians lived
nomadic or semi-nomadic lives. Town living had been almost unknown
in Trans-Jordan. The capital city, Amman, an outgrown village, had a
population of 30,000 in 1943; four other communities with a combined population of 75,000 were designated as cities.[8] In contrast, at
the same time there were eleven cities in Palestine with populations
ranging from 11,000 to 60,000, and ten towns with populations between
4,000 and 10,000.[9] Thirty-four per cent of the Palestinians lived in
cities in 1944, while 22 per cent of the Trans-Jordanians were city-
dwellers.

A middle class had flourished in Palestine as a result of commercial
activities and the development of a sophisticated bureaucracy under
the British Mandate. A large labour force, whose 15,000-20,000 members
were represented by two unions, exerted an appreciable influence on the
economic and political life of the country.[10] Trans-Jordan had neither
a developed middle class nor a sizeable labour force. Its merchants and
civil servants were drawn from the ranks of Palestinians, Circassians and
Syrians.

Palestinian schools had enrolled 52 per cent of all school-age children,
while the schools of Trans-Jordan had enrolled only 28 per cent in the
mid-1940s.[11] There were three physicians for every 10,000 Palestinians
in 1939, as compared with one physician for the same number of Jordanians. The infant mortality rate for Palestine was 115 per 1,000 as compared with 181 for Trans-Jordan.[12] Palestinians in 1946 read four daily
newspapers with a combined circulation of 31,000, ten weekly periodicals, and five monthly or quarterly journals.[13] There was only one news-

paper published in Trans-Jordan at that time.

The nomadic structure and low educational level in Trans-Jordan inhibited the development of modern institutions and political consciousness among the people. The principal actors in the country's political process were the Amir (Abdullah), a few civil servants formerly connected with the Ottoman administration, a military establishment created and headed by General Glubb, and the tribal chiefs who rallied to Abdullah's support. The regime survived without much serious opposition from its inception until 1950, when the West Bank was officially annexed to Trans-Jordan. Abdullah's role has been described as 'largely that of a superior sheikh given a modern quality by the trappings of a constitutional monarchy'.[14]

There had developed among the Palestinians a highly political element as a result of their contact with the West and their struggle against Zionist efforts to establish a Jewish state in their country. The merger of the two banks consequently produced instability in Jordan, because the Palestinian majority was determined to challenge the basic foundations of Abdullah's regime. They brought with them broad demands for equality and participation. The tribal segment of the population of Trans-Jordan, who were generally loyal to the Hashemite throne, resented the urbanised and educated Jordanians and Palestinians, making the latter group draw closer together out of a sense of common grievance and deprivation.

2. Communal Conflict and Political Development: The Formative Years

The Palestinians of the West Bank sought to modify the patriarchal system of power under Abdullah and to introduce the concept of parliamentary democracy. In less than five years, the political structure of Jordan had been so modified as to permit Palestinian politicians a presence on various levels of the civilian bureaucracy, from which they launched a serious campaign aimed at the reorientation of the regime's domestic and foreign policies. They introduced ideological political parties, lobbied for a democratic constitution, and established links with their counterparts on the East Bank.

The constitutional gains of the 1950s represented the fruits of the combined efforts of the liberal bourgeoisie of Palestine and Trans-Jordan. Whereas the opposition parties, accounting for one-third of the members of Parliament in the mid-1950s, represented the two banks, the government-sponsored parties were based strictly on the East Bank. They comprised elements from the tribes, the land-owning aristocracy, the civilian and military bureaucrats, and the propertied classes.

The opposition parties of the national bourgeoisie advocated a re-orientation of Jordan's foreign policy that would include abrogating the Anglo-Jordanian Treaty[15] and bringing the country's foreign policy in line with that of the non-aligned Arab states. They drew their support from intellectuals, students, workers, liberal professionals, businessmen, peasants and refugees. They exercised their first act of defiance on 3 May 1951, when a virtual vote of no confidence was cast by a majority in the House of Representatives. However, their disapproval of the government's budget so angered the King that he dissolved Parliament by decree. After his assassination, the opposition pressed for and obtained a new constitution in which the executive branch was deprived of arbitrary power. A simple parliamentary majority was empowered to request a Cabinet to resign. Civil liberties were protected by the constitution, and the judiciary was given an independent status. A second short-lived victory followed when young Crown Prince Hussein returned from London to be inaugurated King on 2 May 1953. He was hoping to establish a consensus based on the support of moderate nationalists from both the Palestinian and the Trans-Jordanian communities. But he soon discovered that the traditional elite that had served his grandfather was not in favour of his liberalism. General Glubb, one of the most important pillars of the elite, expressed misgivings about Hussein's first Prime Minister:

> Fawzi Pasha had modern ideas about democracy. He was in favour of freedom of speech, freedom of press. Not only did he approve of their principles, but he set himself to pass laws depriving his own, and any future government of the right to deny them.[16]

Indeed, it was this fear that was instrumental in mobilising the traditional elite against the liberal government and its nationalist supporters. The young monarch could not resist their pressure; he requested the Cabinet to resign on 2 May 1954, after it had been in office for exactly one year.[17]

This incident marked the beginning of a cyclical pattern in which the two dominant political groups vied for power, a pattern that characterised Jordanian politics during the 1950s.[18] There was a showdown in 1955, when the liberal opposition of Palestinian and Trans-Jordanians launched a well co-ordinated attack on the government's foreign policy, which aimed to link Jordan to the Western-sponsored Baghdad Pact. Not only did this group register opposition to the Baghdad Pact, which it viewed as an extension of NATO, but it also demanded the expulsion of General Glubb from Jordan, the immediate termination of the Anglo-Jordanian Treaty of Alliance, and the substitution of a financial subsidy from the non-aligned Arab states for that which Britain provided in accordance with the treaty. In essence, the opposition demanded that Jordan reorient its pro-Western foreign policy and seek alignment with Egypt, Syria and Saudi Arabia, who were attempting to expel Hashemite Iraq from the Arab League for having adhered to the Baghdad Pact.[19]

Hussein did not hesitate to rely on his army's guns to suppress the dissidents during this critical juncture, nor to dissolve Parliament or enforce the Defence Regulations, which enabled the government to ban public assemblies. He nevertheless deemed it advisable to respond to some of the public demands. The opposition secured the dismissal of General Glubb and the dismissal of Jordan's fourth Parliament, which had been installed in office after a rigged election.[20] The liberal opposition of Palestinian and Trans-Jordanian nationalists assumed power in what appeared to be the country's *first real parliamentary experiment.* Together with the Communists and Ba'athists from both banks, they secured sixteen seats in Parliament in the autumn of 1956. Suleiman Nabulsi, a liberal wealthy Jordanian of Palestinian origin, was commissioned as leader of the nationalist bloc to form a Cabinet. His government abrogated the Anglo-Jordanian Treaty of Alliance, ended the British subsidy, and signed a military pact with Egypt, Syria and Saudi Arabia.

Now in the saddle of political power, the opposition was quite patently winning the contest. Hussein became concerned that the monarchy was about to be replaced by a republic dominated by nationalists and Communists. With American assurances that the integrity of Jordan was vital to the national interest of the United States,[21] the King and his temporarily retired supporters, including Jordanians and Palestinians, restored the *status quo* and reasserted royal absolutism. Jordan became a police state in mid-1957. Hussein dissolved Parliament and all political parties, ordered large-scale arrests, and enforced martial law for the next fifteen months.

The events of the 1950s illustrate the extent to which the regime was unable to consolidate its political structure or to deal with political opposition. The East Bank constituted the natural base for its power. But the East Bank groups and classes were much less united in their support of Hussein than they had been in support of Abdullah. Absent from Hussein's power base were the national bourgeoisie and liberal professionals of Trans-Jordan who had opted for an alliance with their Palestinian counterparts. The civilian and military bureaucracies were not completely loyal, as evidenced by the purges of the 1950s. The tribes remained loyal to their employer and benefactor but appeared at times disenchanted with the regime's occasional tolerance of views and actions of the liberal nationalists. At the same time, Palestinian opposition to the regime was almost unanimous irrespective of class or education. As a dispossessed nation, the Palestinians were committed to oppose Israel's backers, who also were the backers of the Jordanian monarchy.

In handling the opposition, the regime had to take into account the fact that it included a segment of the East Bank community. It had to be tempered in such a way as to avoid any further narrowing of the regime's power base. East Bank dissidents had to be co-opted. In view of all this, the regime refrained from dealing the opposition the crippling blow that it was to resort to in September 1970. The opposition of the 1950s was national, cutting across regional lines, whereas the 1970 opposition was predominantly communal. The former was but a single chapter in political development; the latter was part of a general rev- olutionary struggle in which an armed Palestinian movement was poised against Hussein's bedouin army.

3. Consolidation of Communalism: the Technocrats of the 1960s

The 1960s ushered in the beginning of the era in which the technocrats began their ascent to political power. With American financial assistance averaging $50 million annually, the bureaucracy almost quadrupled in size in less than a decade, and the government became the principal employer in the country. The technocratic class began to lavish jobs and subsidies on potential supporters in an attempt to rebuild the power base that had been seriously weakened by the cyclical ruptures of the 1950s. Such benefits were no longer distributed by the army chief of staff to tribal leaders. The technocrats followed different methods, more sophisticated, and in tune with the changing times. New institutions such as the Tribal Council and the Bureau of Agricultural Loans served as conduits for the financial subsidies.

With the technocrats in command, the principal elements of the East Bank community were drawn close to the power structure. Tribal chiefs and land-owners on the East Bank, who served as intermediaries between the regime and the rural sector, presided at the distribution of jobs and subsidies, thus evading a possible situation in which peasants and workers would rise against a coalition of technocrats and land-owning aristocracy. Retired army officers and soldiers were offered positions in the civil bureaucracy at all levels.[22] The civilian and military bureaucracies were integrated under a single chief. The Prime Minister combined his duties with those of the Minister of Defence.

In brief, the technocratic class made the integration of the East Bank community with all classes represented, a top priority in its endeavour to rebuild a power structure and to establish 'law and order'. While control of jobs and money enabled it to draw the support of the rural sector, government spending, subsidised from the outside, enabled it to attract the support of urban entrepreneurs who aspired to be junior partners of foreign capital and who were dependent on government licensing to import and export. The technique proved effective in disarming the national bourgeoisie, which had been attracted to radical ideas in the 1950s, as well as the peasantry and working class, which might have linked with its Palestinian counterpart at a later stage in a class-based confrontation with the regime. The new technique was thus instrumental in driving a wedge between Palestinians and Trans-Jordanians who had previously articulated their interests without regard to regional or communal differences. The sixties witnessed the rise of a regional division of labour. Communalism was consolidated, while integration, which was desired by neither party, suffered a greater setback.

The entry of the Palestinian upper class into the Jordanian power structure came too late to guarantee it a secure position or influence in that structure. Its presence in the decision-making level of the bureaucracy remained of secondary importance. It was undoubtedly enriched as a result of governmental spending in the 1960s when new avenues were opened in commerce and industry, but, unlike the case with its Jordanian counterpart, wealth did not lead to political power. Its ties with the lower classes of Palestinian society were weak, due to the ineffectiveness of the tribal factor in Palestine.

Other strata of Palestinian society had less reason than their Trans-Jordanian counterparts to curry favour with the regime. Neither the urban bourgeoisie nor the peasants and workers were dependent on governmental employment to the same degree. Their interests as well as their liberal inclinations tended to steer them towards Pan-Arabism and anti-imperialism. Their heroes resided in Cairo and Damascus, and not in Amman, which they considered more or less a seat of occupation. West Bank farmers derived their income from relatives employed abroad, mainly in Kuwait and other oil states, as well as from their own farms. They were not accustomed to look to the Amman government for agricultural loans and price support, as did the peasants of the East Bank.

Palestinian workers, who made up the bulk of Jordan's industrial proletariat, were mainly refugees living in camps and shanty towns in and around Amman. They were expected to survive on meagre incomes, whereas Trans-Jordanian workers were more often than not retired soldiers collecting two salaries. Under these conditions interest articulation along class lines was out of the question. Workers and peasants from the East Bank drifted towards the Amman government, whereas Palestinian workers and peasants sought closer ties with Egypt and Syria and later embraced the Palestinian resistance movement.

The regional lines were drawn so precisely in the 1960s that the national coalition of opposition parties and groups of the 1950s virtually ceased to exist. So effective was the technocrats' technique of co-opting the various strata of East Bank society that opposition in the Hashemite realm became synonymous with the word 'Palestinian'. In fact, the 1957-8 uprisings and the subsequent suppression were the last in which a sector of East Bank society was also a target of the regime. The principal episodes of political opposition in the 1960s were strictly Palestinian affairs. And it was the absence of the East Bank factor from the opposition movement which paved the way for the massacre of September 1970. The technocrats took full credit for both — isolating the Palestinians and then attempting to deal them a crippling blow.

The massacre of 1970 was preceded by two confrontations demonstrating an absence of communal and regional integration. The first incident involved the agreement by Egypt, Syria and Iraq to establish a federal state on 17 April 1963, and the subsequent demonstrations in Jordan demanding that Jordan join the federation. These events brought about the resignation of Wasfi Tal's government on 27 March and the ouster of Samir Rifa'i's government on 20 April on a vote of no confidence.[23] Both in the street as well as in Parliament, Palestinians constituted the overwhelming opposition to the regime. Their sympathies were clearly with the 'advocates' of Arab unity.

The second confrontation involved the emergence in 1964 of the Palestine Liberation Organization, which was another project of the 'progressive' Arab states. If Hussein were to contribute to the achievement of the PLO goals, he would be presiding at the disintegration of his own dynasty. No sooner had the PLO been established than its troubles with Jordan began over the right of the PLO to tax Palestinians and to enrol them in the Palestine Liberation Army. For the first time the two communities had to face squarely the issue of sovereignty. Their dispute became an open conflict in 1966, when the Amman government ordered the PLO offices closed in Jordan. Ahmad Shukairy, the then

leader of the PLO, called for the establishment of a Palestinian republic
in the Kingdom of Jordan, and in November 1966, following an Israeli
attack on a West Bank village (al-Sammu), he urged all Palestinian members of the Jordanian Cabinet to resign.[24] Demonstrations staged in the
major Palestinian cities of the West Bank to protest the regime's inaction
in the face of Israel's attack on al-Sammu were put down by force, and
order was restored. It should be noted, however, that the regime's
opponents were predominantly Palestinians. Communalism had been
consolidated.

4. The Transformation of the Palestinian Community: from Political Conflict to Armed Confrontation

Israel's decisive military victory in June 1967 over the forces of Jordan,
Egypt and Syria contributed to a change in Palestinian relations with
Jordan and Israel. The Palestinians, whose struggle had remained political in nature during the fifties, now embarked on an activist, militant
course. They took up arms in pursuit of their goals and opted for
violence against the forces that had dismembered their country. This
was a radical departure from traditional Palestinian relations with Jordan
and Israel, the two states who shared the occupation of Palestine. Having
been galvanised into action by the 1967 War, the Palestinians began to
develop their own institutions in the political, military and social welfare
areas, and to compete with the Jordanian regime for allegiance of the
populace. Their failure to establish a revolutionary situation on the
Israeli-occupied West Bank left the East Bank as the logical base for their
operations against Israel.[25] This was bound to set them again on a col-
lision course with Jordan. King Hussein openly criticised them as early
as 4 September 1967, on the grounds that their operations from the East
Bank provoked Israeli retaliation: 'I regard it as a crime that any quarter
should send so-called commandos to engage in activities which can only
assist the enemy in his attempts to break the spirit of resistance to the
temporary occupation.'[26]

The commandos made it known that they would not permit the
regime to impede their operations. Their confrontation with Israeli
regulars at the Palestinian village of Karameh on the East Bank (March
1968) gave them prestige all over the Arab world. In Jordan, they began
to appear as a viable alternative to the Hussein regime. The internal
struggles of Jordan were no longer a domestic affair; they acquired a
wider Arab character. The loss of the Trans-Jordanian sector of the
opposition was compensated for by support from throughout the Arab
world. It was impossible for Hussein, at least for the time being, to crush

the Palestinian opposition, although Jordan's technocracy never ceased to advocate a total confrontation. Only when Arab support of the Palestinians began to waver would Hussein follow the technocrats' advice. For the time being the King was forced to bargain with the Palestinians, to an extent that jeopardised his sovereignty,[27] and he thus alienated the extreme right-wing sector of East Bank society. On 25 April 1968, he dismissed two Cabinet Ministers who had expressed their opposition to the use of Jordanian bases as a staging area for guerrilla attacks against Israel.[28] Further concessions to the commandos followed the confrontations of November 1968, and February and June 1970. The clashes of November 1968, which erupted right in the heart of Amman, were ended with compromise settlement in which the commandos stated their acceptance of the regime's authority, but which left them with 'a recognized sphere of political and military autonomy'. Malcolm Kerr underscored this autonomy as follows:

> The slogan 'no victor and no vanquished' was an odd slogan to describe relations between a government and its subjects; but it was an odd situation. 'No victor and no vanquished' really meant that by tacit agreement, this question was still in abeyance. It was to remain so for another two years.[29]

In fact, by August 1969, Hussein felt compelled to endorse publicly autonomy for the Palestinians, although he conceded that such an option could not be exercised until the occupation of the West Bank had come to an end:

> Our Palestinian brothers shall have the right of self-determination after the occupation has been removed. Until then all of our land, including the occupied parts, shall remain united under one flag, and we shall not allow disunity to enter our ranks.[30]

Meanwhile the struggle between the King and the commandos continued. The crisis of February 1970, which was precipitated by the regime's assertion of its rights to ban the carrying of weapons in cities and to require registration of all vehicles with the Jordanian authorities, ended in another political victory for the commandos. Rasoul al-Kilani, Minister of the Interior since June 1969, who tried to impose the new security measure, was dismissed on 23 February for the second time at the request of the commandos. Al-Fateh, the largest of the Palestinian organisations, issued a communique saying that 'we will not let ourselves be disarmed and we are certain that the noble soldiers of the Jordan army will stand by our revolution.'[31] After meeting with representatives of all the commando organisations, the King agreed to 'freeze'[32] his Minister's order, and he dismissed the affair as an 'unfortunate error' resulting from a 'misunderstanding'.[33]

The pact lasted for a few months, until 6 June, when a new confrontation erupted between the army and the commandos. At least 100 were killed and more than 250 injured during five days of fighting in and around the capital.[34] But again Hussein acceded to commando demands for the dismissal of top military and civilian officials and members of the ruling family who were associated with the new technocracy, which was beginning to see Hussein as 'too soft' on Palestinian radicalism.[35]

For them, the commando presence in Jordan was a violation of the principle of state sovereignty. They feared the Palestinians would ultimately supplant the Hashemite monarchy and establish a revolutionary republic in Jordan. Moreover, in the short run, they saw the commandos as the main obstacle to a political settlement with Israel. Liquidation of the Palestinian movement was seen as the wisest course, but Hussein was not yet ready for such a drastic measure. For the time being, he chose to ignore their counsel and listened to the more moderate wing of the East Bank component of his power structure, which was being gradually challenged by the technocrats. This faction advocated a conciliatory policy towards the commandos and sought a peaceful settlement between Israel and the Arab states. Although their roots were firmly entrenched in the Hashemite regime, they gravitated towards the Egyptian concept of a political settlement with Israel.[36] *They had hoped to divide the guerrilla movement and co-opt the moderate faction*, under Yasser Arafat's leadership, as a party to the negotiations. Their moderate counsel continued to prevail throughout the successive confrontations of 1968 and 1969.

5. Jordan, The Palestinians and Inter-Arab Politics

The resurrection of Security Council resolution 242 by Secretary of State William Rogers in December 1969 introduced a new element in the relations between the Palestinian movement and the Arab states. The Rogers Plan drove a wedge between the Palestinians and their Arab allies, whose support, as well as the internal balance of power, has prevented Hussein from adopting the confrontational posture advocated by the technocracy. Now the way for that course had been opened by the United States.[37] The moderate Prime Minister Abdul-Moneim al-Rifai was dismissed on 16 September 1970, and a Cabinet composed of army officers was appointed by the king. The next day war broke out. The attempted liquidation of the Palestinian movement was performed under the direction of Prime Minister Wasfi Tal, a representative *par excellence* of Jordan's technocracy. In a reply to the King's orders to take a 'firm and decisive line' against the commandos, Tal said, 'In our response there will be no hesitation, no tolerance and no compromises.'[38] It took the regime eight months to disarm the Palestinian guerrillas and to effectively terminate their political and military presence in Jordan. All this had been accomplished while an inter-Arab force was supposedly charged with finding a formula which would allow continued guerrilla action without infringing on Jordan's sovereignty. The Cairo Agreement, which was negotiated at an Arab summit meeting one day before the death of Nasser, stipulated that both guerrillas and army leave the cities.[39] The guerrillas were gradually driven to a narrow strip bordering the occupied West Bank where they were dealt a crushing blow in July 1971. All efforts to bring about a Jordanian compliance with the Cairo Agreement under the auspices of Saudi-Egyptian mediations ended with failure.

Although Hussein was showered with reproach by his Arab colleagues, some of whom even broke diplomatic relations, the general consensus of Arab regimes was that Black September did much to enhance their negotiating position *vis-à-vis* Israel.

Having achieved the cessation of guerrilla action in Jordan and renounced the Cairo Agreement, Hussein proceeded to attempt a Jordanisation of the Palestine question. His efforts were directed towards undoing what the PLO had gained in its endeavour to become a legitimate spokesman of the Palestinian people since 1969. On 15 March 1972, Hussein announced his plan for a so-called 'United Arab Kingdom' which envisaged autonomy for the Palestinians living on the West Bank.[40] He created a new portfolio for Occupied Territories Affairs in the Cabinet, which was formed by Zaid Al-Rifai in May 1973. The Minister holding the new portfolio became responsible for the distribution of travel and commercial licences to residents of the West Bank, as well as subsidies and grants to West Bank municipalities. These grants and the salaries paid to former Jordanian civil servants represented, in part, Hussein's bid for West Bank loyalty. Hussein continued his bid for restoration of the West Bank to his realm when the Arab Summit meeting opened at Rabat on 27 October 1974. He delivered a long speech giving his own version of Jordanian history from 1916 to 1974. The dominant theme of his speech was the allegation that the Palestinians have become an

integral part of Jordanian society, and that it was no longer possible to
separate the two people. On one occasion he asked rhetorically:

> Who are those citizens who will be dropped from membership in the
> state which they helped to construct? Are they the Palestinians who
> came from west of the river to the east in 1924 to help in building
> the nation? Or are they the ones who sought refuge in 1948 among
> their own people? Or those who immigrated in 1967 or were driven
> out by an oppressive occupation? Or are they only the Palestinians
> who reside in the West Bank but not in the East? Or Palestinians
> who hold Jordanian citizenship and live outside the boundaries of
> the Hashemite kingdom of Jordan?[41]

Quite plainly, Hussein was asking the conferees at Rabat to renounce
their decision of a year ago at Algiers making the PLO sole legitimate
representative of the Palestinian people. His statement represented an
unequivocal claim that Jordan was the only legal representative of *all*
the Palestinian people. The Arab heads of state simply disagreed; their
Algiers mandate to the PLO was affirmed.

Now as always, Jordan is ruled by its monarch with no place for free
democratic political activity, especially political parties. Thus the activity of the Palestinian organisation is all underground, very small and
highly vulnerable to the intelligence networks. The nature of relationships between the Jordanian government and the PLO is characterised
by mutual distrust and veiled enmity. For although the King has publicly
accepted the PLO as the sole legitimate representative of the Palestinian
people, the activities and other statements of Jordanian officials indicate
quite well that the Jordanian regime would like to re-annex the West
Bank to its rule. A sovereign independent Palestinian state in the West
Bank and Gaza, if it ever happens, may be a political and economic
magnet drawing away from the East Jordanian Palestinian population.
Should this happen, East Jordan will suffer and weaken accordingly. In
some ways its traditional regional 'police' function over the Palestinians
will have been lost as the new Palestinian state itself will perform that
function.

III. Lebanon

The Palestinian community in Lebanon numbers about one-third of a
million people. Accurate population figures for Lebanon are simply unavailable; the last official census, which was conducted in 1932, became
one of the principal elements justifying a confessional political system.

Confessionalism allocates political power in accordance with the numerical ratio each sect represents in the citizenry.[42] The Lebanese traditional leadership supported this system and formalised it in the National
Pact of 1943. They agreed upon a formula for a division of power in
the political, social, economic and military structures. Their arrangements did not provide for any possible changes in the ratios of the
various religious groupings in the country, hence a population census
would have been inconsistent with these delicate arrangements which
created a rather precarious distribution of power. Given the lack of an
official census, figures on the Palestinians in Lebanon abound. The
Bureau of Palestinian Affairs, which was established in the Ministry of
the Interior in 1949, reported that Palestinians numbered 180,000 in
1952 and 223,000 in 1968,[43] while the Research Center of the Palestine
Liberation Organization estimated that Palestinians were divided nearly
evenly between camp dwellers (106,440 in 1972) and those living on
their own in private residence.[44] Only a small fraction of the Palestinians living in Lebanon have been able to acquire Lebanese citizenship.[45]
These are mostly wealthy Christians who received the citizenship during
the presidency of Camille Chamoun between 1952 and 1958. The greatest majority of Palestinians remained stateless; they were treated as
foreigners. Like other foreigners, they have rights of property ownership, investment and employment, by permit. They were placed under
the jurisdiction of the General Bureau of Palestinian Affairs in the Ministry of Interior, which regulates their affairs relating to travel, matters
of personal status, and movement from one camp to another.

Because a large segment of the Palestinians were farmers and unskilled,
they were employed cheaply and exploited accordingly. According to
one report, nearly 30,000 workers constituted in 1971 a pool of cheap
farm labour.[46] It is estimated that 60 per cent of Palestinians residing in
Lebanon are workers (both skilled and unskilled) in agricultural, industrial
and artisan jobs. In south and north Lebanon, Palestinians worked mostly
in agricultural wage labour, especially on citrus and other plantations.
In Beirut and its eastern suburbs, the Lebanese industrial development
emerged through the labour of poor Palestinians who had to compete
with other exploited groups such as Syrians, Kurds, and poor Lebanese
Sh'ites who fled incessant Israeli bombing of the south. Because of
official restrictions on the employment of foreigners, all these groups
living in what became known as the 'Misery Belt' provided black-market
labour at wages far below the officially sanctioned minimum wages.
Many workers preferred this arrangement to the complex and lengthy
process of obtaining a work permit which offered neither social security

nor insurance benefits nor a regular wage increase, and which became
invalid when its holder was laid off the job. Moreover, employment in
large institutions is governed by the rules of the confessional system
which makes allocations in accordance with sectarian affiliation; hence
it is largely closed to Palestinians.

Table 5.1 reveals the comparatively low percentage of Palestinians
who held work permits in 1969.

Table 5.1:   Percentage of Work Permit Holders by National Groupings

Nationality	Number of Residents	Percentage of Work Permit Holders
Jordanian	16,890	4.0
Iraqi	7,027	2.5
Egyptian	5,148	26.5
American	6,095	10.5
Palestinian	225,000	1.0

Source: Sulafa Hijjawi, 'The Palestinians in Lebanon', *Journal of the Center for
     Palestinian Studies* (Baghdad), no. 22 (May/June 1977), p. 44 (in Arabic).

Despite all this, the Palestinians in Lebanon did enjoy a certain measure
of psychological security. Their occupational and class structure is basically similar to the Lebanese structure as they become integrated economically into the country. The Palestinian middle class, or petty
bourgeoisie, is substantial. It is estimated to be about 30 per cent of
the Palestinian population, superceded in wealth and influence by a
Palestinian bourgeoisie of 2-3 per cent. The Palestinian bourgeoisie and
middle class, white-collar workers as well as small entrepreneurs, have
played a pivotal role in the capitalist economic development of Lebanon.
Palestinians were prominent in building the Lebanese banking institution
(e.g. Intra Bank, Arab Bank, etc.), airline companies (MEA and TMA),
cinemas, design, construction, auditing, marketing and other institutions
of technical services. Furthermore, they were active in building the
boutiques and entertainment businesses of Ras Beirut, the most cosmo-
politan part of Lebanon. Additionally, Palestinians, in part because of
their knowledge of English, became employed in those American businesses
that made Beirut their Middle Eastern headquarters. For the above reasons
the Palestinian community in Lebanon has a substantial, highly educated
and highly skilled middle class.

1. Communal Conflict and Ideological Development, 1967-1978

The Palestinian role in Lebanon, unlike that in Jordan, was restricted
to the private sector. Their dynamic role in the private economy of
Lebanon was matched by their political activity on several levels: in
pan-Arab parties and movements, and in organising student, worker and
white-collar unions both before and after the rise of the armed Palestinian movement. And just as significant, they made a vital contribution
to the intellectual ferment which had both a national and regional
impact. These political and quasi-political activities developed in the
context of rapid transformation of Lebanese society in the last eleven
years (1967-78). The rise of the Palestinian movement coincided with
the structural crises of Lebanese society that polarised the country and
gave birth to two contradictory political tendencies: the Lebanese left
and right. The socio-political polarisation of the Lebanese population
as a consequence of internal Lebanese dynamics inevitably became enmeshed with the Palestinian movement (and vice versa) which probably
acted as a catalyst for the savage and bitter Lebanese civil war. The Palestinian question and its solution became permanently linked with the
Lebanese problem and its solution – witness southern Lebanon now.

As early as 1969 and starting with the Israeli attack on Beirut Air-
port, the Lebanese government sought to control, if not suppress, the
popular Palestinian guerrillas. Following a period of social unrest in
early 1969, which witnessed many a strike among students, agricultural
and port workers, and teachers, the authorities began to tighten the
reins by first establishing a so-called *cordon sanitaire* of soldiers around
the southern region in which Palestinian guerrillas had established their
bases, thus cutting them off from supplies and food. A second step was
the rounding up of numerous suspected dissidents, Palestinians and Lebanese alike, which led to the bloody events of 23 April 1969. Spontaneous demonstrations erupted in major Lebanese cities protesting against
repression and asserting the right of the guerrillas to freedom of action.
More than thirty were killed and a hundred wounded in these demonstrations. Rightist Lebanese politicians who had earlier endorsed the
cause of the Palestinian fighters began to perceive the matter in the context of Lebanese domestic politics. The President of the Republic contributed to the ensuing polarisation when he proclaimed on 31 May
1969 that the military presence of the Palestinians was 'totally rejected'.[47]

Later during the year, refugee camps witnessed an armed insurrection
following bombardment of these camps by the military, and the city of
Tripoli was the scene of violent street fighting. In both areas insurrection-

ists challenged the central government by declaring 'autonomy' in areas
they came to control after they succeeded in expelling the authorities.
The inconclusive conflict resulted in the Cairo Accords (November 1969),
which have become ever since the basis for regulating Lebanese-Palestin-
ian relations. Thus the weakness of the Lebanese state became for the
Palestinians the functional equivalent of the 'red bases' or the 'liberated
zones' of, say, Vietnamese revolutionaries.

The Cairo Accords formalised a relationship whereby the Lebanese
government and PLO jointly supervised Palestinian refugee camps, and
according to which the Lebanese government accepted and recognised
a Palestinian military presence in the country for the first time.[48]

Palestinians organised and mobilised themselves; they grew stronger
not only militarily and organisationally (more so than in Jordan), but
also politically and diplomatically. Of course, what helped them in Lebanon was that at least half the population, the patriotic (nationalist)
and progressive, supported them and learned from them. Thus, a Lebanese progressive-Palestinian alliance was forged as the country polarised.
Hence, it is not surprising that the civil war started in spring 1975, with
the rightist Phalangist attack on a Palestinian bus in a Beirut suburb.
The Palestinians became enmeshed in a Lebanese war in spite of themselves. The Phalange rightists strategy was intended from the very
beginning to drag the Palestinians into the civil conflict by redirecting
the focus of the conflict to the relationship between the Palestine national movement and the Lebanese government. They regarded containment of the Palestinians as crucial to the task of dealing with the social
unrest. A series of provocations by the rightists throughout the latter
part of 1975, culminating in the massacre of 'Black Saturday' on 6
December, the siege of the Tal Al-Zaater refugee camp, the capture of
the Dbaye camp, and the Quarantina and Maslakh massacres in early
January 1976, thrust the Palestinians, who had kept more or less to the
periphery, into the midst of the battle. Hence the counter-offensive of
January 1976, by the Palestinian-leftist alliance leading to the Syrian
proxy intervention aimed at forestalling a Palestinian-leftist victory.[49]

The Syrian and other foreign intervention stopped the potential and
probable victory of the Palestinian-Lebanese leftist alliance. The civil
war ended without resolving the issues that triggered it. The Syrian-
Lebanese rightist alliance that ended the war and contained both the
Palestinians and the Lebanese nationalist/leftist movement is now under
strain as a result of the regional changes; the rise of the Likud to power
in Israel and its interventionism in Lebanon. Some readjustments in
regional political forces are currently in order. The new Lebanese state

being constructed under Syrian auspices is still far too weak to re-impose its authority on anyone in Lebanon. Furthermore, the instransigence and hostility of the Lebanese right does not augur well for stability and peace in the country despite the recent Chtaura Agreement which reaffirmed the Cairo Accords with some modifications.

The Palestinian situation in Lebanon, for those active in the movement as well as for individuals who have never been involved, has become more complicated and uncertain. The situation will remain uncertain until the outline of the Lebanese system becomes clear. Moreover, the threat of another round of civil war in which the Palestinians could become involved again is not out of the picture.

Finally, the Lebanese state, new and old, as well as the Lebanese establishment and ruling class, would favour most strongly a regional political settlement in which the Palestinians gain an entity of their own on the West Bank. This would be the basis for moving the Palestinians *en masse* out of Lebanon. Short of that, the Lebanese right has called for another dispersal of the Palestinian residents in Lebanon to other Arab countries. (In this way the Lebanese right hopes to reimpose its rule over the rest of Lebanon and to liquidate the Lebanese left.)

In conclusion, the situation in Lebanon is principally dependent now on the resolution of the outstanding regional issues, especially the question of a Palestinian entity.

IV. Kuwait

Palestinians began to emigrate to Kuwait soon after the Zionist take-over of their country in 1948. It was a steady pattern of immigration which received a quantitative boost soon after the 1967 War and the expulsion of more Palestinians from the West Bank and Gaza.

They are the largest immigrant community, amounting to more than 200,000, or more than half of all Kuwaiti nationals in a country with 1.13 million people. Together with the Lebanese, they have lived in Kuwait longer than any other Arab expatriate group and are more firmly established—holding key positions in nearly all official establishments alongside the private sector. They played the most crucial role in building the modern Kuwaiti state, being widely represented in banking, the technical services, education and the various industries. Indeed, Palestinians are the principal civil servants in the country. For example, until recently, the Ministry of Electricity was dominated entirely by Palestinians while over 50 per cent of the personnel of the Health and Education ministries was also Palestinian. They even had a role in building the army through their work in Kuwait's defence ministry. In medicine,

Palestinian doctors constitute about 40 per cent out of the estimated 1,000 medical doctors currently practising in Kuwait. In the oil industry, Palestinians in Kuwait work at highly skilled levels, especially in production and maintenance of machinery.

Together with the Lebanese, the Palestinians find employment at all levels and are not part of the ethnic division of labour which prevails in the country. For example, Egyptians are prominent in the professions, particularly teaching and medicine, besides performing menial tasks; Indians work as house-servants and in lower-grade clerical functions; Pakistanis and Iranians specialise in tailoring and construction work and Syrians occupy jobs in the retail trade and business.[50]

In Kuwait the Palestinian middle class is the largest among the communities in 'diaspora', and is also the largest segment of the middle class of all people resident in Kuwait. It is estimated that 35 per cent of the Kuwaiti Palestinians are middle-class, with an additional 5 per cent of big entrepreneurs: merchants, constructors, etc. Few if any industrial capitalists exist. The remaining 60 per cent are skilled and unskilled workers in all sectors of the economy, but especially in services, and petty bourgeois shop-owners.

The Palestinian right to residence in Kuwait is granted on an individual basis, not as a collective privilege as in the Levant Arab countries. A Palestinian can reside in Kuwait on a temporary basis as long as he has employment. If he becomes unemployed he has only 15 days before he is deported. Thus, a strong feeling of insecurity exists. Young Kuwaiti Palestinians who leave the country to study abroad cannot go back to live in Kuwait unless they obtain work permits, even if they were born there. The number of Palestinians who acquired citizenship in Kuwait is very negligible; the Naturalization Decree of 1959 restricted citizenship to those who lived in Kuwait continuously since 1920 and their descendents. But to ensure against mass naturalisation, the decree stipulated that only fifty persons are to receive citizenship in any given year.

Like all foreigners, Palestinians have no right to own immovable property in Kuwait. The Imports Law of 1964 confined the right of importation to citizens, partnerships providing all members are citizens, and stock companies in which Kuwaiti capital is not less than 51 per cent.[51] Likewise, the Law of Industries of 1965 limited the right of establishing industrial firms to Kuwaiti nationals who may be owners, managers or the majority on boards of directors. In fact, licences are withheld from any firm that fails to employ at least 25 per cent citizens. Moreover, Kuwaiti graduates are exempted from civil service entry examinations and certain degree requirements. They have exclusive rights to certain top executive administrative and academic posts.[52] In addition, pension privileges, social security benefits, unemployment compensations, as well as mortgage loans and other such benefits, are the exclusive preserve of Kuwaitis.[53] In retirement, the government as well as the private sector provide for the expatriate a single pay-off amounting to one month's salary for each year of work. At this point the expatriate's residency is revoked and his only option is to return home. Palestinians who have no home to return to and who have struck deep roots in Kuwait and bred children and grandchildren become resentful with so much at stake.

Although these discriminatory parochial measures affect all non-Kuwaitis, the Palestinians, as the largest single group and victims of fragmentation and dispersal, tend to view themselves as the principal victims. After all, their situation is unique, for, unlike other foreigners, they view themselves as being there to stay. Most Egyptians and Syrians employed by the government are technically 'on loan' for a specified period by their respective governments to assist in the development of Kuwait. As non-Arabs, Indians and Pakistanis have no aspirations to be treated as citizens. Koreans and other Far Easterners go to Kuwait on contracts. The Palestinians, on the other hand, have no state to protect them and no nation to house them. When the Kuwait government decreed in June 1978 that Kuwaiti landlords may increase rents by 100 per cent and evict tenants from buildings constructed over twenty-five years before for the purpose of remodelling, Palestinians living in the battered districts of metropolitan Kuwait City (Hawalli and Nugra) perceived the measure as being directed against them – a more sophisticated method of deportation.[54]

Palestinian-owned property, investments and businesses are registered in the names of Kuwaiti nationals to assure compliance with the law. These so-called 'dummy' partners receive a share for merely lending their names. Thus despite its size, its economic significance and its organisational base, the Palestinian community is insecure and tenuous, as it is throughout the rest of the Gulf and Peninsula.

In Kuwait the Palestinians have no right to engage in internal Kuwaiti politics and actually have no role. Besides, political parties are not allowed in Kuwait. However, the Kuwaiti government permits the PLO and Fateh to organise and politically mobilise the Palestinian community there. Demonstrating, however, is not allowed. The PLO runs its own schools; a fact that helped the mobilisation of the Palestinians enormously. However, because of the fears generated by the Lebanese war, the Kuwaiti government forced the reintegration of Palestinian students with Kuwaiti and other students in the public schools. Indeed, a governmental tightening of its grip over the Palestinian community in Kuwait has developed as a consequence of the Lebanese tragedy and Kuwaiti fears of Palestinian trouble. In fact, the government has occasionally rounded up suspected Palestinians for quick deportation in an effort to break up a tightly knit, highly motivated and politically conscious group. The last such incidents occurred two years ago at the height of the Lebanese civil war. So insecure was the Kuwaiti establishment at that time that the Ruler ordered the Articles of the Constitution suspended, Parliament dissolved and periodicals censored. Professional associations and popular organisations known for liberal and progressive leanings were also dissolved. The government was apparently convinced that the Lebanese fall-out could undermine law and order. Again, the Palestinians viewed themselves as the principal virus against which such 'preventive' measures had to be undertaken.

It may appear paradoxical, however, that in foreign affairs Kuwait has strongly and consistently supported the efforts and positions of the PLO. Kuwait has been more consistent and more principled in this political, financial and diplomatic support than any of the other peninsula states. Many examples can be cited to support this observation. But the Lebanese tragedy has had its impact on Kuwaiti-Palestinian relations. It is clear that Kuwait would support the PLO in its effort to achieve a sovereign Palestinian state. It remains an open question, however, as to how many Palestinians would want to leave Kuwait to return to what would inevitably be a less affluent life in an independent Palestinian state.

V. Syria

The size of the Palestinian community in Syria is quite small, especially by comparison with the total Syrian population (250,000 out of 8,000,000 or 3 per cent), most of them registered as refugees. Of these, about 50,000 reside in camps. This is unlike a Palestinian majority in Jordan, over 20 per cent in Kuwait and about 10 per cent in Lebanon. Syria's treatment of the Palestinians derives from its long history of support for pan-Arab movements and ideology and from its anti-imperialist stances. In some ways, Palestinians became most integrated into Syrian society at all levels and rarely suffered discrimination in jobs, rights to ownership or political activity. Palestinians are represented in all walks of Syrian life, including top-level command of the Syrian Ba'ath Party.

Their economic role is neither visible nor very significant, for two

main reasons: first, their number, which constitutes a small percentage
of the total population, and second, the economic policies of the state,
which favour regulation, controls and various restrictions. Unlike Lebanon, where a free-enterprise system enabled enterprising Palestinians
to prosper and achieve upward mobility, Syria's control of imports and
exports and strict currency regulations create a climate which is not conducive to business. Fewer gaps thus exist in the social structure of the
Palestinian community in Syria.[55]

However, their political role is important. They have participated
actively in the political life of Syria over the past quarter-century. Syria,
government and people, have always supported the Palestine cause.

Various Syrian governments have supported Palestinian guerrillas
materially and politically. Syria permits Palestinians to operate training
camps and mobilise the refugee camps politically but only to Palestinian
organisations who are in agreement with the Syrian regime's policy: these
have been principally the Saiqa, Fateh, and the Democratic Popular Front
for the Liberation of Palestine.

Palestinians serving with guerrillas or the PLO were not required to
serve in the Syrian armed forces. But with the Syrian intervention in
Lebanon and the sudden Syrian-Palestinian War, all Fateh and other activists were arrested and the training camps closed and material aid stopped. Now some of the Palestinian armaments are open again. A Syrian-
Palestinian *rapprochement* has been taking place and may get strengthened the more Syria feels isolated by the process of Middle East political
settlement. The Syrian-Palestinian bridges were never burned despite
the short and costly war in which they were engaged. Furthermore,
Syria still remains most determined to include the Palestinians in a political settlement in Geneva, and for a sovereign West Bank-Gaza state to
be created. The degree of the Syrian regime's support for these minimal
Palestinian rights depends on its international situation and on the internal opposition to the Assad government. Syria seems unimpressed by
semantic and/or cosmetic solutions proposed by Israel. The future
remains most uncertain.

VI. Iraq

The Palestinian community in Iraq is numerically insignificant, about
40,000 out of a population of 12 million, or a mere 0.33 per cent of the
total population. Population figures for the Palestinians in Iraq are unreliable. The Republican government which assumed power in 1958
did not consider as refugees those who arrived since that date, hence the
census taken by the Bureau of Palestinian Affairs in 1969 shows a figure

of 13,743 Palestinians, which did not include those who entered since 1958, particularly the refugees of the 1967 War.[56] Most of those who arrived since 1967 reside illegally in Iraq, having no work permits or governmental subsidies.

Unlike Jordan, Syria and Lebanon, there are no refugee camps in Iraq. Instead of the United Nations Relief and Work Agency, various governmental agencies assumed responsibility for caring for the Palestinian refugees. The Ministry of Defence was in charge of their affairs until 1950 when that responsibility was transferred to the Ministry of Social Affairs. The Bureau of Palestinian Affairs in the Ministry of Social Affairs has been budgeting a sum of 200,000 dinars (equivalent to $600,000) per year since 1952, some of which is distributed in the form of a regular monetary allowance while some is spent on housing.[57] No more than a third of those registered with the bureau receive the monetary allowance, and nearly two-thirds benefit from public housing.[58] The Revolutionary Command Council of the Ba'ath regime decreed on 17 August 1969 that housing projects be constructed for Palestinians residing in Iraq.[59] Families began to move into these publicly owned houses in 1970 free of charge. A large number of Palestinians, however, still live in shelters and emergency housing prepared for them by the defence ministry in 1949.

Like Kuwait, Iraq does not permit Palestinians to own immovable property; however, discrimination in employment rarely exists. Palestinians were accorded equality by law with Iraqi citizens in appointments, promotions and retirement benefits.[60]

The social structure of the Palestinian community in Iraq is characterised by the existence of serious gaps. The original refugees and their descendants, who constitute the majority of Palestinians in Iraq, provide a pool of unskilled and semi-skilled cheap labour. They were unable to practise their skills as farmers due to the Iraqi government's policy which discouraged their settlement on farm land and which prohibited them from owning land and property. Having arrived with the Iraqi army, which participated in the Palestine War of 1948, from villages near Haifa, these refugees converged on the big cities of Baghdad, Basra and Mosul, where they were unable to compete with educated urban and indigenous inhabitants. Unable to pursue the only work they knew, they were placed at the mercy of employers who exploited them as cheap labour. A second group, which emigrated in the early 1950s, engaged in insignificant vocations as small shopkeepers, barbers, cleaners, tailors and small restaurant-owners. With the growing industrialisation of Iraq after the oil boom, a section of this petty bourgeoisie abandoned their small businesses and became factory workers. A third group of Palestinians, who immigrated to Iraq in the late 1950s in pursuit of a better life, is constituted of a bourgeoisie of big merchants and contractors, while some are engaged in the professions, the civil service and clerical jobs.

Palestinians remained largely absent from the press and cultural life in general, unlike their counterparts in Jordan, Kuwait and Lebanon. Their political role also remained insignificant despite the fact that various Iraqi governments supported the Palestinian cause. Between 1949 and 1958, Palestinians were fairly active in Arab nationalist politics in accordance with the prevailing assumption that the liberation of Palestine would have to be a general Arab undertaking. They gravitated towards the Arab Nationalist Movement, the Ba'ath, the Communist Party and other nationalist groups. With the fall of the monarchy, a large segment embraced the Nasserite cause. Succeeding regimes in Iraq, however, insisted on political conformity and showed even less tolerance of dissent than did the monarchy.

During the Qassem era the regime inaugurated a Palestine Liberation Brigade within the army, with officers and soldiers recruited from among the Palestinians. The mission of the brigade, which was assumed to be a nucleus for a thoroughly Palestinian army, has rarely exceeded participation in parades for visiting Arab delegations. By 1963, when Qassem was overthrown, the brigade was integrated into the Iraqi army and was renamed the First Brigade. Many Palestinian officers and soldiers dropped out, and the brigade was sent to northern Iraq to take part in the campaign against the Kurds.

The present Ba'ath government in Iraq has been an advocate of people's war but is presently at odds with the Palestine Liberation Organization. The PLO office in Baghdad is controlled by a pro-Iraqi who has been sentenced to death by the PLO. His close association with the Iraqi government enabled him to establish a political machine which presides at the distribution of patronage to sympathetic Palestinians. Jobs, housing, scholarships and other benefits are dispensed to reward allies and punish enemies.

In the military sphere the government sponsors the Arab Liberation Front, one of the several Palestinian guerrilla organisations, which, together with the political machine, constitutes an important avenue of social mobility for Palestinians in Iraq.

Given Iraq's isolation in the region as well as its enmity to the Ba'ath government of Syria, it is unlikely that the present Iraqi leadership will take a firm stand on the Palestine question and the Arab-Israeli conflict. Iraq is a 'rejectionist' but it has so far rejected the rejectionists who consist of Syria, PLO, Libya, Algeria and Democratic Yemen. In the meantime, it is one of the few Arab countries which have not recognised the United Nations Security Council resolution 242, which calls on Israel to withdraw from Arab territories occupied in 1967 in exchange for recognition of Israel. In the present circumstances, it is unlikely that Iraq would support the PLO in its efforts to achieve a sovereign Palestinian state.

VII. Summary and Conclusion

We have dealt in this chapter with Palestinian reality in exile. More specifically, we have discussed the Palestinians as political minorities in selected Arab host countries, namely, Jordan, Kuwait, Lebanon, Syria and Iraq. It is evident from our discussion that the numerical ratio of Palestinian communities in these Arab countries varies tremendously: from about 60 per cent in Jordan to less than one-third of 1 per cent in Iraq. Moreover, it is also clear that this numerical variation does not alter the minority status of the Palestinians, either in terms of their own perception, or in terms of the objective conditions under which they have to exist.

The persistent and complex minority status of Palestinians in Arab host countries is unchanged by their varied population ratios, occupational structure, educational level, class structure or economic integration. Palestinians have become 'minorities' with the dismemberment of Palestine and remain so in the context of the continuing Palestine-Zionist conflict, the Arab-Israeli conflict, and the local and regional interests of Arab regimes. In other words, although Palestinians in Arab countries are objectively not ethnic minorities, they are treated by the regimes with suspicion and largely as subjugated minorities who are denied full freedom of action.

Palestinians in exile in Arab host countries have been residentially and socially segregated. Residentially, Palestinians have been living together in refugee camps or in city districts and neighbourhoods which have been almost exclusively Palestinian. This is a consequence of two factors: the typical residential segregation of the traditional Arab city, and the pragmatic placement of Palestinian populations as a result of sudden and massive migrations. They are absorbed into special or new sections of the cities. And as the waves of flight and migration out of the different regions or districts and cities of Palestine took place at different times, this pattern of population movement brought kin groups, clans, friends and acquaintances to the same refuge. This pattern thus meant the transfer of whole Palestinian villages, districts or larger kin groupings more or less to the same residential areas in exile.

This fact enabled the Palestinians in exile to recreate much of their pre-diaspora social relations. It helped them retain their Palestinian dialects, social customs, even their distinctive folklore. Significantly, Palestinians typically intermarried with each other and not with the Arabs of the host countries. The tragic experiences in the loss of their livelihood – their property – and of their country, and the traumatic disruption of their lives came to be collectively memorialised annually and frequently. These occasions reinforced their collective consciousness of themselves as Palestinians. Thus, despite their relative and differential integration in the respective economies of the host Arab countries, their residential segregation and the institutionalisation of their collective memory enabled the Palestinians to reproduce in exile their social and cultural relations. Most significantly, however, these factors sustained and reinforced their identity as Palestinians. There is no doubt also that the treatment by the host governments of the Palestinian exiles, as circumscribed or subjugated socio-political minorities, helped sustain their identity and their collective consciousness. In turn, these factors helped the Palestinians organise an independent liberation movement in order to liberate both person and land from Zionism. Finally, their socio-political minority status can be altered only when they create their autonomous and independent social, political and economic institutions in their homeland of Palestine.

Notes

1. Of course, the Palestinians who remained in their homeland after the establishment of Israel did become an ethnic, linguistic and religious minority. In Israel, the so-called Israeli Arabs have been treated by Israel antagonistically as a colonised group subject to all kinds of discriminatory and prejudicial laws and attitudes. See E. Zureik, *The Palestinians in Israel, A Study in Internal Colonialism* (Routledge and Kegan Paul, London, 1979); see also S. Jiryes, *The Arabs in Israel* (Monthly Review Press, New York, 1976).

2. P. van den Berghe, *Race and Racism* (J. Wiley, New York, 1967); see also F. James Davis, *Minority-Dominant Relations* (Arlington Heights, Illinois, 1978).

3. See S. Farsoun, 'South Africa and Israel: A Special Relationship', paper given at Conference on Socio-Economic Trends and Policies in Southern Africa, United Nations African Institute for Economic Planning, Dakar. Conference took place in Dar-es-Salaam, 29 November-1 December 1975. Excerpted in S. Farsoun, 'Settler Colonialism and Herrenfolk Democracy' in R.P. Stevens and A. Al-Messiri, *Israel and South Africa* (New Brunswick, NJ, 1977).

4. See I. Abu-Lugod (ed.), *The Transformation of Palestine* (Evanston, Illinois, 1971); D. Waines, *A Sentence of Exile* (Wilmette, Illinois, 1977).

5. S. Ryan, *Israeli Economic Policy in the Occupied Areas: Foundations of a*

New Imperialism (Middle East Research and Information, Washington, DC, Project Report No. 4).

6. It is these majority policies in the political and economic content, together with the collective responses on the part of the minority, which influence individual and personal perceptions, attitudes and personal relations.

7. The population of the East Bank prior to the merger was estimated at 400,000; the population of the West Bank at the same time was 850,000.

8. A. Konikoff, *Transjordan: An Economic Survey* (Jerusalem, 1946), p. 18.

9. *Survey of Palestine* (Jerusalem, 1946), pp. 137-9, 148-51.

10. *Survey of Palestine*, pp. 763, 766.

11. *Survey of Palestine*, p. 717; Konikoff, *Transjordan*, p. 27.

12. Nasser H. Aruri, *Jordan: A Study in Political Development* (The Hague, 1972).

13. Mohammed Y. al-Husseini, *al-Tatawor al-Ijtima'i wa al-Iqtisadi fi Filastin al-Arabiya* (*Social and Economic Development in Arab Palestine*) (Jerusalem, c. 1946), pp. 193-4; *Survey of Palestine*, p. 716.

14. George Harris, *Jordan* (New Haven, Conn., 1958), p. 73.

15. *Proceedings of the Jordan House of Representatives* (Arabic), (Amman, 1954-5), p. 32.

16. John B. Glubb, *A Soldier With The Arabs* (London, 1957), p. 347.

17. H. al-Majali, *Muthakkarati* (*My Memoirs*) (Amman, n.d.), p. 142.

18. For a discussion of this period, see Aruri, *Jordan*, pp. 111-50.

19. For an account of how Hussein perceived the Baghdad Pact, see King Hussein, *Uneasy Lies the Head* (London, 1962), pp. 108-9; Peter Snow, *Hussein: A Biography* (Washington, DC, 1972), p. 72. For a somewhat different account, see Elizabeth Monroe, *Britain's Moments in the Middle East* (Baltimore, 1963), p. 188.

20. See al-Majali, *Muthakkarati*, pp. 147-48; Glubb, *Soldier*; George Lenczowski, *The Middle East in World Affairs* (Ithaca, NY, 1962), p. 458.

21. *Documents on American Foreign Relations*, 1957 (New York, 1958), p. 231; *New York Times*, 26 April 1957.

22. For an interesting discussion of class conflict in Jordan, see *Ba'd Qadaya al-Sira' al-Ijtima'i fi al-Urdun* (*Social Conflicts in Jordan*) (Haifa, c. 1973).

23. For an account of inter-Arab politics at this time, see Aruri, *Jordan*, pp. 180-3.

24. V. Vance and P. Lauer, *Hussein of Jordan: My War With Israel* (London, 1969), pp. 29-30.

25. With the influx of additional Palestinian refugees from the West to the East Bank after the 1967 June War, Palestinians came to constitute two-thirds of the population of the East Bank.

26. *al-Dustour* (Amman), 5 September 1967, quoted in Fuad Jabber, 'The Arab Regimes and The Revolution', *Journal of Palestine Studies*, vol. 2, no. 2 (Winter 1973), p. 86.

27. 'The commandos were building an incipient state of their own in Jordan,' and a political force which paralleled the monarchy (Malcolm Kerr, *The Arab Cold War, 1958-1970* (London, 1971), p. 141.

28. One of the dismissed, Minister of Interior Hasan al-Kayed, had made a statement in February declaring that the government had intended to strike at the guerrillas 'with an iron fist' (*New York Times*, 26 April 1968). He was removed, along with the Defence Minister Habes al-Majali and the former Chief of Intelligence Rasoul al-Kilani. The latter was a national security adviser to the King at the time of his dismissal.

29. Kerr, *Arab Cold War*, p. 141.

30. *New York Times*, 3 August 1969.

31. *Christian Science Monitor,* 12 February 1970.

32. *New York Times,* 13 February 1970.

33. Snow, *Hussein,* p. 211; *New York Times,* 16 February 1970.

34. *New York Times,* 11 June 1973.

35. This group consisted of General Nasser Ibn Jamil, the King's uncle, Gen. Zayd Ibn Shaker, the King's cousin and chief of intelligence. Others who were associated with this group but who were not in power at the time included Gen. Habes al-Majali, who at times served as defence Minister and army chief of staff, Wasfi Tal, an intelligence officer and later Prime Minister, Salah Abu-Zayd, a propagandist and Minister of Information, and Zayd al-Rifa'i, chief of the royal court and Prime Minister since June 1973. It represents the views and interests of the overwhelming majority in the army, the landlords, big businessmen and tribal leaders, and comprises the technocrats of the 1960s.

36. This group represents a segment of the Jordanian bourgeoisie that viewed the rapid rise to power of the technocrats as a threat to its own position. Principal figures include Abdul-Moneim Rifa'i and Bahjat Talhouni, both members of prominent Jordanian families with a long record of service to the dynasty. The two men served as premiers throughout most of the period of confrontations between the commandos and the army.

37. *New York Times,* 12 September 1970.

38. 'The Palestinian Resistance and Jordan', *Journal of Palestine Studies,* vol. 1, no. 1 (Autumn 1971), p. 163. Wasfi Tal was assassinated on 28 November 1971 in Cairo by Palestinian commandos.

39. *The Times* (London), 28 September 1970.

40. *New York Times,* 15 March 1972.

41. *The Bases of the Jordanian Position: the National Declaration Presented by King Hussein at the Rabat Summit Conference* (Press Department, Amman, October 1974), pp. 28-49.

42. For a brief discussion of confessionalism, see Michael Suleiman, 'Origins of the Lebanese Civil War' in N. Aruri and F. Moughrabi (eds.), *Lebanon: Crisis and Challenge in the Arab World* (Association of Arab American-University Graduates, Detroit, 1977), pp. 2-4.

43. Sulafa Hijjawi, 'The Palestinians in Lebanon', *Journal of the Center for Palestine Studies* (Baghdad), no. 22 (May/June 1977), p. 44 (in Arabic).

44. Elias Khouri, *Palestinian Statistics* (PLO Research Center, Beirut), p. 21.

45. About 3,000, according to Hani Mendis, *al-Amal wa al-Ummal fi al-Mukhayan al-Filastini.*

46. 'Agricultural Report of the Lebanese Communist Party' in Hijjawi, 'The Palestinians in Lebanon', p. 42.

47. *Palestinian Documents* (PLO Research Center, Beirut, 1969), p. 218.

48. Unofficial text of the Accords was published in *al-Nahar* (Beirut), 20 April 1970.

49. See Naseer Aruri, 'The Syrian Strategy and the Lebanese Conflict' in Aruri and Moughrabi, *Lebanon,* pp. 21-5; S. Farsoun and W. Carroll, 'The Civil War in Lebanon', *Monthly Review,* vol. 28 (June 1976).

50. 'Expatriates, No Pot of Gold', *Financial Times* (London), 27 February 1976 (Survey on Kuwait), p. 22.

51. Text in *al-Kuwait al-Yawm; al-Jarida al-Rasmiya (Kuwait Today: The National Gazette),* no. 84, 18 May 1965, pp. 35f.

52. Kuwait, Ministry of Guidance and Information, *Kuwait Today: A Welfare State* (Nairobi, Kenya, n.d.), p. 158f.

53. Ibid., pp. 18-24.

54. See *al-Raye al-Amm* (Kuwait daily newspaper), 29 June 1978.

55. D. Peretz, 'Palestinian Social Stratification: the Political Implications',

Journal of Palestine Studies, vol. 7, no. 1 (1977), p. 62.

56. I. Sakhnini, 'al-Filastiniyun fi al-Iraq' ('The Palestinians in Iraq'), *Sh'un Filastiniya*, no. 13 (September 1972), p. 90.

57. *al-Waqa'i al-Iraqiya* (*Iraqi Chronicles*), no. 530, 1 June 1961. See also ibid., pp. 91-2.

58. Sakhnini, 'al-Filastiniyun', pp. 92-5.

59. *al-Waqa'i al-Iraqiya*, no. 1772, 28 August 1969.

60. Ibid.

6 PALESTINIAN WOMEN: PATTERNS OF LEGITIMATION AND DOMINATION

Yvonne Haddad

Over the last four decades Palestinian history and politics have received extensive coverage from scholars of the Middle East; Palestinian women, however, have been virtually ignored as a topic of study. Anthropologists, sociologists and feminists have generally concentrated on the role and status of women in Egypt and Lebanon because of the availability of research funds for such studies, the presence of several universities, and the general trend-setting influences of these two countries over the rest of the Arab world.

A major reason for the paucity of studies on Palestinian women is the difficulty in identifying, studying and drawing conclusions about persons who represent one geo-cultural area, but who are actually living in diaspora. Palestinians are now located all over the world. Their receptivity to the cultural influences of host countries varies, depending on such factors as the initial area of residence, social class, level of education, type of employment and the degree of Westernisation at the time of dispersal. Also important in the determination of receptivity are the degree to which the host culture is similar to, or different from, pre-1948 Palestine, the openness displayed by that culture to the new Palestinian immigrants and the level of social and educational facilities provided.

This chapter will attempt to describe the role and status of women in the traditional Palestinian home and the influence of the 1948 dispersion on the Palestinian family. It will utilise the few studies that have been made. Substantial additional research needs to be done in various areas of the world on the dispersed Palestinian communities in order to provide further data for a more comprehensive assessment.

I. The Traditional Role and Status of Palestinian Women

One significant element in Palestinian society is the *hamula*, an aggregate of extended family related through a common ancestor. All members of each *hamula* are mutually responsible for one another. The social order is maintained through communal strictures that sanction supervision of accepted customs and mores in the private lives of the members. Any deviation from the social norms by any individual members brings shame

147

to the collectivity. In cases of murder, rape or other infractions against other families each member of the *hamula* is liable to be an object of revenge for his kin. (In cases where ransom is agreed upon, all males participate in paying the amount designated.) This custom places the burden of social conformity not only on each individual for himself but for each member of the *hamula.* Thus individuality is fulfilled through participation in the community and in supervising the behaviour of other members of the group.

The *hamula* also functions as the social mechanism for solving personal problems. What the collectivity sees fit is acted upon. Any intimation of trouble to outsiders is frowned upon and considered a disgrace (*fadiha*). Thus the members of the group work together to maintain the social order. In the context of the *hamula*, the female is restricted to defined patterns of behaviour and is expected to adhere to them. Deviation from the norms is liable to bring shame. Shameful behaviour is punished through repudiation, and infractions by females have to be cleansed by their males. In the case of a bad reputation, the errant female is killed in order to maintain the purity of the family name and the honour of the group. Thus the *hamula* is the centre of corporate responsibility and accountability. Since individual infraction leads to corporate shame, the errant individual is sacrificed for the sake of the group.

The role and status of Palestinian women in the *hamula* system has been defined by centuries of cultural patterns and social restrictions and justified by religious sanctions. It has also been maintained by local and alien governments ruling the Palestinians, who have utilised this trad-itional structure as a system of social control in order to avoid conflict and facilitate the administration of the conquered territories.

Palestine has had a predominantly Muslim culture, although there is a sizeable Christian minority. The culture that has evolved, as is true of the Middle East in general, is informed by various religious ideas and regulations but is one in which the same norms and mores generally apply to all women. Certain specific regulations hold only for Muslims, but the assumptions underlying them bear on the general understanding of the place of women in the Palestinian culture.

Both Islam and Christianity perceive male and female in the generic sense as equal before God. Both religions, however, advocate a difference in status when the role of the wife is discussed *vis-à-vis* her husband. She is to be obedient to him and to look after his physical, emotional and material needs in the home context. Centuries of religious commitment have solidified cultural customs so that this obedience has become, in the Palestinian case, a pattern of identity. Although the twentieth-century observer may perceive injustice in these patterns, most of the people[1] involved seem to have been oblivious to any infractions on their rights. Rather, they appear to have internalised and appropriated their roles and sought to maintain them in the society at large.

Islam as a way of life has developed a system of religious law (*Shari'a*) which defines and regulates all aspects of life. This law is seen as a blueprint of God's order for humanity. Living in accordance with the *Shari'a* provides the society with the best possible social, economic and political system. In this order, the role of the wife is seen as one that is below that of the husband. This is due to the fact that the Qur'an says that 'men are in charge of women because God has made the one superior to the other, because they spend on them out of their wealth. So the virtuous women are the obedient, guarding the secret which God has given' [Sura 4:34].

The superiority of males over females has been explained by modern conservative writers[2] as due not only to the fact of economic dependency, but also to basic pervasive differences between males and females, which are biological, psychological, intellectual and physiological in nature.[3] They exist because God has created humanity of two kinds, male and female. If he did not have specific roles and requirements for them, he would not have created them different. Thus femininity and masculinity share in the cosmic order and must be accepted as part of God's purpose for mankind. For women to seek roles inconsistent with those designed for them is seen as a rebellion against God's will.

Muslim apologists will insist that Islam raised the standard of the woman in the world by giving her rights she did not possess before. These include the right to inheritance, the right to maintain possessions, the right to keep her name, the right to choose a husband and the right of upkeep (i.e. freedom from economic worries).

Religious parameters on women's rights, however, have placed the Muslim woman in a special position. For although her rights of inheritance are guaranteed, she only inherits one-half of the portion of the male. This is seen as more than adequate since she is at no time responsible for her own upkeep. Palestinian customs in attempting to be consistent with religion have tended to define the role of the woman from birth until death as one of dependence on males for maintenance and protection. The woman is never autonomous nor is she ever responsible for herself. At all times she is to be in custody of her closest male relative, whether that be her father, brother, husband or son. This has led to the tendency of females of marriageable age and those that are married to renounce their inheritance rights in favour of their brothers in order to keep the property in the family and thus ensure the good will and support of the family in case of divorce.[4] The family of the girl is also responsible for her in the case of widowhood or separation. This dependency puts a great deal of pressure on the married woman to do her best in order to stay married, regardless of the abuse she may receive from her husband and his kinfolk. Thus the right that she has to keep her maiden name acts as a constant reminder that she is living in her husband's house on his sufferance and can stay there as long as she fulfils her duties and obeys him.

The same Qur'anic verse quoted above gives the husband the right to punish his wife and beat her if necessary in case she is disobedient.[5] A contemporary Arab Muslim has written the following on the subject:

> It is permitted for the man to beat his wife if she disobeys him in bed, if she leaves the house without reason, if she refrains from applying cosmetics when he wants her to use them or if she neglects her religious duties.

He describes the mode of administering the beating in the following words:

> He should not drag her, break her bone or harm her in such a way as to leave a scar. He should avoid the face for it is the center of beauty. He should spread the punishment to different parts of the body and not concentrate it in one area lest he maximize the harm.[6]

The duty of obedience to the husband used to be impressed on the wife during the wedding ceremony where she learned that he is her lord.[7] She was to treat him with respect, kissing his hand on special occasions such as feast days.[8] Between 1958 and 1962 persistence of the primacy of the males was witnessed by this author in some traditional families from the rural areas of Palestine where the husband was served the food first. Only when he had finished his meal did the wife and the young children eat. During feasts and celebrations, the males were served first. Later the leftovers were consumed by the females in the privacy of the kitchen.

The Muslim man, according to scripture and as part of the Islamic legal structure, has the right to marry more than one wife, while the female is restricted to one husband.[9] He also has the right to divorce his wife whenever he wants, while the female may have the right to divorce her husband only under very stringent conditions, including a clause in the marriage contract giving her the right to do so. Furthermore, whereas for the man a triple verbal repudiation makes the divorce effective immediately, the woman must have specific reasons, such as impotence, desertion, maltreatment and lack of support. She has to go through the courts, a process that may take years because of the general sympathy towards the male. This, coupled with the stigma that divorce ascribes to women, lead many to accept their lot of gaining contentment only through obedience and meekness in service.

Many of the characteristics of Palestinian culture were determined not by religious law but by customs prevailing as part of the Middle Eastern milieu. Thus the role of the female as wife was perceived throughout as involving obedience and commitment to the husband. The husband's duties in return were those of being the provider and protector of his wife.

For the Arab, the birth of a daughter is not a joyous event,[10] nor does it call for a celebration.[11] The girl 'brings nothing but headaches' as the common saying goes. Her vulnerability makes her in need of constant protection. Her behaviour is supervised by the members of the *hamula* to ensure her upright moral character and therefore the corporate honour.

Male pride and honour in society (*'ird* or *sharaf*) are not contingent on achievements or personal identity, but are dependent on the men's ability to control and supervise the behaviour of their females. Honour is external to the man in that he is held accountable for the behaviour of the women in his family. The highest values in the maintenance of this honour are the chastity and abstinence of his women. Women are perceived as weak and easily deceived; any contact between males and females is potentially dangerous as leading to sexual relations. Veils, enforced seclusion and segregation have been carefully maintained for the protection of family honour. This restriction on female mobility in its extreme form does not allow a woman to leave the home except in the company of her husband or by his permission in the company of other females.[12]

Honour is challenged not only by flagrant promiscuity but by the slightest inference of misconduct on the part of the woman. In some of the rural areas a female brings dishonour on her family simply by being addressed by a male; even a casual greeting on the street can be perceived as a compromise. Fear of having their women assaulted by Israeli forces was the primary reason for 30 per cent of those leaving the West Bank in 1967.[13] One Palestinian described his experience with the phrase *shirridna bi-'irdna* ('We have dispersed maintaining our

honour'[14]). He had maintained his honour by protecting his women
from misuse by the occupying forces.

The dependence of the woman on the male in Arab society was described by Qasim Amin, one of the earliest exponents of the liberation
of women in Egypt. He wrote:

> Woman, from the time of her birth to the day of her death is a slave
> because she does not live by and for herself; rather, she lives through
> and for the man. She needs him in all her affairs. She does not go
> out unless he guards her. She does not travel without his protection.
> She does not think but through his brain; she does not look but
> through his eyes; she does not move but that motion proceeds from
> him. Thus she is not an independent human being; rather, she is a
> thing attached to man.[15]

This attachment persists throughout her life. Relief and fulfilment
come through her role as a mother of sons. Not only is the female aware
throughout her childhood and adolescence that males are superior;
when she is married, people wish her and the groom male progeny. It is
only when she gives birth to a son that her true identity is achieved.
Henceforth, she will always be known as the 'mother of ——(name of
her eldest son)'. Through his birth she solidifies her marriage[16] and gains
respect in the community.

The relationship between mother and son is extremely close; it is one
of mutuality and intimacy, sanctioned and advocated by society. Segregation of the sexes, fear of sexual exploitation and the general tendency to frown on any overt expression of emotion towards husbands
enhances the mother-son relationship into one that is normal, acceptable
and right.[17] The context of the extended family provides for the maintenance of the closeness throughout the mother's life. This relationship
endows the mother with special powers as she operates behind the
scenes. Usually she is instrumental in the choice of a wife for her son.[18]
She supervises the household and sees to it that the wife does not replace her in her son's affection.[19] As her husband ages, she assumes the
powers of running the household through the authority of the son.
Meanwhile, the daughter-in-law labours patiently, and obediently awaits
her liberation through her own male progeny.

II. Modernisation and Social Change through Education and Employment

Social customs and norms in the Arab world underwent a marked change
in the twentieth century. The process of change in Palestine was initiated

by the presence of Western residents and the opening of mission schools
in different cities. These schools provided training in Western norms
and mores while the residents provided live models to be emulated. It
was mainly the urban elite who began to emulate the Westerners and
to institute change in their cultural patterns.

Education became the vehicle through which new ideas were trans-
mitted to the younger generations. Under Ottoman rule, the Palestinians
in theory had compulsory elementary education, although very few
schools existed. Those that did were in the major urban areas and were
too few in number to provide adequate education for the population.
In 1914, there were only 1,480 girls in primary schools in Palestine. In
private Muslim schools, there were a total of 131 females.[20] With the
institution of the British Mandate over Palestine, a few more schools
for girls were opened. British policy was based on providing education
for the maintenance of a civil servants' cadre rather than development
or humanitarian reasons. There was no universal education under the
British. In fact, 41 per cent of applicants to schools were rejected
because of lack of space.[21] In 1931, parents demonstrated against the
educational policy of the Mandate government and sought more schools
for their children.[22] Only 5 per cent of the budget was spent on
education.[23] This led parents to send their children to private schools.
In 1931, 70.5 per cent of the student population attended British,
French, German, Italian, American and Swedish schools.[24]

Parents' interest in the education of their daughters is evidenced by
the steady increase in the number of girls attending schools. There were
3,591 in 1925; 4,942 in 1931; 9,712 in 1935; and 15,303 in 1944.[25]
The majority of these girls attended elementary schools. Few registered
for classes in secondary education. This was in part due to lack of facilities; but the predominant reason was the hesitation of parents to send
teenage daughters outside the home.[26] By 1946, only 34 per cent of
urban and 20 per cent of rural school-age children were able to attend
schools.[27] Thus the majority were denied educational opportunities.

After 1948, Palestinians who were dispersed throughout the world
appear to have placed a high premium on education. The stress on
education and training was reflected in the female population, as the
number of educated girls increased substantially, especially among the
middle and upper classes. Parents encouraged their daughters to go to
school as education was perceived as a permanent portable commodity
that could be put to use in whatever place a person settled. The loss of
property in Palestine enhanced the feeling that education was a better
investment, a permanent possession that could not be usurped by alien

colonising forces. Furthermore, education became an avenue of liberation from dependency, from poverty, hunger and want. It was the
means to a better income, to enhancement of status and fulfilment
through a sense of achievement and mastery of destiny. Consequently,
a greater number of families allowed their daughters to travel alone
away from home to acquire university education.

Despite the apparent value of education as a means of social mobility,
university education for women is not encouraged among the conservative segments of the population because its atmosphere provides for
mixing of the sexes which places the female increasingly in compromising
situations without providing proper supervision for the protection of the
family's honour. Restrictions on female mobility have led to a lag in
women seeking employment[28] as well as in educational opportunities.[29]
Parents continue to place their highest priority on the education of the
son as a source of pride, prestige and identity for the family, as well as
an investment, since he will be their sole source of income in old age
because of the lack of social security.

Among the other factors influencing the preference for the education
of sons over that of daughters is the general utilitarian attitude of Arabs
towards education. The question is often asked, 'What would she do with
it?' Since this attitude takes for granted that the destiny and fulfilment
of every girl is through marriage, benefits that may accrue from her
education are perceived as the projected property of her husband's
family while her own parents would lose her as a source of free labour
in housekeeping and child-rearing. It also affirms the traditional role of
the wife as housekeeper and the husband as the provider.

Claims that higher education may be an asset in finding an educated
husband are usually countered by the assertion that too much education
may in the long run prove counter-productive and an impediment to
marriage. This is especially true among the lower classes, since educated
professional men of that class tend to seek partners among members of
the middle class, while those with lesser education prefer less educated
women who make more obedient wives.

The number of female university graduates among Palestinians is
higher than that among other Arabs.[30] The Arab nations, since independence, have made great strides towards providing education for females
through literacy campaigns and educational institutions. Despite that,
20 million out of 24 million Arab children had an illiterate mother in
1974.[31]

Palestinians who remained under Israeli rule in 1948 appear to have
progressed least in the areas of liberalisation of the family laws and

female education, although for obvious social as well as demographic and political reasons polygamy has been outlawed in Israel. Statistics show that not only is the educational level of Palestinians outside Israel higher[32] than those who are under Israeli rule, but that the earning power and occupational attainment of Palestinians outside Israel is superior.[33] Despite Israeli claims to the contrary, Palestinians who remained were dispossessed through various means, including expropriation of their land. Their wives and children are employed as pickers, in some instances in the same orchards they previously owned. They have been reduced from land-owners to wage-earners. Thus they were not only alienated from their land, but also from their source of income, their dignity and their identity. The exploitation of Arab women as cheap labour has not freed them; rather, it has led to their enslavement as they assume two jobs, one in the labour market and one at home, since the low wages they receive and the high taxes they pay do not provide for labour-saving devices at home.

The exploitation of Palestinian women in Israel extends to those who live in the occupied territories, as can be seen in this newspaper interview with one of the leaders of a kibbutz:

'Why are you employing these Arab women?'
'It is more profitable. They receive lower wages.'
'Did it occur to you to promise social insurance to these workers?'
'It is not customary here. We have no agreement with the contractor, and we pay him, that's it. We want to be able to expand the farm, to build, to buy cars, machines, and T.V. sets. Before the Six Day War we did not enjoy this kind of life. It has been made possible only through cheap labor.'[34]

Further exploitation of Palestinians is due to Israel's policy of not providing adequate education for them in order to keep them in low-paying jobs. Uri Lubrani, a former adviser to the Prime Minister said in a newspaper interview, 'If there were no pupils the situation would be better and more stable. If the Palestinians remained hewers of wood it might be easier for us to control them.'[35] This is reinforced by the Israeli policy of periodic expulsion of educated and professional Palestinians, mainly from the occupied territories, in order to keep the indigenous people without any leadership.

Studies of Palestinian women[36] in Israel tend to emphasise Arab cultural restrictions without exposing the exploitative policies of the government, such policies as the maintenance of indigenous institutions such as the *hamula* in order to control the population. When young men are kept in preventive detention rather than provided with education or gainful employment, their dependency on the extended family is increased.[37]

The Palestinian family in Israel has survived as the primary institution of belonging. The more hostile the environment became, the stronger the family bond grew. Maintenance of traditions became necessary for the purpose of continuity and protection. The vulnerability of the female in an alien and hostile environment increased her dependency and need for protection.

The conservative nature of the Arab Israeli community can also be attributed to the fact that during 1948, most of the Westernised trend-setters left for other Arab countries. Thus those who stayed behind felt truncated, as most of their institutions were severed. The fact that the coloniser and oppressor was identified with the West increased the vigilance of Arab fathers. They were anxious that their women not emulate the 'loose' ways of the Sabras, who were identified as offspring of Western settlers.

In recent years, more female Arab cheap labour has been integrated into the Israeli labour force. They work in textile and food-processing factories, while most of the Galilee area women work as share-croppers, and some of the young unmarried females work in factories. They are not allowed to keep their earnings since they are not responsible for their own upkeep. Young men, on the other hand, are allowed to save their salaries in order to collect enough money to get married. Some fathers attempt to postpone the marriage of their daughters for fear of the loss of her income which supplements their own.[38] Because of lack of adequate housing which is within reasonable reach of young Palestinians, the marriage rate among the Arabs has dropped compared to that of the Jews.[39]

As we have seen, the exploitation of Palestinian women is not restricted to areas under Israeli occupation; it is also prevalent in other areas. This is by no means a uniquely Palestinian characteristic, but is rather part of the general Arab cultural framework. While there are educated liberated females, they continue to depend on the males because of cultural restrictions. The variety of roles they have assumed makes it hard to generalise about developments.

The urbanised Westernised Palestinian elite tends to imitate Western standards. They can be found in the major metropolitan areas of the Arab world, but are most noticeable in Western Beirut, where their women date freely and participate fully in the 'male' world. Similar patterns exist among immigrants from Ramallah in the United States and among groups of assimilated Palestinians in Canada,[40] who participate fully in Canadian life and appear to all practical purposes to have severed all connections with the traditions and customs of the old country. Not only are their daughters allowed to mix, they can also choose any profession they want.

Meanwhile, the most conservative areas where Palestinians have clung to traditional customs appear to be in the refugee camps that exist on the periphery of urban areas such as Amman and Beirut. These camps have operated as ghettos where Palestinians continued to maintain their identity without mixing with members of the host countries. The concentration of relatives has acted to re-enforce old patterns and maintain traditional customs. This isolation has led to the persistence of old customs and mores. These appear to be operative among groups that have tended to congregate together and uphold the norms of traditional Palestinian culture.

Studies have shown that university education is very rare among female camp residents. The highest level they seem to aspire to is the attainment of a high school diploma. A substantial number never go beyond junior high education due to the lack of UNWRA schools in the camps, and the necessity of leaving the camp in order to acquire an education. Meanwhile there is a great deal of emphasis on education among the young. The number of illiterate females is higher among those who are forty years or older.[41]

Those who seek higher education tend to concentrate on 'feminine' topics. At the University of Jordan (where it is estimated that 90 per cent of the students are of Palestinian origin) there are more females than males in the Faculty of Arts, Shari'a (religious studies) and nursing.[42] There are no women enrolled in the agricultural schools despite the fact that, traditionally, the greatest number of agricultural labourers were female.[43] The introduction of mechanised farming has changed it into a 'masculine' occupation. Meanwhile, 80 per cent of professional women in Jordan are employed by the Ministry of Education where they constitute 45 per cent of the employees, while most of the officials and executives of the Ministry are male.[44]

Other professions acceptable for females include employment as 'nurses, secretaries, typists and social workers'. Some are self-employed as hairdressers, seamstresses or managers of retail outlets.[45] Honour and respectability continue to be operative in defining female professions. Parents of females residing in refugee camps are concerned about their working outside the camp. The family reputation is placed above economic need. The majority would rather be poor than allow their daughters to be singers or dancers.[46] Similarly, recent Palestinian immigrants from Israel to Canada are adamantly opposed to their women being employed as waitresses.

Surveys among Palestinians in Kuwait and Lebanon show that economic necessity has produced some changes in Palestinian attitudes towards women working and becoming assistant providers for the family, as shown in Table 6.1. There is no doubt that, in part, these contrasts are shaped by the more conservative climate of Kuwait, compared to that of Lebanon.

Table 6.1:   Attitudes towards Palestinian Women Entering the Labour Force (per cent)

	Kuwait	Lebanon
Approve of women working	25	52
Approve in limited range of jobs	51	38
Against working women but will tolerate	12	—
Totally opposed and other	12	10

Source: Based on figures provided by Bassem Sarhan, 'Family and Kinship Among Palestinians in Kuwait', Workshop on Family and Kinship, Kuwait, Nov. 27-30 1976, p. 47 (unpublished).

Strictures on females are not confined to their choice of profession but seem to extend in some cases to the permission to develop hobbies. Of Palestinians interviewed in the Kuwait sample only 35 per cent gave unconditional approval of females indulging in the pursuit of hobbies, while 13 per cent were totally against it. Thirty-two per cent said that they would favour certain hobbies such as drawing and some respectable sports, but were adamantly against dancing and swimming. Of those questioned 19 per cent would allow dancing and swimming only in secluded segregated areas.

Acceptable female professions as well as other stereotypical female roles are defined and enforced in women's magazines that are published in the Arab world. Their features include topics such as 'Domestic Arts', 'Today's Dish', 'Marriage: Reasons for its Success and Failure', 'How to Stay Vivacious', 'Your Lips are the Prettiest of What You Have.'[47] In fact, articles dealing with the contemporary role of women or with equality occupied an insignificant 0.009 per cent of magazines. Equality received more coverage in 1975 as articles on the subject were given a little less than 1 per cent of printed space.[48] Information about liberation, equality and the role of the modern woman can be found in official publications of the Arab feminist movements and of revolutionary groups.[49]

Change in the role and status of Palestinian women appears to have come through education, employment and political participation. All three areas are the concern of Palestinian women's organisations.

III. Women's Organisations

Very little is known about the organised efforts of Palestinian women in the service of their communities. Published material[50] makes cursory references to the existence of women's organisations in various parts of Palestine. These organisations were mainly initiated at the beginning of the century. Like other women's associations in such Arab countries as Syria, Lebanon and Egypt, they appear to have gathered their impetus and gained their sanction from the public acceptance of the appeals of social reformers like Muhammad Adduh, Saad Zaghlool and Qasem Amin, who saw in the liberalisation of social sanctions on women's activities in the public sphere a defence against Western labelling of Islam as an 'inferior religion' because of the customary seclusion of women.

The members of the women's organisations seem to have been conscious of social status and to have been mainly drawn from the middle and upper classes of the urban areas of Palestine. Thus their efforts were aimed at providing care and relief for the less fortunate in the society, and at raising the standard of the 'lower classes' by promoting better education, new skills and modern methods of child care and home economics.

Among the earliest societies formed were those associated with the different churches.[51] The rise of nationalist consciousness at the turn of the century, however, is reflected in the formation of women's associations dedicated to political ends as well as to the customary social services. Membership in these associations was not based on religious affiliation. Rather it reflected the growing nationalist attempts to transcend the traditional fragmentation of the community according to sectarian and denominational lines, and thus included both Christian and Muslim women.

Among the earliest active organisations was the Arab Ladies' Association of Jerusalem, formed in 1919, which sent a delegation to Damascus to congratulate King Faisal on his accession to the throne.[52] Other societies included the Arab Union of Haifa which, in the thirties under the leadership of Mrs Nassar,[53] attempted to integrate its efforts with

those of other women's associations in Palestine in the service of the
nationalist cause. Also active in the political field was the Arab Women's
Society of Jaffa. Palestinian nationalist women's organisations promoting education for girls and relief for the needy were in existence in
Nablus, Tulkarem, Jenin, Acre, Ramallah, Bethlehem and other smaller
towns.[54]

The political activities of women's associations were mainly the
concern of the urban educated upper classes. In 1921, the First Palestinian Women's Congress[55] urged anti-British demonstrations and organised
committees aimed at opposing Zionist settlement and British occupation.
Eight years later, the Arab Women's Committee participated in a protest
demonstration in the form of a motorcade in Jerusalem. They also submitted a memorandum to the British government protesting the Balfour
Declaration, the Zionist immigration, the maltreatment of Arab prisoners by British authorities, and the ordinance of collective punishment.
In 1933, the members of the Congress participated in a march of veiled
women to protest Allenby's visit to Jerusalem and the failure of the
British to implement the promise of liberation.[56] In 1936, the women
urged all citizens to strike in protest of British policies[57] and called
for the boycott of Jewish products.[58]

It was fashionable then for well-to-do women in the urban areas to
belong to women's organisations, take part in social activities, and to
voice their support for nationalist causes. The majority of the Palestinian women, however, live in rural areas and their participation thus has
taken a different form. Unhampered by the seclusion restrictions of the
urban areas, many of them took part in the efforts to resist the British
and Zionist settlers by going out on missions with their men and helping
with supplies of ammunition and provisions.[59]

The women's organisations have reflected an attempt on the part of
educated females at participating in the affairs of the modern world
rather than a feminist revolt against oppression or domination. Their
activities centred on social services, as they restricted their operations
to 'feminine' concerns such as child welfare, literacy campaigns and
training in such skills as sewing, spinning, weaving and embroidery.
Their centres were located in urban areas, the most active being Jaffa,
Haifa, Nablus and Jerusalem prior to 1948. With the dispersion of the
Palestinian people, their activities were disrupted in certain towns or
temporarily suspended in others.

After 1948, there were no records of activities overtly organised by
Arab women in Israel. The Israeli policies of deporting professional Arabs
from the occupied areas and of intimidating the Arab population by

restricting freedom of speech and political expression and banning organised activities have been applied to Palestinian female activists as well. Meanwhile, women's associations were organised in most of the major towns on the West Bank (a few continued to exist in Gaza). Their programmes expanded to meet growing needs precipitated by the dispersal of the Palestinian people. Several began operating orphanages and nursery schools to provide child care for working mothers. This was necessitated by the economic situation that forced women to work. It also reflected the breakdown in the extended family and the lack of availability of older female relatives in the household to care for the children.[60]

Other activities these societies undertook included establishing old people's homes, family planning clinics, and schools for the blind, the deaf and dumb, and the retarded. After the occupation of the West Bank by Israel in 1967, several organisations exhibited interest in preserving and maintaining Palestinian culture and identity.

Under Jordanian rule, Palestinian women continued to restrict their political activities to protest marches, whenever these were allowed by the authorities. They perceived their role primarily as supporting the men in the struggle and urging them to take some initiative for the solution of their problems. A few individuals, on the other hand, did participate with total commitment, including Nadia al-Salti[61] and Raja Abu Ammasheh.[62]

The formation of the Palestinian Liberation Organization in 1964 marks the first time in Arab history that a handful of women were allowed at the meetings of a political organisation (traditionally considered the domain of the male). In 1965, the General Union of Palestine Women was established. Like former women's organisations, it was concerned with raising the standard of women and called for the eradication of illiteracy and care for the Palestinian family. One clause in its charter called for 'participation of the Arab Palestinian woman in all aspects of the organization and struggle, and for her equality with the male in all rights and privileges for the purpose of liberating the homeland'.[63]

Between 1967 and 1978, a new development in women's political struggle occurred as they participated in armed and unarmed activities in the public as well as the private efforts of the revolution. The image the PLO tried to foster is the mother who urges her sons and daughters to full commitment for the struggle for the liberation of Palestine,

the fighter who took 'death packages' to the enemy, the organizer who led secret cells, carrying messages and hiding revolutionaries, the instigator and political advocate who helped organize demonstrations against Zionism and the relief worker aiding the families of the martyrs and the imprisoned.[64]

Meanwhile, female participation in the PLO structure verges on little more than tokenism, as no female is elected to the general body of the PLO on her own merit. Those who attend the meeting of the deliberative body do so in their capacity as representatives of the Women's Organization.[65] Furthermore, early female activities were 'feminine' in nature as they concentrated on support services such as collecting contributions, knitting sweaters, training women in sewing skills, visiting fighters, caring for families of prisoners and martyrs and working for the Palestine Red Crescent. The role changed from support to participation in all activities after 1970 when women were trained to be fighters. This was the case particularly in Jordan. The situation in Syria, Lebanon and Egypt varied depending on the interest of the women and the support the men in their families gave them.[66]

The Popular Front for the Liberation of Palestine organised women in the occupied areas. Their initial assignments were in the resistance efforts, including political insurrection, distribution of pamphlets, smuggling of arms and providing a haven for freedom fighters. The women were later given military training and were sent out on missions with the men.[67]

The women who joined the ranks of the Palestinian revolution were mostly drawn from the young educated middle class. Efforts to reach the lower classes failed as the males in this group frowned on mixing. In the anxiety of the leadership of the revolution not to alienate the fathers and brothers, it compromised on its expressed aim. The revolution perceived itself not only as one to liberate Palestinian land, but it also aimed at liberating the Palestinian person from patterns of oppression that blind him or her to caution and fear. It was to be a movement of national, political, social and economic liberation. Female members of the Palestinian resistance movement, however, felt that the organisation failed them because it did not at first encourage their full participation. Women had to prove their effectiveness under fire and thus earn the respect of the men.[68] There appears to be an express need for further development in the role of the woman so that she may become more effectively involved in the political organisation as well as policy matters. For although the Palestinian revolution has brought about changes in the attitudes of some of the males whose role it is to guard and protect the females in their families, these changes do not appear to be universal but rather are restricted to the participants.[69] Some have expressed fear that once the revolutionary phase is over, the woman may be relegated back to her traditional role. Any liberalisation of customs that restrict female mobility and participation will have to be gained through the approval of the males. As Leila Khaled wrote,

> A large part of women's liberation must take place through the liberation of the male . . . It is a matter that involves all efforts aimed at liberating society from all forms of oppression and tyranny on the national, economic and social levels, as well as on the level of customs and worn out traditions which we find at the root of male chauvinism.[70]

IV. The Role and Status of Palestinian Women since 1948

The creation of the state of Israel in 1948 brought 900,000 Palestinians under the rule of other Arab governments. Only 160,000 remained under Israeli occupation.[71] Most of the dispersed Palestinians were farmers who through force were alienated from their only means of subsistence, the land,[72] as most had lived in agricultural villages.[73] The loss of the land led to total dependence on outside agencies (e.g. UNWRA) for support. In this manner, the rural woman was freed from working in the fields, but the economic deprivation that ensued necessitated her seeking employment as a maid or servant to help supplement the family income. For although employment was not available for most males, both males and females were exploited with cheap wages.

This situation created a disruption in the traditional family patterns. Not only were some of the females forced to enter the public world and work in households other than their own, their work became an indispensable source of income for the family. This did not necessarily grant the women any extra freedom or status, rather it intensified their exploitation and domination by the males.

Some studies show an apparent erosion in the authority role of the male;[74] he is no longer the sole provider, as wives, sons and daughters participate in the effort of maintaining the family. Also operative is the fact that a substantial number of Palestinian families were split up due to the dispersal of 1948. Furthermore, there is a general tendency towards the nuclear family.[75] The absence of the mother-in-law (mother of the husband) from the scene appears to have enhanced the role of the female without jeopardising the role of the male. The wife assumed the role of companion and confidant, and became a contributor to family decisions.[76] The absence of the mother has also enhanced the role of the husband in that he is no more caught between contending factions of different generations. His word has become more significant in family decisions. He is now the source of strength, protection and guidance and appears to have a more important role in the family.

Diseprsal has also shown the fortitude of the Palestinian family. The co-operation and sacrifice of the members, one for the other, enforced the cohesive nature of the family. It appears to have been strengthened as an interdependent unit for survival in an alien and sometimes hostile environment. It became the only haven in a fickle world.

The parents provide a link to the past, to a homeland and an identity. The family functions as a unit of stability in a situation of flux where the exigencies of life are controlled by forces outside of oneself and where a person's existence and destiny are manipulated by unseen men in Cairo, Tel Aviv, Washington and Moscow. Where people from the same villages or of the same kin group congregate together, a sort of 'neo-*hamula*' is restructured.[77] In this case, older members help maintain the traditional mores and moral codes. There is some evidence of movement towards the liberalisation of some of the old customs. However these differ from one female to another, or one town to the next. Differences appear to be contingent on the educational background of the group,[78] the concentration of kin in the area and the length of time of dwelling in one place.[79]

It is clear that some changes have taken place as a result of the dispersal which intensified the process. Change, development and modernisation have been taking place in most Arab countries. Since gaining their independence from Western domination, most of them (e.g. Jordan, Syria, Tunisia, Lebanon, Iraq, Egypt, etc.) have expended extensive efforts on liberalising laws that impinge on the role of women and the status of the family. These include (for different countries) such laws as those restricting polygamy, granting women the right to vote and hold public office, instituting equal pay for equal work, and providing maternity leave with pay. Great strides have also been taken in providing education for females and in literacy campaigns among adults.

Women have assumed roles in public life traditionally held to be the domain of the male. There are women doctors, lawyers, engineers, judges[80] and Cabinet members (one each in Syria, Iraq and Egypt). These developments have received substantial criticism from conservative circles, but have been adamantly defended by nationalist leaders as a necessary development of society in order to achieve parity with the West and to participate fully in the modern world.

Most of these 'liberated' women come from the urban middle class.

The recently urbanised appear to be reluctant to take advantage of educational and employment opportunities because of the uncertainty about the propriety of women participating in a man's world and the fear of dishonour and shame.

This general Arab trend seems to be operative among Palestinian women, too. The dislocation of the Palestinian people, however, appears to have accelerated the liberation process among some women due to the greater mobility that ensued as Palestinians spread out in search of employment.

Palestinian women are working all over the Arab world. A substantial number are employed as teachers in different parts of the Arabian Peninsula. In fact, among the first female teachers in Kuwait in 1937 were Palestinians. By 1965, there were 2,258 Palestinian women working in Kuwait. Statistics for 1968-9 show that there were 3,590 Palestinian women teaching in Saudi Arabia while Bahrain had 121, Abu Dhabi 77 and Qatar 243.[81] Excluding agriculture, participation of Palestinian women in the labour force is approximately nine per cent, equal to that in Syria and Egypt.[82] The inclusion of female agricultural workers raises the proportion to such levels as 20.6 per cent of the Palestinian labour force in the occupied areas and 14.4 per cent in Israel.[83]

Education continues to be an important vehicle of attaining a measure of freedom and becoming a contributing member of society. Among famous Palestinian women are the authors Thurayya Malhas, Fadwa Touqan, Salma al-Khadra al-Jayyusi, Asma Toubi, Samira Azzam and Najwa Qaawar Farah. A painter of note is Samia Taqtaq. Educated middle-class women make up the majority of female freedom fighters.[84] Efforts to reach the lower classes failed because of the restrictions on female mobility.[85]

The Palestinian revolution has been perceived by some, including the women who have participated in the armed resistance and struggle, as a true liberation. In her willingness to fight at the side of the male and die in the cause of liberating the homeland, the female has risked her reputation, that which is of greatest value, and has thus earned equal rights with men in all aspects of life. Studies of males involved in the liberation movement do not bear out these female expectations. Males continue to perceive their role as protectors of the female.[86]

Studies show that there is a great deal of support for female participation in the resistance effort (97 per cent of Palestinians in Kuwait and 96 per cent of those in a Lebanese refugee camp); however, a substantial number (42 per cent in Kuwait and 43 per cent in Lebanon) insist that this support should be restricted to social services only.[87] Meanwhile, it is important to realise that the roles females have performed are not an innovation for Islam, nor are they new. From the time of Muhammad, Muslim women have had the right to participate with males in the war effort.[88] Furthermore, war conditions permit different norms of operation, as women are allowed to give refuge to males during disturbances. Thus hiding freedom fighters does not compromise a woman's honour, as it is permitted by custom and precedent.[89] Given the resistance of many males to the participation of females in the struggle and the precedent of females in the resistance movement in Algeria and Jordan,[90] traditional norms may be re-imposed should the revolution be successful or should it fall on hard times.[91] Thus the appearance of female freedom fighters has not necessarily settled the question of female liberation once and for all. There is a real danger that conservative elements may be successful in reinstituting traditional norms once the extenuating circumstances are over.

The future of the liberation of Arab women will continue to be affected by universal education and the influence of mothers over their sons in defining feminine and masculine roles. Available research on young Palestinian females shows that while they are psychologically predisposed to engage in revolutionary activity at a level comparable to that of boys, if not more so, they face discouragement from the male members of the family.[92]

As in other Arab countries, the Palestinian women's liberation movement was launched through their participation in the political resistance to foreign occupation. Her outcry against discrimination, displacement and forced colonisation by an alien people brought her out of the respectability of seclusion and into the public arena.

The liberation of women continues to have international political overtones. There is an awareness that true liberation for both males and females can come only when national liberation is attained. Thus freedom is perceived as the liberation of the total community from oppression, poverty, hunger, ignorance, fear and alienation from the land. It is liberation from political subjugation to, or domination by East or West, rather than a freedom of the individual from the restraints of culture and community. Thus the freedom that is sought is not licence to act or live independently; rather it consists of the female being taken seriously as a responsible agent capable of living up to communal expectations and of providing a contribution to the total development of the group.

The participation of women in the liberation movement is not anti-male in nature. The roles of male and female are perceived as complementary and supportive of one another as they both labour for their mutual liberation. Girding up this trend is the long history of female dependency on the male for support and protection coupled with the necessity of male approval for any change to occur. In this rejection of the Western model of female liberation, Arab women are rejecting sexual liberation (except for a handful of what some consider to be 'libertine' females, e.g. Ghada Samaan and Leila Baalabaki). The movement is an affirmation of equal identity and capacity rather than sexuality. It seeks to prove that the female is able to participate fully in the social, political and economic aspects of life without short-changing her dedication to honour or compromising her chastity and abstinence. In a sense, it seeks to prove that women can share fully in public life without being sexually 'available' and without being compromised. Thus the internalisation and appropriation of the 'honour' mores is utilised as the agent of liberation rather than that which causes one to be singled out as a vulnerable sex object in need of constant supervision.

In internalising and appropriating 'honour' restrictions, the modern Palestinian woman is rejecting the early champions of female liberty, i.e. the Western colonisers and the missionaries who advocated Western customs and ideals as normative for all human beings. To appropriate Western norms as the elite did at the turn of the century is to abdicate responsibility and the freedom to be Palestinian and to decide and fashion Palestinian priorities and destiny.

The group continues to function as the primary identity for the female. She functions as a member of that group where her personality is developed and enhanced through participation in the collective good. Thus she strives to maintain the mores and expectations of the group through mutual co-operation and participation. Her self-fulfilment is achieved in being accepted as an equal while maintaining her family honour, at no time compromising herself, her mission or the trust that others have placed in her. Through this submersion of the self in seeking approval the female continues her role as a follower.

Appendix: Palestinian Women's Organisations*

1921 – *The Arab Women's Society of Nablus*: a service-oriented association aimed at improving the condition of women by providing services in education, health and welfare. Among its operations are the *Women's Society Hospital*, which was established in 1965, specialising in general surgery, internal medicine, gynaecology, obstetrics and paediatrics. The

*Adapted and translated from Ghazi al-Khalili, *Al-Mar'ah al-Filastiniyyah wa-al-Thawrah* (Beirut, 1977).

School for Girls was established to provide a home for daughters of martyrs and for needy female orphans. The *Cultural and Sporting Club* was established in 1945, and concentrated on cultural activities and sports. It also participated in literacy campaigns. The *Modern Nursery School* was established in 1958 to provide educational services for children (aged 4 to 6) of working mothers, and the *Center of Light for Blind Girls* was established in 1962 to provide education and care for blind girls aged 6-20.

1925 – *The Association of Women's Rennaisance of Ramallah*: aimed at wiping out illiteracy and teaching females weaving and embroidery. It has recently begun to offer aid to the needy and has established a school for the retarded.

1928 – *Women's Auxiliary for Child Welfare and Motherhood of Nablus*: this association provided instruction in child care and motherhood.

1929 – *The Arab Women's Congress of Jerusalem* aimed at wiping out illiteracy among women. By 1953 it was providing four literacy classes. It also established a workshop for sewing and embroidery.

1939 – *The Arab Women's Society of Ramallah* (affiliated with the Arab Women's Society of Nablus) operated a workshop for weaving, spinning and embroidery. In 1962, it established a home for the elderly.

1944 – *The Women's Auxiliary for Child Welfare of Beit Jala*: it operated a clinic for childhood diseases and a centre for developing embroidery. In 1965, efforts were expended in enlarging the embroidery centre and adding a sewing centre to it. The association also operated a club for girls and one for families.

1945 – *The Association of Child Welfare of Ramallah*: its efforts were geared to child care. It ceased operations for a period but resumed its efforts in the 1960s by opening a nursery school for 100 children.

1947 – *The Arab Women's Society of Bethlehem* (affiliated with the Arab Women's society of Nablus). It established two centres to provide first aid and health services for freedom fighters. In 1953, it organised a centre for child care and a kitchen to provide meals for poor students.

1947 – *Zahrat al-Uqhuwan*: organised in Jaffa to provide services for warriors, including supplies of food and ammunition. The women helped in digging trenches and erecting barricades. Its members sought to participate in the military struggle but were not allowed. Some of the members in Nablus did participate by fighting with the Syrian forces.

1948 – *Institute of the Arab Child of Jerusalem*: established after the massacre of Deir Yaseen to care for Palestinian children. It operated a nursery school as well as a primary and a secondary school.

1949 – *Home for Refugee Girls of Jerusalem*: it started by offering its care services for children of working mothers. Since 1967, it began operating a primary and a secondary school.

1955 – *The Arab Women's Society of Tulkarem* (affiliated with the Arab Women's society of Nablus): it aimed at raising the standard of living of the Arab women. It established a school for the retarded in 1975 and a home for children. It also operated a nursery for 140 children of working mothers.

1956 – *The Arab Women's Society of al-Bireh*: aimed at raising the standard of rural women. It opened a school for sewing and weaving; it established a nursery and a nursing home for elderly women.

1956 – *The Hebron Women's Association* aimed at raising the standard of women. It operated a centre for motherhood and child welfare and a workshop for sewing and weaving.

1956 – *The Arab Women's Association of Beit Sahur*: it established a nursery school and a kindergarten.

1960 – *The Women's Benevolent Association of Qalqilya*: it was established to care for children of the martyrs, needy orphans and to eradicate illiteracy among women. It operated a nursery school for 150 children and a workshop for spinning and sewing, as well as a school for the deaf and the dumb.

1961 – *The Association for the Rennaissance of Rural Women Of Dora*: provided literacy classes and workshops for sewing and embroidery. In 1970, it opened a workshop for spinning and weaving wool and began operating a nursery.

1963 – *The Women's Benevolent Association of Jericho*: operated a nursery school and a sewing centre as well as a health clinic for children.

1964 – *Halhoul Women's Benevolent Association of Hebron*: operated a nursery school, a workshop to teach sewing and weaving, and a club for girls. It also provided instruction for 20 deaf and dumb students.

1965 – *Association for Welfare and Family Planning of Nablus*: it sought to provide services for families making available scientific and medical information for birth control and family planning.

1965 – *Association for Family Revitalization of al-Bireh*: one of the most active associations which started operations by opening a workshop for sewing, weaving and literacy. In 1967 it began publishing a magazine on culture and society *Majallat al-Turath wa-al-Mujtama'*. It operated a nursery school for 154 children, a library (3,000 volumes) and a literacy campaign in the villages. It also provided courses in foreign languages, a summer school and a secretarial school. It awarded scholarships for needy students and aid victims of the June 1967 War. It also helped in having 26 orphans adopted. It operated a shirt and pyjama factory and a canning plant. Since 1972 a committee has been established to care for the preservation of Palestinian heritage through research, publications and a modern museum of culture.

1969 – *The Association for Family Planning and Welfare of Hebron*: aimed at providing help for families and through medical guidance for family planning and birth control.

Notes

1. Professor Hadia Shakeel of Toronto University in a private conversation has reported to the author about an interview she had with the president of the Women's Association of Jaffa (1936-48) who said, 'We never thought of liberation; it never occurred to us that we were oppressed!'

2. For a detailed discussion of the subject see Yvonne Haddad, 'Traditional Affirmations Concerning the Role of Women as Found in Contemporary Arab Islamic Literature' in J.I. Smith (ed.), *The Role and Status of Women in Contemporary Muslim Societies* (Bucknell University Press, forthcoming).

3. Miqdad Yalgin, *Al-Bayt al-Islami: Kama Yanbaghi an Yakun* (Cairo, 1972) pp. 63-6; cf. ʿAbbas Mahmud al-ʿAqqad, *Al-Marʿah fi al-Qurʾan* (Cairo, 1959?), pp. 8-19; cf. Muhammad al-Ahmadi Abu al-Nur, *Manhaj al-Sunna Fi al-Zawaj* (Cairo, 1972), p. 57.

4. Aharon Layish, 'Women and Succession in the Druze Family in Israel', *Asian and African Studies*, vol. 11 (1 Nov. 1976), pp. 109-11; cf. Janet Zollinger Giele and Audrey Chapman Smock, *Women: Roles and Status in Eight Countries* (New York, 1977), p. 47.

5. Incidents of wife-beating also occur among Palestinian Christians. The author is aware of two such cases among immigrants to Canada.

6. ʿAbbas Mahmud al-ʿAqqad, *Al-Marʿah fi al-Qurʾan* (Beirut, 1967), p. 203.

7. Hilma Granqvist, *Marriage Conditions in a Palestinian Village* (Helsingfors, 1935), vol. II, p. 167.

8. Abdulla M. Lutfiyya, *Baytin: A Jordanian Village* (The Hague, 1966), p. 60.

9. Modernist reformers such as Muhammad Abduh have interpreted the scriptures as limiting marriage to one wife since the Qurʾanic verse traditionally interpreted as sanctioning polygamy makes its practice contingent on justice in treating the wives. The Qurʾan also says that 'you will not be just' thus categorically denying the practice. Statistics show that despite legal rights that may imply the contrary, the Arab family is a strong and enduring unit. In 1950, Egypt had 263,033 marriages and only 74,611 divorces (a much lower rate than that of the US and other Western countries). As for polygamy, 1947 statistics show that only 0.03 per cent of Egyptian households had four wives, whereas 96.14 per cent had only one wife (3.62 per cent had two wives, 0.21 had three wives).

10. One mother boasted to the author, 'I gave birth to three daughters, thank God, only one has survived.'

11. It has been noted that whenever there is a pause of silence in a conversation, someone will say, 'A girl is born.' This reflects the common disappointment at the birth of a girl. This is to be contrasted with the 'luluing' (expressions of joy) that accompanies the birth of a son.

12. For a discussion of shame and its function in maintaining social order, see J.G. Peristiany, *Honor and Shame: The Values of Mediterranean Society* (Chicago, 1966) and Greer Litton Fox, '"Nice Girl": Social Control of Women Through a Value Construct', *Signs* (Summer 1977).

13. D. Barakat and H.P. Daw, *al-Nazihun Iqtila' wa-Nafi* (Beirut, 1968), p. 46.

14. Peter C. Dodd, 'Family Honor and the Forces of Change in Arab Society', *International Journal of Middle East Studies*, vol. 4 (1973), p. 43.

15. Qasim Amin, *Al-Mar'ah al-Jadidah* (Cairo, n.d.), p. 35.

16. Failure to give birth to sons is a common cause for divorce and for polygamy. It is common for a traditional wife who has not produced male heirs to urge her husband to marry a second wife.

17. What a Muslim anthropologist wrote about the situation in Morocco is generally true throughout the Arab world:

Marriage, which in most societies is invested with a kind of initiation ritual function allowing the adult son to free himself from his mother, is in Morrocan Muslim society a ritual by which the mother's claim on the son is strengthened. Marriage institutionalizes the Oedipal split between love and sex in a man's life. He is encouraged to love a woman he can't engage in sexual intercourse with, his mother. He is discouraged from lavishing his affection on the woman he does engage in sexual intercourse with, his wife.(Fatima Mernissi, *Beyond the Veil* (New York, 1975), p. 69).

18. A common Palestinian phrase used by the mother-in-law to express displeasure at the behaviour of her daughter-in-law is 'ya-naga 'ayni' ('the choice of my eyes'). While affirming the power structure in the home where the mother makes the decisions, it reminds the daughter-in-law of the possibility of other choices and of repudiation.

A study of Palestinians residing in Kuwait, revealed that 71 per cent continue to entrust the mother in the choice of a wife. Bassem Sarhan, 'Family and Kinship Among Palestinians in Kuwait', Workshop on Family and Kinship, Kuwait, 27-30 November 1976, p. 47 (unpublished).

19. For a discussion of the Qur'anic and Hadith sanctioning of mother-son relationship, see Haddad, 'Traditional Affirmations'.

20. A.L. Tibawi, *Arab Education in Mandatory Palestine* (London, 1956), p. 20.

21. Sa'id Hamadeh, *Al-Nizam al-Iqtisadi fi Filastin* (Beirut, 1939), p. 49.

22. Khalil Totah, 'Education in Palestine', *Annals of the American Academy of Political and Social Science*, vol. 164 (Nov. 1932), p. 156. Totah reports that in 1931, only 51.18 per cent of applicants were accepted. The British authorities provided education that year for 19,346 boys and 4,942 girls.

23. Hamadeh, *al-Nizam*, p. 45.

24. Totah, 'Education', p. 159.

25. Tibawi, *Arab*, p. 49.

26. Ibid., p. 53. Tibawi reports that in 1925 there were 54 girls in urban teacher training. By 1935, the number had risen to 94. There were also 13 girls in rural teacher training in the Rural Women Teacher's Training Center at Ramallah (opened in 1935) where the emphasis was on 'domestic science and mothercraft'. The statistics for that year reflect the beginning of secondary education as there were 33 girls studying in Secondary I and II classes. The figures for 1944 reveal little increase. (There were 100 girls in the urban teacher training, 34 in rural teacher training and 161 in secondary I and II,) Hamadeh, *Al-Nizam*, p. 49 reports that there were no secondary schools in Arab villages.

27. Adnan Mohammad Abu Ghagaleh, *Arab Cultural Nationalism in Palestine During the British Mandate* (Beirut, 1973), p. 89.

28. Statistics of the Jordanian Ministry of Labour show 4,101 employment certificates for males wishing to work abroad, while the number for females was 31. In 'am al-Mufti, *Department of Women's Affairs: A Working Paper Setting Forth the Aims and Functions of the Department* (Amman, 1977), p. 2.

29. Statistics in Jordan show that the number of female students at universities in 1950-1 was 22. After the University of Jordan was established, the number of women rose to 2,669 in 1974-5. See Abdulla al-Khatib *et al.*, 'The Role of the Jordanian Woman in the Fields of Education, Social and Medical Care' (Amman, 1976); cf. Nabil Ayyub Badran, *al-Ta'lim wa-al-tahdith fi al-Mujtama' al-'Arabi al-Filastini* (Beirut, 1969), pp. 137-8, where he shows that Palestinian students at the American University of Beirut and International College in 1946-7 numbered 342 males and 4 females.

30. Arab women are attending universities in greater numbers. In 1974, the percentage of females were the following: 49 per cent Kuwait, 30 per cent Iraq, 28 per cent Jordan, 25 per cent Algeria, 25 per cent Egypt, 32 per cent Lebanon, 21 per cent Tunisia, 18 per cent Syria, 14 per cent Morocco, 10 per cent Libya, 10 per cent Sudan, 6 per cent Saudi Arabia.

31. *Al-Watan al-'Arabi 'Am alfayn*, p. 34, cited by Khalili, *al-Mar'ah*, p. 53.

32. Sami Mar'i and N. Dahir, *Facts and Levels in the Development of Arab Education in Israel* (Haifa, 1976), p. 55.

33. Elia Zureik, 'Toward a Sociology of the Palestinians', *Journal of Palestine Studies*, vol. VI, no. 4 (Summer 1977), p. 11.

34. *Maariv*, 4 April 1971, cited by Amal Samed, 'Palestinian Women: Entering the Proletariat', *Journal of Palestine Studies*, vol. VI, no. 1 (1976), p. 166 (reprint from MERIP Reports, no. 50).

35. *Haaretz*, 4 April 1961.

36. Khalil Nakhleh, 'Anthropological and Sociological Studies on the Arabs in Israel: A Critique', *Journal of Palestine Studies*, vol. VI, no. 4 (Summer 1977), pp. 41ff.

37. Samed, 'Palestinian Women', p. 161.

38. Ibid., p. 164.

39. Yahiel Harari, *The Arabs in Israel* (Givat Haviva, Israel, 1974), p. 15.

40. All the material on Palestinians residing in Canada is based on interviews conducted by Professor Hadia Shakeel of Toronto University among the members of the Palestinian community in Toronto and with Mr Khaled Mu'ammar, president of the Palestine Arab Club of Toronto, Canada, which she has kindly made available to the author.

41. Ghazi al-Khalili, *Al-Mar'ah al-Filastiniyyah wa-al-Thawrah* (Beirut, 1977), p. 224.

42. Adwiyya Alami *et al.*, 'Woman's Work: Trends and Motives', (Department of Women's Affairs, Amman, 1976), p. 13.

43. Abdulla al-Khatib *et al.*, 'The Role of the Jordanian Woman in the Fields of Education, Social and Medical Care', typescript (Amman, 1976), p. 8.

44. Ibid., p. 15.

45. Alami, 'Woman's Work', p. 15.

46. Khalili, *al-Mar'ah*, p. 250.

47. Aida Najjar *et al.*, 'The Role of Mass Media in Attracting Women for Development', typescript (Amman, 1976), p. 10.

48. Ibid., p. 10.

49. The following magazines published by the different Palestinian revolutionary groups provide articles on the new roles of women: *Filastin al-Thawrah, Al-Thawrah al-filastiniyyah, Al-Hadaf, Al-Hurriyah, Ila al-Amam, Al-Tala'i', Al-Tha'ir*

al-'Arabi, Nidal al-Sha'b, Al-Filastiniyyah al-Tha'irah, Al-Nashrah Al-Dakhiliyyah.

50. Among the rare exceptions are Matiel E.T. Mogannam, *The Arab Woman and the Palestine Problem* (London, 1936); Khalili, *Al-Mar'ah*; and Ghada Karmi, 'Palestinian Women: A Force for Liberation', *Palestine Digest*, vol. 8, no. 4 (July 1978).

51. These include the Christian Public Charity Society for Ladies in Haifa which was established in 1911 as a charitable institution. (It appears that their goal of operating an old people's home was never implemented.) Other Church-related women's groups that existed in Jerusalem in 1936 included the International Women's Alliance, the Society for the Education of Girls, the Mar Mansour Society (affiliated with the Roman Catholic Church) and the Society for the Needy and the Sick (affiliated with the Greek Orthodox Church). Societies in Jaffa included the Arab Women's Association (credited with being the first organisation formed), and the Infant Welfare Center (Mogannam, *The Arab Woman*, p. 59).

52. Ibid., pp. 55-62.

53. Ibid., p. 62. Granddaughter of the founder of the Bahai faith described by Ms Mogannam as 'an ardent Nationalist'.

54. Ibid., p. 63. For a list of some women's organisations and their activities in the West Bank see the appendix.

55. It was formed by Emilia Sakakini and Zalikha Shibabi. See Khadijah Abu Ali, *Muqaddamat Hawl waqi' al-Mar'ah wa-tajribatuha fi al-Thawrah al-Filastiniyyah* (Beirut, 1975), p. 44.

56. For details of a first-hand report and photographs see Mogannam, pp. 70ff; cf. Khalili, '*Al-Mar'ah*', pp. 77-9; cf. Ijlal Khalifah, *al-Mar'ah wa-Qadiyyat Filastin* (Cairo, 1974), p. 39; cf. *Wathaiq al-Muqawamah al-Filastiniyyah al-'Arabiyyah Did al-Ihtilal al-Baritani wa-al-Sihyawniyyah* (1918-1939) (Beirut, 1968), p. 160; cf. 'Abd al-Qadir Yasin, *Kifah al-Sha'b al-Filastini Qabl al-'am 1948* (Beirut, 1975), pp. 141, 144.

57. *Watha'iq*, pp. 384, 386, 428.

58. Yasin, *Kifah*, p. 22.

59. Khalili, *Al-Mar'ah*, p. 77. Cf. Khadijah Abu Ali, *Muqaddamat*, p. 45.

60. About 90 per cent of nurseries in Jordan belong to charitable institutions. Khatib, 'Role of the Jordanian Woman', p. 19.

61. She was arrested for blowing up a building in Amman in 1958. Khalili, *Al-Mar'ah*, p. 96.

62. Considered a martyr since she was killed in Jerusalem while leading a demonstration against the Baghdad Pact (ibid., p. 96).

63. Rashid Hamid, *Qararat al-Majlis al-watani al-Filastini* (Beirut, 1975), pp. 44, 45 as cited by Khalili, *Al-Mar'ah*, p. 105.

64. Khalili, *Al-Mar'ah*, p. 107.

65. Ibid., p. 114, reports that at the first conference of the PLO 10 out of 422 representatives were women. The fourth conference had one female representative (to one hundred males), the fifth conference had one, the sixth conference had two, the ninth had three, the eleventh and twelfth had four each.

66. Ibid., pp. 116-17.

67. Ibid., p. 124. Among the leaders of the female resistance were Wadad Qumri, Leila Khaled, Rashida Ubaydo and Aisha Audeh.

68. Ibid., p. 141.

69. In a study of 34 women who were active members of the revolution, 18 said that there was a positive change in their status in their family as a result of their participation in revolutionary activity. Others saw no alteration. What is significant is that none reported a negative response. This may be due to the fact that female participation at any level implies the tacit approval of her relatives. Abu Ali, *Muqaddamat* as cited by Khalili, *Al-Mar'ah*, p. 142.

70. Leila Khalid in *Al-Thawrah wa-Qadiyyat Taharrur al-Mar'ah*, cited by Khalili, *Al-Mar'ah*, p. 127.

71. Khalili, *Al-Mar'ah*, p. 83.

72. In 1922, 71 per cent of the population lived in rural areas. Nabil Ayyub Badran, *al-Ta'lim wa-al-tahdith fi al-mujtama' Al-'Arabi al-Filastini* (Beirut, 1960), p. 71.

73. In 1944, 66 per cent of the population of Palestine lived in agricultural villages. Shahadeh Yusef, *al-waqi' al-Filastini wa-al-harakah al-niqabiyyah* (Beirut, 1973), pp. 28-9.

74. Eighty-five per cent of those questioned in Kuwait believed that the authority of the father decreased due to changes since 1948. The reasons that led to this weakening in his position are perceived to be: (1) dispersion-separation of members of one family; (2) evolution of world and times – this is the time of liberation; (3) education of children – the extensive standard of education and teaching; (4) the economic factor – the improvement of the family's material conditions and the reliance of the parents on the children economically; (5) development of individual freedom and democratisation within the family; (6) dissolution of the extended family (Sarhan, 'Family', p. 39).

75. Eighty-three per cent of Palestinians surveyed in Kuwait advocated that the son should form his own family unit when he gets married. Only 15 per cent insist on having the son and his bride dwell with the parents (Sarhan, 'Family', p. 25).

76. Sixty-one per cent of those surveyed see the enhanced position in the role of the Palestinian wife, while 73 per cent of heads of households said they always consult their wives on important matters (ibid., pp. 37, 40).

77. Sixty-nine per cent of those interviewed asserted that belonging to a large family provides them with a sense of security (ibid., p. 54).

78. The camp residents, whose original home town was Tarshiha, were more liberal than others due to the presence of a school in that town before 1948 and the relatively high percentage of literate people among them (Khalili, *al-Mar'ah*, p. 220).

79. Because of the custom of mutual support, relatives have tended to congregate in certain areas. When one member of the family emigrated, began to work and became successful, he usually sent for his next of kin to participate in the new life.

80. The appointment of female judges led a conservative author to raise the question, 'How can half a witness be a judge?' (a reference to the Qur'anic verse that requires two female witnesses for each male). Muhammad al-Ghazzali, *Min Huna Na'lam* (Cairo, n.d.), p. 200. Dr Joyoushi of Syria ridiculed this conservative attitude in a lecture she gave at Damascus University. She said, 'No law is broken when eight women ride in an automobile because eight women equal four persons.'

81. Elias Khouri, *Ihsa'at Filastiniyyah* (Beirut, 1974).

82. Nawal Al-Sadawi, *Alwajh Al-Ari Lil-Mar'ah Al-Arabiyah* (Beirut, 1977).

83. Jaqueline Farhood Jeriysati, 'Al-Sha'ab Al-Filastini', *Palestine Affairs*, nos. 41/42 (1975), pp. 399-431.

84. Khalili, *Al-Mar'ah*, p. 230. There were 65 women in Israeli gaols in 1970. The warden of the gaol reported that

the cleanest and best-looking prisoners are the Arab girls. The Jewish prisoners are here for criminal offenses and many of them are prostitutes. Many of the Arab girls, on the other hand, are the elite of the West Bank Society, most of them come from prosperous and respectable families. They are from the intelligentsia, graduates of university or teachers' colleges (Zeev Schiff and Raphael Rothstein, *Fedayeen* (London, 1972), p. 176).

85. Ibid., p. 126.

86. Ibid., p. 150.

87. Sarhan, 'Family', p. 15 and Khalili, *Al-Mar'ah*, p. 183.

88. Muhammad A. Al-Abrashi, *Makanat al-Mar'ah fi al-Islam* (Cairo, 1970), p. 21.

89. Al-Bahi Al-Khuli, *Al-Islam wa-Qadaya al-Mar'ah al-Mu'asirah* (Kuwait, 1970), p. 27.

90. Women involved in the Palestinian revolution in Jordan during 1970-1 opted to get married in order to avoid the reintroduction of control by their parents (Khalili, *Al-Mar'ah*, p. 189).

91. Parents' disapproval of female participation in the revolution tends to increase during periods of stress or adverse conditions, as they fear physical abuse of their daughters by the authorities which would detract from the family's honour (ibid., p. 142).

92. Sylvie Mansour, 'The Sense of Identity among Palestinian Youth', *Journal of Palestine Studies*, vol. VI, no. 4 (1977), pp. 71-89.

7   PALESTINIAN INTELLECTUALS AND
     REVOLUTIONARY TRANSFORMATION

Khalil Nakhleh

I. Conceptual and Methodological Framework*

While the concern of this chapter is with revolutionary intellectuals, it is important to distinguish between what constitutes an intellectual category and a revolutionary intellectual category. In general, the concept of 'intellectual', as used here, encompasses both 'basic types' of intellectuals, elaborated by Gouldner,[1] namely the intelligentsia whose cerebral activities are fundamentally 'technical' and 'intellectuals whose interests are critical, hermeneutic, emancipatory, and often practical-political'.

Exposure to modern education through formal training and study is the major vehicle through which these types of cerebral activities are achieved.[2] The systematic acquisition of knowledge through modern education provides the recipient with a specific type of 'technocratic' or 'intellectual' consciousness. This is not the same as 'revolutionary consciousness', since the majority of intellectuals are uncommitted to a revolutionary transformation of the *status quo*.

'Revolutionary transformation' refers to the process by which the existing oppressive, undemocratic, discriminatory and exploitative *status quo* in Palestine and other Arab countries can be changed. It must be revolutionary since it seeks a radically different social order and social formations. It is 'transformation' because a change of this magnitude cannot be accomplished through gradual historical modifications of the existing order.

Now, to focus on the role of Palestinian intellectuals in this process of transformation, we need to isolate that category of Palestinians who acquired 'intellectual consciousness' through education, and that segment of it who translated that into a 'revolutionary consciousness'. While the two consciousnesses are not synonymous, it is argued here that 'intellectual consciousness' is a necessary but not sufficient factor for generating 'revolutionary consciousness'.

Let us look first at the 'function' of intellectuals and the nature of

*I would like to thank my good friend Guy Levilain for making extensive comments on an earlier draft of this paper.

176

'revolutionary consciousness' which they might generate. In his *Prison Notebooks* Gramsci writes:

> All men are intellectuals . . . but not all men have in society the function of intellectuals. When one distinguishes between intellectuals and non-intellectuals, one is referring in reality only to the immediate social function of the professional category of the intellectual, that is, one has in mind the direction in which their specific professional activity is weighted, whether towards intellectual elaboration or towards muscular nervous effort . . . There is no human activity from which every form of intellectual participation can be excluded . . . Each man, finally, outside his professional activity, carries on some form of intellectual activity.[3]

Gramsci's preoccupation is with those functions which effect a revolutionary transformation of the *status quo*. What concerns us here is the dialectical relationship between two major functions performed by intellectuals in any political struggle: the production of revolutionary consciousness, and being 'the dominant group's "deputies" exercising the subaltern functions of social hegemony and political government'.[4] The two functions are contradictory: the first aims to overthrow the dominance and legitimation of the ruling group while the second aims at its maintenance. Put differently, the intellectuals who are in the 'production of revolutionary consciousness' are pitted against the intellectuals who are the 'managers of legitimation' for the existing order; hence, there is a battle for consciousness and for hegemony – what consciousness and whose hegemony?

The importance of the intellectuals in this regard is obvious. They are the ones 'who play the main part in articulating and giving expression to the terms of that battle'.[5] Yet, the contradictory functions of intellectuals in the battle for consciousness urge us to consider Gramsci's classification and discussion of this point. IIe spoke of 'organic intellectuals' as the ones who are able to give the lower classes 'homogeneity', 'self-consciousness' and 'organization', which are necessary prerequisites for the generation of hegemony.[6]

The successful production of revolutionary consciousness requires the interaction of a number of processes: (1) the production of an 'advanced theory' of challenge to the existing ideological dominance, which is comprehensive, systematic, long-term and persuasive;[7] (2) the attempt at delegitimising and eroding the hegemony of the existing order; and (3) the forging of organic alliances with the oppressed strata of the society.

The production of ideas which acquire dominant qualities is related, of course, to the forces which control material production. Marx and Engels wrote in *The German Ideology*:

> The ideas of the ruling class are in every epoch the ruling ideas: i.e., the class, which is the ruling material force of society, is at the same time its ruling intellectual force. The class which has the means of material production of mental production, so that, thereby, generally speaking, the ideas of those who lack the means of mental production are subject to it.[8]

However, as Miliband rightly warned,[9] the ideological predominance of the 'ruling class' is not immutable; it has always to contend with 'many-sided and permanent challenge' which 'produces a steady erosion of that predominance'. Part of this challenge results from the process which Marx and Engels themselves delineate in the *Communist Manifesto*:

> in times when the class struggle nears the decisive hour, . . . a portion of the bourgeoisie goes over to the proletariat, and in particular, a portion of the *bourgeois ideologists*, who have raised themselves to the level of comprehending theoretically the historical movement as a whole.[10]

Even though, as Lenin argued in *What is to be Done?*, the role of these ideologists is indispensable in providing 'the most advanced theory' to guide the vanguard party, they nevertheless cannot be trusted as true revolutionaries: as are actual party members. Lenin argued further, as did Gramsci after him, that the context of effective revolutionary activity is the party, providing that '*all distinctions as between workers and intellectuals . . . must be effaced*'.[11] As the true vanguard, 'we must go among all classes of the population as theoreticians, as propagandists, as agitators, and as organisers'.[12]

To summarise so far: following the classical expositions of the role of intellectuals in revolutionary movements, we have established the two major contradictory functions which they perform in the 'battle for consciousness'. First, they act as the 'managers of legitimation' of the dominant class; and second, they are the producers of revolutionary consciousness whose purpose is to erode that ideological predominance.

In terms of this theoretical framework, I intend to examine in the following sections the contradictory functions of Arab intellectuals, and

Palestinians in particular, in the initiation, management and sustenance of the Palestinian revolution.

II. Arab Intellectuals

Socio-historical Assessment

In an attempt to assess the failure of the revolutionary process in Italy at the turn of the century, Gramsci maintained that

> the success of a revolutionary movement at any given time will ultimately depend upon the nature and scope of the political consciousness that informs it. And this can be part of the gradual and diffuse historical flow of ideas, involving an organic fusion of the 'personal' and 'cultural' realms with the political.[13]

Here, I shall dwell on the functions of Arab intellectuals, mainly the precursors of Palestinian intellectuals, in providing the necessary political consciousness which informs the Palestinian revolutionary movement. Methodologically, this is justifiable because of the historical continuity in ideas between the leading pre-1948 Arab intellectuals and those Palestinian intellectuals who have helped articulate the present revolutionary direction.

The religious, class and regional heterogeneity of Arab culture has led a variety of scholars to focus on the 'social setting' which gave rise to Arab intellectuals and the political consciousness they generated.[14] A few individual examples notwithstanding,[15] collective action of Arab intellectuals under the Ottoman occupation, until the first decade of the twentieth century, was basically of a reformist nature. All resolutions of the First Arab Convention of the Decentralization Party in June 1913 in Paris, for example, revolved around the rights of the Arabs in the Ottoman Empire, recognition of the Arabic language and general semi-autonomous rule within the framework of the existing *millet* system. An Arab separatist movement which would have required a cohesive, anti-*status quo* ideology did not emerge until a few years before the total demise of the Ottoman Empire as a result of the First World War.[16] In other words, until the antagonism of Turkish nationalism towards Arabs became flagrant, Turkish Muslim domination over the Arabs was acceptable. The most radical demands in that context were those of the young Arab Society (*al-Fatat*), which was founded in 1909 in Paris by a group of Arab Muslim students who were studying there. *Al-Fatat* sought to achieve Arab independence within a bi-racial framework, but without the dismemberment of the Ottoman Empire.[17]

So far, Arab intellectuals under the Turks have been presented as the 'managers of legitimation' for the Turkish Muslim dominant stratum. Yet, taking the modification of the existing social order which they sought at face value, one finds a glimpse of a progressive consciousness. The aims of the Decentralization Party stated, in part, the following:

> We desire an Ottoman government, neither Turkish nor Arab, a government in which all the Ottomans have equal rights and equal obligations so that no party or group may deprive any other party or group from any of its rights or usurp them, for reasons of either race or religion, be it Arab, Turk, Armenian, Kurd, Muslim, Christian, Jew or Druze.[18]

By advocating democratic secularism, this position reflected a progressive consciousness. However, it is clear that, were this change to be realised, the intellectual group advocating it would have been buoyed into power, since they were members of the economically dominant classes. Hence, there was a total absence of any new economic consciousness in terms of material production and the distribution of wealth in the society.

The differences between Muslim and Christian intellectuals during *al-Nahda*,[19] which corresponded in part to the type and context of formal education they recieved, were mainly differences on which model of development and which world-view to adopt: traditional Arab culture with a variation in the emphasis on Islam, or Western European culture with more emphasis on its patterns of social thought than its Christian religious world-view. Undoubtedly, the tensions between these two models, which were represented by different intellectuals, generated new consciousnesses in the Arab intellectual milieu. However, the important point here is whether this debate led to a mere change in allegiance and infatuation by another existing social order (in this case, West European), or to a radical consciousness regarding control over the means of material production, the role of religion, minorities, etc.?

Until World War One, Arab intellectuals developed no coherent political ideology which could inform their collective action in the transformation of Arab culture.[20] With the extension of European political, economic and cultural domination over most of the Arab world after the disintegration of the Ottoman Empire, Arab intellectuals — Christians and Muslims alike — were faced with a new situation of foreign rule. They were bypassed again in matters pertaining to their self-determination and national existence. Therefore, from the 1920s to 1948, certain intellectuals who received their formal education in the West developed

the ideological framework of Arab nationalism for the purpose of inform-
ing the development of Arab culture during this stage. The development
of the new 'national consciousness' reflected the realisation by those
intellectuals of a need for a comprehensive ideology. As an ideology,
however, Arab nationalism, as perceived by these intellectuals, was not
very well developed; it had many unresolved problematics with which
it had to contend (e.g. the role of religion, non-Arab minorities in Arab
countries, flagrant imbalance in the distribution of wealth, absence of
democratic principles, subjugation of women, etc.). The most severe
drawback, as I see it, was the fashioning of the ideology of Arab nationalism along the model of European nationalisms, with a unilinear
evolutionary vision of historical and cultural development.[21] While the
purpose of this ideological framework was to create unity where diversity
abounded, its explicit motive was to reach the same level of development
as Europe's. In other words, here too leading Arab intellectuals function-
ed as the 'managers of legitimation' of a social order whose ideas they
internalised through formal education, but whose immediate political
domination they resented.

What has been termed as 'liberal Arab nationalism' evolved into a
more radical form of Arab nationalism following the loss of Palestine in
1948.[22]

The flow of ideas from intellectual centres in Lebanon, Syria and
Egypt to Palestine (at least until 1948) compelled us to assess the
transformational nature of the consciousness which was being produced
by Arab intellectuals in general. While it was non-revolutionary, it
attempted to articulate a direction for the development of Arab culture
which was entirely under foreign and non-democratic rule. Keep in
mind, moreover, that the intellectuals who were prominent in the articulation of Arab nationalism were members of the dominant elite—
academic and political.

Palestine, in the meantime, was also under foreign rule, but with a
much dimmer hope for political autonomy and sovereignty. In the
next section, we shall focus on the specific functions of Palestinian
intellectuals, before and after the loss of Palestine.

III. Palestinian Intellectuals

1. Pre-1948

The nature of the threat in Palestine shaped in large measure the type of
consciousness articulated by Palestinian intellectuals. Unlike other Arab
countries between the 1920s and 1948, when the struggle was for national
independence, the major threat in Palestine was directed against its very

national existence.[23] The sequence of diplomatic and strategic successes
of the Zionist movement regarding the transformation of Palestine into
a Jewish 'national home', which was manifested through mounting
Jewish immigration into the country, made acute the stress on the
Arabism of Palestine. Influenced by the already existing formulations
on Arab nationalism in Lebanon, Syria and Egypt, the Palestinian
intellectuals' emphasis on the Arab character of Palestine and the positive and pride-generating dimension of Arab history became a classic
illustration of this consciousness. Due to their small numbers and the
immediacy of the threat, Palestinian intellectuals had to conduct
initially a rear-guard action; they had to develop, once they became
fully aware of the implications of the threat, frameworks for counteracting it. The proliferation of political parties, intellectual associations,
clubs, organisations, etc. at this period of Palestinian struggle is
indicative of an absence of an ideological framework which could
have been translated into a unified political action. By one
estimate,[24] Haifa alone had about forty clubs and associations of this
type in the mid-thirties.

Regardless of the absence of a cohesive ideology, it is clear that Palestinian intellectuals during this period rejected the implications of the
Balfour Declaration and argued against a change in the character of Palestine. They did that 'in a flood of polemical tracts, booklets, articles
and essays. The origins, aims and techniques of the Zionists were described, analyzed and condemned, and in some cases countermeasures
were suggested.'[25] Shadowed by a predominant ideology of kinship
loyalty, Palestinian political struggle was directed within the context
of six Arab political parties in 1936.[26] The major ones, namely the
Palestine Arab Party, the National Defense Party, and the Independence
Party, represented land-owning and religiously privileged kinship groups,
and an educated rising bourgeoisie with technocratic consciousness.
The Independence Party, which was formed by professional intellectuals from provincial privileged families,[27] was the only one to
emphasise the ideology of Arab unity. In other words, this party postul-
ated a connection between the particular struggle in Palestine and the
general Arab struggle.[28] Perhaps this may be explained in that its founder
was prominent in the early Arab national movement. But why did it
attract other intellectuals?

The Independence Party was not a populist party. It included, however, many of the well known nationalist elite in Palestine. As a counter-
force to the kinship-based parties, it provided the professional intellectuals with the potential for ascendancy and for influencing the course of

events. Additionally, unlike the kin-based parties which operated on the principle that British colonialism could be won over to the Palestinian side, the Independence Party was nationalist and anti-colonial. Therefore, Palestinians who studied law and medicine, for example, in Lebanon and Syria, under the influence of Arab nationalism, were more attracted to this type of ideological framework.

Another segment of Palestinian intellectuals – basically, non-professionals with only high school education – sought to extend leftward the cultural and political consciousness of the Palestinian people. Operating outside the parameters of existing Arab political parties in the mid-thirties, they formed a variety of associations and clubs. The first such organisation was established in the summer of 1937 by a group of high schools students in Jerusalem and Bethlehem.[29] This new Arab Students' Organization (*Jamiyyat al-Tullab al-'Arab*) decided to organise summer schools to combat illiteracy among adults. Many students were attracted to it. In its founding statement, the organisation described the project in terms of 'fulfilling the national obligations that history imposed upon them'.[30]

To reflect its more encompassing nature, the founders of the organisation decided in 1938 to change the name to the League of Arab Students (*Rabitat al-Tullab al-'Arab*). Moreover, new chapters were opened in Jaffa and Haifa. The explicit aims of the League were:[31]

(1) to serve the people by fighting illiteracy and by providing medical aid and assistance to the needy; (2) to disseminate a feeling of self-respect amongst the Arab students, to strengthen the bonds of friendship and comradeship amongst them and to foster their national consciousness. It also strived to foster culture, art and sport, etc.

The League decided also to publish the monthly *al-Ghad*. Even though the published positions of the League showed no overt confrontation with the prevalent political questions of the time, they reflected an understanding of the pervasive nature of national consciousness, coupled with, of course, an emphasis on the revival of Arab culture in its Palestinian variety.

In an attempt to include other Palestinian intellectuals outside the circles of high school students, the League's name was changed in 1941 to the League of Arab Intellectuals (*Rabitat al-Muthaqqafin al-'Arab*), under the leadership and noticeable influence of members of the Palestine Communist Party (PCP), such as Abdalla Bandak. The writings of other intellectual members and sympathisers of the PCP, such as Emile Habibi,

Emile Touma, Tawfiq Toubi and Boulos Farah, appeared in the League's publications.

Two concurrent organisations were formed: the Ray of Hope Society (*Shu'a' al'Amal*) by Touma and Farah and the Peoples' Club (*Nadi al-Sha'b*) by Habibi in Haifa. These organisations disseminated anti-Fascist and pro-Soviet information, and demanded democratic rights for the Palestinian people. Further, they worked for an Arab trade union movement. Consequently, a federation of Arab trade unions, including urban workers in Shell, Iraq Petroleum Company and Haifa refineries, etc., was formed, and it led to the forging of a close alliance between the intellectuals in these associations and the workers in the federation.

The younger generation of Arab members in the PCP pushed 'for a more openly Arab nationalist position'.[32] The collapse of the Arab-Jewish Party on the question of Zionism, political tactics, etc. was a welcome development for the young Arab Communists. With that development, and with the inroads they realised in the Arab labour movement, they were able to form in 1944 a new nationalist organisation with a strong base among intellectuals and urban workers – the National Liberation League ('*Usbat al-Taharrur al-Watani*).

The National Liberation League became a political party with two main components: former PCP members and left-wing intellectuals, and workers. It sought from its inception (which preceded the formation of the Supreme Arab Authority) 'to create a left-wing democratic branch of the Arab national movement in Palestine'[33] and, thereby, to struggle against the non-democratic domination of traditional kinship groups.[34]

The League's membership was open to every Arab Palestinian who concurred with its platform which had the following political, economic and social goals: (1) abolition of the Mandate; (2) establishment of a democratic government in independent Palestine; (3) opposition to Zionism and its aspirations; (4) strengthening of bonds with the Arab peoples; (5) raising the standard of living for workers and peasants; (6) support for labour legislation and progressive tax policy; (7) democratisation of municipal government; (8) development of schools and free compulsory education for all; and (9) dissemination of culture and the strengthening of the position of the intellectual.[35]

According to Yehoshua Porath's analysis, the League's position was distinguished from that of other Arab nationalists in respect of two points: (1) it distinguished between Zionism and the Jewish population in Palestine, and, following the Soviet Union's position, (2) it demanded that the Palestinian problem be submitted to the Security Council and not negotiated with Britain.

Palestinian intellectuals had been influential in the development of
the Arab labour movement in Palestine since the early thirties. It is
interesting to note that some of the League's goals were explicated
already in the First Arab Labor Conference which was held in Haifa on
11 January 1930.[36] The conference emphasised: (1) Marxist and class
analysis of the conflict, and it attacked Zionism and the British Mandate;
(2) that 'there is no difference between Arab capitalism and Zionist
capitalism'; and (3) that it was for an independent Palestine within the
framework of Arab unity, and it denounced Zionist immigration.

In an assessment of the type of consciousness the League produced,
Porath writes:[37] 'By its very existence it performed a signal service to
the Arabs of Palestine for it constituted their first modern political
organization of another basis than that of traditional family loyalties.'
Obviously, the type of question which concerns us is not who had the
most influence in articulating these positions—members of the PCP
or the intellectuals; rather, what type of intellectuals were attracted to
the position of the PCP, and why? How much of a radical consciousness
such a position sought to articulate in relation to the struggle of the Palestinian people?

Setting the connection to the Soviet Union's line aside for a moment,
the general organisational approach by this segment of Palestinian intellectuals was to effect an organisation with a mass base which could
compete in the articulation of Palestinian aspirations with existing kin-
based parties. Clearly, the names which were influential in this development—Toubi, Farah, Habibi, Touma, Bandak, etc.—did not belong to
the ruling families; neither did they expect to ascend to positions of
influence via their kinship affiliation. Democratic principles and solid
party organisation were the only guarantee for reaching the masses of
workers and young intellectuals, most of whom were not members of
these urban-based families. The notable point here is that none of these
intellectuals during this entire period was of the professional elite, nor
were they members of the dominant religious stratum; most, if not all,
have had high-school education, and they came from the petty bourgeoisie
urban background (small merchants, teachers, etc.).

As an Arab party, the League was successful in making inroads among
the rural Palestinian peasantry. The goals pertaining to the abolition of
the Mandate, the independence of Palestine and the opposition to Zionism and immigration were shared by other nationalists, and represented
an accurate articulation of the demands of the Palestinian people. However, the relentless emphasis on the democratic principles, against the
traditional lines of kinship and religious loyalties, and the discrimination

between the Jewish population of Palestine and the Zionist movement represented a recognisable level of progressive consciousness. The League's positions did threaten the existing social order at a time when the latter relied for its perpetuation on some of the most powerful and charismatic traditional leaders. It must be added, however, that the League's programme did not offer a blueprint for what an independent Palestine would look like. In other words, an overall vision with a cohesive ideological base was missing.

Another segment of Palestinian intellectuals (e.g. Darwazah, al-'Aref, etc.), most of whom were of middle-class or land-owning families and who received university education, produced literature which played a role (at least in the literate segment of the population) in sharpening and articulating the terms of the struggle. While these, however, were plugged into the existing elite structure of educators, professionals or government bureaucrats, they 'left their imprint on those who were exposed to their writings in a variety of ways':[38]

(1)   they 'supplemented religious with nationalist motivation';
(2)   they 'tried to remove from their readers' consciousness the memory of the political fragmentation that befell the Arab World';
(3)   they 'helped to introduce an element of bitterness toward the west among the masses of the Palestinians';
(4)   they 'considered nationalism as a program of action'.

Whereas indeed they contributed to the sharpening and clarification of the Arab nationalist consciousness of the struggle, they were unable, due to their position in the bureaucracy and their class interests, to articulate and sustain the needed revolutionary consciousness. They were too well attached to the existing social order; by staffing its bureaucratic slots, they acted, at least in part, as its legitimators.

2. Post-1948

a. The Statistical Reality. The loss of Palestine in 1948 rendered the educational option very attractive and imperative. Education for the politically deprived Palestinian became an indispensable mobile asset.

Due to severe geographical dispersal and a variety of statistical methods and levels of efficiency, it is difficult to present an accurate statistical picture of present-day Palestinian university students and graduates. A hint, however, can be provided. According to the director of student manpower in Beirut, it is estimated that over 80,000 Palestinians are registered (1977-8) in institutions of higher learning in the Arab world, Europe and the United States.[39] A study published in 1977 reveals that 70,000 Palestinians are university graduates, of whom 50 per cent are employed in education, 17 per cent in engineering, 10 per cent in medical fields, and 15 per cent in management.[40] These numbers, according to the authors, constitute 10 per cent of total Arab 'high level manpower'.[41]

Projecting to the year 2000, and taking into consideration 'female emancipation and the increase in university facilities in the Arab world', it seems that over 400,000 Palestinians will be enrolled in colleges and universities. This will represent 50 per cent of the 18-24 age category.[42]

In an earlier and more ambitious survey of 'high level Palestinian manpower',[43] based on 10,000 replies from Palestinians who had successfully completed 16 or more years of study, it was found that about 61 per cent were graduates in humanities, social sciences, law and education, and about 36 per cent for the other subjects.[44] Some conclusions of this study are: (1) the number of Palestinian graduates 'is perhaps greater than that of the Israelis'; (2) 'the ratio of present Palestinian university students to the total Palestinian population is higher than the ratio for any Arab country'; and (3) 'teaching, engineering, management, and medicine represent the four most important professions practiced'.[45]

Statistical data on the educational level of the Palestinians in Israel are more readily available. Data from 1975 show that of the Arab population aged 14 and over only 1.0 per cent received 16+ years of schooling and 3.9 per cent received between 13 and 15 years of schooling.[46] A breakdown by degree shows that 87.5 per cent of all Arab students in Israeli academic institutions are studying for a BA degree, 10.9 per cent for an MA degree, and 0.4 per cent for a PhD.[47] Translated into absolute numbers, this shows 990 Arab university students: 11 diploma students, 4 PhDs, 108 MAs, and 867 BAs with 322 first-year students.[48]

Since these data, however, pertain only to Palestinians registered in Israeli universities, the figures provided here have to be viewed as representing a much lower estimate than the actual situation. It is a known fact that many young Palestinians leave Israel in pursuit of other educational opportunities. Some return, especially from East European countries, while others become a part of the constant brain drain. Data from two Palestinian villages in Western Galilee, gathered in 1976,[49] illustrate this situation clearly. The two villages, whose combined population in 1976 was about 9,000, had a total of 278 university-educated people: 11 PhDs,

29 MDs, 17 MAs, 86 BAs, 3 other, and 132 students in colleges and universities.

b. Palestinians under Occupation: Israel. The Zionist success in transforming Palestine into a Jewish state produced two results pertaining to the political function of Palestinian intellectuals. The first was the loss of the majority of professional-bureaucratic intellectuals (traditional intellectuals in Gramsci's terminology) who were active in articulating certain dimensions of Palestinian struggle under the Mandate. The second, Zionist success pushed Palestinian struggle, abruptly and ruthlessly, back to square one. Put differently, the issues which 'traditional' intellectuals articulated as members of an intact, yet threatened, majority and as members of a well-entrenched, professional and land-owning stratum have to be articulated now by a demoralised, culturally oppressed and dismembered minority.

Clearly, the nature and immediacy of the threat have been altered. Yet, some basic issues remained constant. The question of liberating the people from foreign and culturally alien rule, whether British or Zionist, remained paramount. The character of that rule, however, was transformed from a colonial to a settler state, with differing legitimising ideologies. Like their situation under the Mandate, Palestinians still lack self-determination, autonomy and sovereignty.

A second major question with which the Palestinians in the newly created situation were faced was the question of cultural and political identity. They have become the remnants of a people, the majority of whom became dispersed in different parts of the world, but without having been allowed to identify with that people. An important dimension of this dilemma was their physical isolation from the flow of ideas, rethinking and political reverberations which were taking place in the various intellectual centres in the Arab world.

In the light of the intricate web of this new and immediate threat, what consciousness did Palestinian intellectuals in Israel produce, and how much did they influence the ultimate goal of liberation and self-determination?

Four types of Palestinian intellectuals have been involved, often with antagonism, in providing the terms for the battle of consciousness pertaining to their struggle. These are: (1) literary figures, or 'the people of the pen', who articulated their views mainly through poetry and short stories; (2) university students, organised through the various Arab Students' Committees in Israeli universities; (3) members of the New Communist List (*Rakah*), whose views have been expressed through the

Party's official publications and through mass rallies; and (4) some well-entrenched nationalists who were educated, often on their own, by Arab nationalism (e.g. Mansour Kardoush), but the expression of whose views became very restricted. This typology includes both categories of Gramsci's intellectuals – 'traditional' and 'organic' – some articulate the interests of their traditional attachments and class loyalties, while others provide form and content to the interests of the strata whose goal is liberation, self-determination and the abolition of existing dominance patterns. Hence we speak of a 'battle for consciousness'.

The main ingredients of this battle are: (1) identity – a struggle against severance from the larger Palestinian people and against cultural dis-solution and dismemberment; (2) land – struggle against dispossession of national existence; and (3) liberation and self-determination – a struggle against living in an exclusivist and racist framework and for defining a new social order which will obviate such cultural non-exist-ence.

Arab writers and poets took the lead in addressing themselves to some ingredients of this battle without being explicitly political. They sought means and forums for the unhindered exposure of their product-ion. They started by forming the 'League of Arabic Poets' in March 1954, which combined Arab and Jewish writers.[50] Including all writers of Arabic – Arabs and Jews regardless of their political ideologies – led to an inevitable split only one year after the 'League' was established. Some Arab members, and all Jewish members, decided against the admission of Arab poets who were members of the Communist Party, or sympathetic to its line. This group wanted poetry detached from the existential political reality of the people. They formed in March 1955 the 'League of the Arab Pen'. In their subsequent publications, they became the 'managers of legitimation' for the existing order. Most of these writers were elementary and high school teachers and were able through their apolitical posture to retain those jobs.

The League held frequent poetry festivals in a variety of Arab locations (e.g. the Kufr Yasif Festival of 14 July 1957). Through poetry, they mesmerised their audiences with emotional poems which they re-cited often in the open, on topics such as the struggle for land, village life, the peasant, and oppression and suppression by the military govern-ment, etc. 'The Arabs in Israel', one of these active poets wrote, 'awaited anxiously these festivals as they did national or religious holidays. They saw in the defiance of their poet brethren their image, and what they desired to be'.[51]

Soon after its success at the Kufr Yasif Festival, the League expanded to include other Arab intellectuals. On 5 September 1957, therefore, it became the League of Arab Intellectuals. In addition to its poet-members, the names of well-known nationalist and Communist Party intellectuals appeared as members. Among its goals were the revival of Arab tradition, the founding of an independent publishing house, the sponsoring of literary panels and workshops, the defence of Arab intellectuals and the rights of the Arab people in the country, and the solidarity with all oppressed peoples.[52]

The celebration of 1 May 1958 in Nazareth, which coincided with the tenth year of Israel's existence, was turned into what may be described as an Arab nationalist holiday, thanks to the poems of defiance and resistance by Arab poets on the one hand, and the oppressive behaviour of the police on the other.

It must be mentioned here that some Arab poets, who occupied a variety of bureaucratic positions in the Ministry of Education, produced for the occasion verse after verse in praise of Israeli independence, the Jewish struggle for its 'homeland', and the ingenuity of the Israeli system in developing the land of Palestine. In other words, they helped legitimate the system which oppressed them and their people. In many cases, these poems, which Arab pupils had to memorise, were included in the curriculum of Arab elementary schools.

'To take part in the African revolution,' Sekou Toure wrote, 'it is not enough to write a revolutionary song; you must fashion the revolution with the people.'[53] Certain segments of Arab intellectuals attempted, at the risk of opposing other segments of the intellectuals, 'to fashion the revolution with the people', or, at least, to help define the parameters of that revolution. However, the Zionist success in pushing back the Palestinian struggle to square one took its toll: square one was defined in terms of basic freedoms for the Arabs within Israel, the official nature of the Arabic language, national dignity, improved educational facilities, abolishment of military government, defence of Arab lands, often at the expense of a serious and sustained theory of the roots of the Palestinian question, a comprehensive Palestinian identity, and the struggle against the uncompromisingly racist nature of Zionism.[54]

While this was true on the whole in terms of the organised effort which existed, significant attempts by certain categories of Arab intellectuals in Israel were initiated for the specific purpose of producing a well integrated and comprehensive ideology of this struggle. Generally, these were young nationalist intellectuals, many of whom believed in the socialist option but felt that a certain degree of opportunism and distortion had become a characteristic of the Communist Party's position.

The Al-Ard movement in the early 1960s was an attempt in this direction. While it combined efforts with the Communist Party and other progressive forces in Israel in its struggle for basic freedoms and equality for the Palestinians, it diverged from the Communist Party in stressing the indivisibility of the Palestinian people and the Palestinian question. In article '3c' of its goals, it sought a just solution for the Palestinian question, commensurate with the desires and aspirations of the entire Palestinian people in regaining its integrity, its legitimate rights for self-determination within the context of the aspirations of the Arab nation.[55]

Deprived of legitimacy within the Israeli system, the Al-Ard movement was killed as a movement but the well integrated consciousness it sought to produce lived on. The consciousness pertaining to the ideological indivisibility of the Palestinian people and their struggle survived. The Arab Students' Committee at the Hebrew University in Jerusalem has played a substantial role in sustaining this consciousness. The heart of their statement on 30 March 1976 concerning the general strike against the expropriation of Arab lands, for example, dealt with the unity of the struggle of the Palestinians in Israel, the West Bank and Gaza, and the diaspora. 'All of these struggles constitute one, integrated, and indivisible struggle,' they wrote.[56]

In addition to, and perhaps because of, the historical role of the Arab Students' Committee in Jerusalem, a new force sustaining this consciousness has been provided recently by the Sons of the Village Movement (*Harakat Abna' al-Balad*). In a co-signed statement on Sadat's visit to Jerusalem, it was reiterated that 'the road to peace must go through the recognition and the realization of the right of the Palestinian-Arab people to self-determination and to return to its homeland'.[57]

Deciding to emphasise a comprehensive consciousness of the struggle, the intellectuals in these movements found themselves confronted by the party intellectuals of Rakah. The irony is that some of the intellectuals in question were the ones who produced the most comprehensive consciousness for Palestinian struggle prior to the United Nations' 1947 Partition Plan and the position of the Soviet Union in support of that Plan. Now, straddled by the present foreign policy line of the Soviet Union and impeded by the need to maintain their legitimate parliamentary representation, they are producing what might be called a fragmentary consciousness of the Palestinian struggle. The 'advanced theory' they are providing is not advanced at all; it postulates the divisibility of the Palestinian people into Palestinians and Arabs of Israel; in effect, it acts as a legitimator for Zionist Israel, albeit within 4 June 1967 borders.[58]

c. Palestinians under Occupation: West Bank. Like the situation with
the Palestinians inside the so-called 'green line', Palestinian intellectuals
in the West Bank, who have been involved in articulating the consciousness of the struggle, are also comprised of different categories: university
students and graduates, members of the Communist Party, and 'traditional' intellectuals with Arab nationalist convictions. Here too the abrupt
and forceful military occupation of this part of Palestine imposed itself
on the type of consciousness which defined the struggle. More effort
has been expended by West Bank intellectuals on the articulation of an
end to military occupation and oppression than to a formulation of a
comprehensive ideology for the entire Palestine question. Put differently,
while the end of Israeli occupation and the autonomous political existence of the West Bank (and Gaza) constituted the main ingredient of
the struggle here, as articulated by intellectuals, little effort (at least
mental) was invested in an analysis of the future of Palestinians in Israel.
In other words, following the pattern of international dominance, these
intellectuals fell into the trap of relegating 500,000 Palestinians to
Israel 'proper', thus defining them outside the heart of the Palestine
question. In that sense, military occupation succeeded again in forcing
the fragmentation of the consciousness of Palestinian struggle.

Arguing that the West Bank and Gaza are 'proper' Palestine, and
coinciding in that with the formal position of the Soviet Union (regarding UN Resolution 242), non-Communist intellectuals met more closely
with the position of the Party's intellectuals in the West Bank and
Israel, in terms of the definition of the struggle. Some of the tactics
which were followed by intellectuals in Israel were repeated here. Bir
Zeit University and Bethlehem University students were instrumental in
utilising poetry as a means of consciousness-raising. 'Poetry reading
sessions, panel discussions, and seminars or study sessions have become
familiar phenomena on a very wide scale in the West Bank.'[59] Also, the
revival of Palestinian folklore through a variety of clubs and associations
has been a successful element in the battle against the dissolution of Palestinian identity under occupation.

d. Palestinians outside Palestine. The successful creation of a Jewish
national home in Palestine in 1948 generated, in addition to bewilder-
ment and despair, the need to rethink Arab structure, and regroup after
al-Nakbah. Palestinian students in Arab universities, mainly in Beirut
and Cairo, took the lead in a slow and tedious explication of the Palestinian question. A tremendous need was felt for creating a sustaining consciousness of the newly created situation, a kind of consciousness which

could inform and inseminate practical organisational efforts.

At the American University of Beirut, a group of active Palestinian students, who had witnessed the destruction of their homeland, founded the Arab Nationalist Movement in the early 1950s. The main uniting theory for the group at the time was anti-imperialism and anti-Western-ism. Since most of these students came from bourgeois background, the Movement at first lacked any class consciousness, and had no developed understanding of Marxism and socialism.[60] With Palestine having been dismembered in front of their eyes, the Movement sought answers in the Arab world—the need 'to develop and educate the national spirit among the Arab students'[61] was recognised, and Arab unity became the panacea for the overwhelming ills.[62]

Habash, Haddad and others took this Movement, which they founded, a long way—both organisationally and conceptually. Since the concern of this essay lies with the latter, the organisational structure of the Movement will not be discussed here.

While Palestine was the permeating theme of the Movement, the objectives of 'unity, liberation, and vengeance' were thrust towards the Arab countries until the defeat of 1967. The prior failure of the unity between Egypt and Syria in 1961 was a crucial factor in the rethinking which took place within the Movement and in its subsequently more pronounced leftward direction. The Arab National Movement, therefore, was radically transformed into the Popular Front for the Liberation of Palestine and the Democratic Front for the Liberation of Palestine.

As the guiding consciousness for a prolonged and radical struggle for the liberation of Palestine, the eradication of Arab reaction, exploit-ation, oppression and opportunism was recognised as a primary com-ponent of this ideology. Consequently, the transformed consciousness which these intellectuals produced provided an ideologically com-prehensive framework for the struggle, whose major components are the indivisibility of the Palestinian revolution (while recognising, of course, the need for different tactics), and the indivisibility of Arab revolutionary struggle.

Contemporaneously, other active Palestinian students in Cairo (Yasser Arafat, Hani al-Hassan, etc.), were also preoccupied with a radical alteration of the Zionist *status quo* in Palestine. However, the paramount concern of these students was (and remains) organisational, rather than conceptual. The explicit objective was the liberation of occupied Palestine, but the persistent question was how to achieve it? A National Liberation Movement for Palestine (*Fateh*) was created, and for a variety of reasons— with ideological flabbiness not the least important—it became the largest

of the resistance movements and the core of the Palestine Liberation
Organization (PLO).

While it is demonstrably true that Fateh's energies were sapped by
organisational and military questions, its theoreticians produced a consciousness for the future of Palestine which, with further development,
will prove to be a radical departure from the *status quo* —both Arab
and Zionist. I am referring to the vision of democratic and secular Palestine where the Muslim, Christian and Jewish inhabitants of the country
can enjoy equal rights without the exclusive domination of one category
of the population over another. To serve as a guiding consciousness for
a successful Palestinian struggle, it is clear, however, that this vision
needs to address itself explicitly to the question of control and distribution of wealth —in other words, the accessibility to and control over
the means of economic production.

Palestinian intellectuals at present play a substantial role in guiding
the struggle. Of the 293 members of the 13th Palestine National Council,
for example, more than 90 per cent were college graduates; and over 15
per cent had PhDs or equivalent degrees.[63] The variety of agencies and
media for mental production have been staffed, controlled and shaped
by vast numbers of intellectuals with formal university education.

Additionally, Palestinian students still constitute a significant pool
for providing potential guidance and rethinking for the struggle. A
recent study of students in Lebanese universities revealed that 94 per
cent of the Palestinian students interviewed 'rejected the prevailing
social values, in contrast to 68 percent of the Lebanese; 63 percent
of the Jordanians, and 70 percent of other Arabs'.[64] On the index of
'political alienation' and 'leftist radicalism', 86 per cent of the Palestinian
students 'indicated that they were dissatisfied with the dominant political
conditions, only 71 percent of other Arabs did so'.[65]

Through mental production and consciousness-raising, segments of
Palestinian intellectuals served a crucial function in sustaining their
people's revolutionary struggle; other segments of Palestinian intellectuals, however, contributed in a large measure to their personal accumulation of capital and influence, often at the expense of the revolution.
Palestinian intellectual skills were repeatedly and massively utilised
during the last twenty years in sustaining the embryonic political and
economic systems of the oil-rich areas of the Arab world, which proved,
on the whole, to constitute serious impediments in the course of Palestinian revolution. Due to the lack of a territorial base for the revolution,
the absence of a comprehensive conceptual framework and the non-
existence of individual and collective revolutionary consciousness, sub-

stantial numbers of Palestinian intellectuals were rendered commodities for conservative and insatiable markets. Thus, they have been channelled into functions which legitimated the existing order of dominance.

IV. Conclusion

A recent study on 'Palestinian nationalism' among camp Palestinians in Lebanon included the following excerpt from an interview with a 25-year-old building worker:

> Teachers told us something about Palestine, but they should have told us more. They should have participated in action, for example in demonstrations, but they hadn't the courage. Most were with the Deuxieme Bureau ... They are good at making speeches, and arguing, but when the Revolution faces difficulties, they will not be there. Only when the difficulties are over, then you will see them in front.[66]

The ubiquitous discrepancy between ideology and praxis is made manifest here. Action was not addressed explicitly in this essay. The focus was on the ideology, or the production of the ideologists, during the Palestinian struggle. An assessment of the comprehensiveness of the type of consciousness propagated by intellectuals was attempted. From this perspective, the question to be answered in this discussion is: what functions do Palestinian intellectuals perform in guiding and sustaining Palestinian struggle?

This discussion has demonstrated the contradictory nature of the intellectual functions pertaining to the Palestinian struggle. Certain categories of Palestinian intellectuals are instrumental in the production of a guiding consciousness for the revolution, while, simultaneously, they act as managers of legitimation for the *status quo* whose transformation was purported to have been the goal of the consciousness they produced in the first place.

By and large, the consciousness which formal Western-style university education incubates is not a consciousness of collective liberation; it is a 'liberation' at the individual level, from job uncertainty, poverty, low prestige and some form of dependence. Such consciousness, if pursued— and it is in most cases, hence the contradiction—jettisons the individual in a direction of 'economic liberation' which contradicts the needed collective liberation. It is unconvincing, as it has been argued recently, that 'the young Arab intellectual' is searching for 'a united world view', for 'fundamentalism and for a holistic ideology'.[67] Recent Arab history, and particularly the course of Palestinian struggle within it, provides with clarity the ingredients for a holistic ideology which is required to guide the struggle. It is more important to ask, however, whether there is an intent on the part of the intellectual to guide the struggle, especially, since the struggle may become economically debilitating, socially indiscrete and personally uncomfortable or fatal.

Formal education provides only the means, but not necessarily the readiness, for pursuing a revolutionary consciousness of liberation. The need, as Gramsci emphasised, is for a category of 'organic' intellectuals, whose interests and hegemony are defined in terms of the interests and hegemony of the dominated segments in the struggle. Nationalist tendencies which are premised on the revival of Arab exclusivism, 'reformed' Arab states, a modified form of Western capitalist democracy, liberal Islam (or Christianity), which logically advocate transformation within the system are the bedrock of the contradiction Arab revolutionary intellectuals manifest, especially in their behaviour towards the Palestine struggle.

I share in Laroui's general assessment:

> All too long has the Arab intellectual hesitated to make radical criticisms of culture, language, and tradition. Too long has he drawn back from criticizing the aims of local national policy, the result of which is a stifling of democracy and a generalized dualism. He must condemn superficial economism, which would modernize the country and rationalize society by constructing factories with another's money, another's technology, another's administration. When it comes to the problems of minorities and local democracy, he must cease from censoring himself for fear of imperiling an apparent national unity. The Arab revolutionary intellectual has too long applauded the call to Arab unity, the while accepting and sometimes justifying the fragmentation that is reality.[68]

The last fifty years of Palestinian struggle for self-determination and sovereignty provide a clear signal for what is to come — and what should be expected — a long and protracted struggle of many dimensions against giant threats of global character. The task of Palestinian revolutionary intellectuals is to chart the relationships among those threats in an over-arching ideological paradigm, without confusing it with the specific tactics, be they short- or long-term, which need to be pursued. The shortcomings of the intellectual involvement in guiding the Palestinian struggle, as discussed in this essay, lie mostly in this domain. Time-bound tactical considerations have replaced long-term and coherent strategy in the absence of an ideological-revolutionary consciousness. The indispensable function which the Palestinian intellectuals must perform in the present revolutionary struggle is not merely the production of radical consciousness, but the tactical translation of that consciousness, through institutional and individual means, to the mass level of the struggle. Only then we can speak of the intellectuals as a segment of the Palestinian revolutionary vanguard.

Notes

1. A.W. Gouldner, 'Prologue to a Theory of Revolutionary Intellectuals', *Telos*, no. 26 (Winter 1975/6), p. 4.

2. See E. Shils, 'The Intellectuals in the Political Development of the New States', *World Politics*, voL II (1960), p. 332.

3. Q. Hoare and G.N. Smith, *Selections From the Prison Notebooks of Antonio Gramsci* (New York, 1971), p. 9.

4. Ibid., p. 12.

5. R. Miliband, *Marxism and Politics* (Oxford, 1977), p. 57.

6. A. Gramsci, *The Modern Prince and Other Writings* (New York, 1968). Gramsci viewed hegemony as 'the predominance, obtained by consent rather than force, of one class or group over other classes'. It is 'a world view of class domination', a 'direction'.

7. V.I. Lenin, *What is to be Done?* (Moscow, 1964), pp. 25-6.

8. K. Marx and F. Engels, *The German Ideology* (New York, 1947), p. 39.

9. Miliband, *Marxism and Politics*, p. 53.

10. K. Marx and F. Engels, *Communist Manifesto* (New York, 1933), p. 20; emphasis added.

11. Lenin, *What is to be Done?*, p. 105; emphasis in original.

12. Ibid., p. 78.

13. C. Boggs, 'Gramsci's "Prison Notebooks"'; *Socialist Revolution*, voL 11 (1971), pp. 106-7.

14. See, for example, H. Sharabi, *Arab Intellectuals and the West: the Formative Years, 1875-1914* (Baltimore, 1969), and Z.N. Zeine, *The Emergence of Arab Nationalism* (Beirut, 1966).

15. Zeine, *Emergence of Arab Nationalism*, pp. 50-1.

16. Ibid., p. 90. See also A.L. Tibawi, *A Modern History of Syria* (New York, 1969), pp. 163-7.

17. Zeine, *Emergence of Arab Nationalism*, p. 95; G. Antonius, *The Arab Awakening* (New York, 1939), p. 7.

18. Zeine, *Emergence of Arab Nationalism*, p. 105.

19. Sharabi, *Arab Intellectuals*.

20. H. Sharabi, *Nationalism and Revolution in the Arab World* (Princeton, 1966), p. 105.

21. See the recent interview with C. Zurayk, one of the formulators of liberal Arab nationalism, in *al-Mustaqbal*, no. 40 (1977), pp. 35-40.

22. See the discussion in T. Ismail, *The Arab Left* (Syracuse, New York, 1976). 'Liberal' and 'radical' are Ismail's terminology.

23. A. Abu-Ghazaleh, *Arab Cultural Nationalism in Palestine* (Beirut, 1973), p. 39.

24. See the interview with Hanna Naqqara pertaining to this stage of the

struggle in *al-Ittihad* (Haifa, 27 January 1978).

25. Abu-Ghazaleh, *Arab Cultural Nationalism*, p. 39.

26. Ibid., pp. 44-5.

27. Porath's detailed study of this period revealed that of the 11 original founders of the Istiqlal (Independence) Party, two were bank managers and financial experts, three lawyers, three journalists, two schoolteachers and one medical doctor. All, however, were not Jerusalemites, and were unrelated to the competing kinship groups: see Y. Porath, *The Palestinian Arab National Movement 1929-1939: From Riots to Rebellion* (London, 1977), p. 125.

28. The Party's principles were: (1) 'total independence for the Arab countries'; (2) 'The Arab countries constitute an indivisible whole'; (3) 'Palestine is an Arab country and it is a natural part of Syria'. The explicit goals of the Party were two: (1) 'The abolishment of the Mandate and the Balfour Declaration'; (2) 'The establishment of a Parliamentary Arab rule in Palestine'. See A. al-Kayyali (comp.), *Watha'iq al-Muqawamah al-Filastiniyya al-Arabiyya* (Beirut, 1968), p. 263 (Arabic).

29. Y. Porath, 'The National Liberation League', *Asian and African Studies* (Jerusalem), vol. 4 (1968), p. 6.

30. Ibid.

31. As quoted in ibid., p. 7.

32. J. Beinen, 'The Palestine Communist Party, 1919-1948', *MERIP Reports*, no. 55 (March 1977), p. 11.

33. Porath, 'The National Liberation League', p. 10.

34. Beinen, 'The Palestine Communist Party', p. 11.

35. Porath, 'The National Liberation League', p. 9.

36. M. Al-Bedeiry, 'Arab Labor Movement in Palestine during the British Mandate', *al-Jadid*, vol. 10 (Haifa, 1976), pp. 25-33.

37. Porath, 'The National Liberation League', p. 21.

38. Abu-Ghazaleh, *Arab Cultural Nationalism*, pp. 100-1.

39. H. Sharabi, a talk on the 'Political Dimensions of Palestinian Identity', 31st Annual Meeting of the Middle East Institute (Washington, 30 September–1 October 1977).

40. A. and R. Zahlan, 'The Palestinian Future: Education and Manpower', *Journal of Palestine Studies*, vol. 6, no. 4 (Summer 1977), p. 104.

41. Ibid.

42. Ibid., p. 105.

43. N. Shaath, 'High Level Palestinian Manpower', *Journal of Palestine Studies*, vol. 1, no. 2 (1972), pp. 80-95.

44. Ibid., p. 83.

45. Ibid., pp. 94-5.

46. Israel, Central Bureau of Statistics, *Statistical Abstract of Israel 1975* (Jerusalem, no. 26), Table xxii/1, p. 559.

47. Ibid., tables xxii/29, xxii/32, pp. 624-5, 627.

48. Ibid.

49. K. Nakhleh, *Nationalist Consciousness and University Education* (Wilmette, 1978), p. 107.

50. H. Qahwaji, *Al-'Arab fi Dhill al-Ihtilal al-Israili* (Beirut, 1972, in Arabic), pp. 281-353.

51. Ibid., p. 285.

52. Ibid., p. 289.

53. Quoted in F. Fanon, *The Wretched of the Earth* (New York, 1963), p. 206.

54. See, for example, the resolutions of the Conference of Arab Intellectuals which was held in Haifa: *al-Jadid*, no. 4 (1960), pp. 6-7 (Arabic).

55. Qahwaji, *Al-'Arab*, p. 458.

56. The statement in question created a very harsh response from the functionaries of Rakah on the grounds that it expressed an 'adventurist' and 'infantile leftist' line. I was present at the private meeting during which these epithets were hurled at the authors of the statement.

57. *Free Palestine*, vol. 5, no. 9-10 (1977), p. 2.

58. See, in particular, *al-Ittihad* (20 June 1978), and the Party's statement on the 30th anniversary of Israel in *al-Ittihad* (16 June 1978).

59. H. Ashrawi, 'The Contemporary Palestinian poetry of occupation', *Journal of Palestine Studies*, vol. 7, no. 3 (Spring 1978), p. 80.

60. W. Kazziha, *Revolutionary Transformation in the Arab World* (New York, 1975).

61. Ibid., p. 20.

62. Ibid., p. 57.

63. I. Abu-Lughod, '13th Palestine National Council', *MERIP Reports*, no. 57 (1977), pp. 10-13.

64. H. Barakat, *Lebanon in Strife – Student Preludes to the Civil War* (Austin, Texas, 1977), p. 125.

65. Ibid., p. 124.

66. R. Sayigh, 'Sources of Palestinian Nationalism', *Journal of Palestine Studies*, vol. 6, no. 4 (Summer 1977), p. 30.

67. A. Dessouki, 'Arab Intellectuals and *al-Nakba*: the Search for Fundamentalism', *Middle Eastern Studies*, vol. 9, no. 2 (May 1973), p. 193.

68. A. Laroui, *The Crisis of the Arab Intellectual, Traditionalism or Historicism*, trans. from French by D. Cammell (Berkeley, 1976), p. 176.

APPENDICES ON PALESTINIAN HUMAN RIGHTS

A. The Defence (Emergency) Regulations, 1945

(The introduction to the Regulations has been written specifically
for this volume by J.G.C. Van Aggelen, PhD Candidate, McGill
University, Montreal, Quebec, Canada.)

Originally the Defence Emergency Regulations were enacted by the
British during their Mandate over Palestine. These regulations were
the answer to the increasing struggle for Jewish settlements against the
will of the Mandate authorities. They served as an instrument to suppress
the Jewish underground movements. Their publication caused a storm
of strong protests among the Jewish settlers. On 7 February 1946, a
protest convention of Jewish lawyers approved two decisions:

(1) the power attributed to the authorities in the regulations the
     Palestinian inhabitants of their elemental human rights (the
     nation Palestine at that time composed both Jews and
     Arabs);
(2) these regulations are against the basic principles of law and
     are a great danger to the freedom of the individual and his
     life and they establish an arbitrary regime without legal control.

The decisions taken at that convention ended with the following
promise: 'All Jewish lawyers in Palestine in cooperation with the national institutes will do everything possible in order to abolish these regulations and to give the individual back his fundamental rights.'
Attorney-General for the Israeli Government Shamgar admits that the
regulations are still in force and Holzmann, who reviewed the situation
after the Six Day War, states that it is right to ask the question 'Why
have not the Defence Regulations been abolished?' He proceeds: 'We
did not *revise* all the Regulations, but the ones we did are enough to
justify the definition which the protest convention of the Jewish Lawyer
League gave: "Regulations which establish an arbitrary regime"'
(emphasis added). His main defence is that there was a never-ceasing
struggle for the abolition of the Defence Regulations. There were a
few cases before the Israeli Supreme Court, but these trials failed and
the regulations were not considered invalid. The Israeli Parliament,

according to Holzmann, tackled steadily their abolition. Minister of Justice Shapira, who held this position before and after the Six-Day War, is quoted as saying: 'We will abolish the regulations, but if someone thinks the law system that will replace them to be a system without teeth and without the possibility to avoid sabotage in the State's security, he is nothing but wrong.'

In *Israel* a three-stage appeal machinery has been set up. The last resort for an appeal against illegal detention is the Israeli Supreme Court sitting as High Court Justice. The Supreme Court may interfere when the authority to detain apparently has been used for purposes other than those set forth by the Regulations.

In the *occupied territories*, however, administrative detention is not effected under the articles of the Defence Regulations, but under orders concerning security instructions. Art. 125 permits the Military Commander to declare a certain area closed, thereby prohibiting both entry and exit except by special permission granted by the Commander. In fact, this provision was an excellent opportunity to get rid of persons who were reluctant to co-operate with the occupying authorities. In his defence of Art. 125, Shimon Peres wrote that this article might serve as a 'direct continuation of the struggle for Jewish settlement and immigration'.

In their entirety, these Defence Regulations consist of 147 articles in 14 sections. The following articles, reprinted here from the original, were adapted, either verbatim or in a slightly varied form, from the Emergency Regulations of 1936, whose intent was to subdue the Arab population after the 1936 Arab Revolt in Palestine. These articles are the most exploited by the military administration in their present suppression of individual and political rights of the Palestinians.

Article 109

(1) A military Commander may make, in relation to any person, an order for all or any of the following purposes, that is to say —
(a) for securing that, except in so far as he may be permitted by the order, or by such authority or person as may be specified in the order, that person shall not be in any such area in Palestine as may be so specified;
(b) for requiring him to notify his movements, in such manner, at such times and to such authority or person as may be specified in the order;
(c) prohibiting or restricting the possession or use by that person of any specified articles;
(d) imposing upon him such restrictions as may be specified in the order

in respect of his employment or business, in respect of his association or communication with other persons, and in respect of his activities in relation to the dissemination of news or the propagation of opinions.
(2) If any person against whom an order has been made as aforesaid contravenes the terms of such order, he shall be guilty of an offence against these Regulations.

Article 110
(1) A Military Commander may by order direct that any person shall be placed under police supervision for any period not exceeding one year.
(2) Any person placed under police supervision by order as aforesaid shall be subject to all or any of the following restrictions as the Military Commander may direct, that is to say—
(a) he shall be required to reside within the limits of any area in Palestine, specified by the Military Commander in the order;
(b) he shall not be permitted to transfer his residence to any other area in the same police district without the written authority of the District Superintendent of Police, or to any other police district without the written authority of the Inspector General of Police;
(c) he shall not leave the town, village or Sub-District within which he resides without the written authority of the District Superintendent of Police;
(d) he shall at all times keep the District Superintendent of Police of the police district in which he resides notified of the house or the place in which he resides;
(e) he shall be liable, whenever called upon so to do by the officer in charge of the police in the area in which he resides, to present himself at the nearest police station;
(f) he shall remain within the doors of his residence from one hour after sunset until sunrise, and may be visited at his residence at any time by the police.
(3) Any person in respect of whom an order has been made under sub-regulations (1) and (2) may be arrested by any police officer or by any member of His Majesty's forces and conveyed to the area in which he should be.
(4) If any person against whom an order has been made as aforesaid contravenes the terms of the said order or of this regulation, he shall be guilty of an offence against these Regulations.

Article 111

(1) A Military Commander may by order direct that any person shall be detained for any period not exceeding one year in such place of detention as may be specified by the Military Commander in the order.

Article 112

(1) The High Commissioner shall have power to make an order under his hand (hereinafter in these Regulations referred to as 'a Deportation Order') requiring any person to leave and remain out of Palestine.

(2) The High Commissioner shall have power by order under his hand to require any person who is out of Palestine to remain out of Palestine. A person with respect to whom such an order is published shall so long as the order is in force remain out of Palestine. An order under this regulation may be made subject to such terms and conditions as the High Commissioner may think fit.

(3) A person with respect to whom a Deportation Order is made shall leave Palestine in accordance with the order and shall thereafter so long as the order is in force remain out of Palestine.

(4) A person with respect to whom a Deportation Order is made, whilst awaiting deportation and whilst being conveyed to any vessel, train, aircraft or vehicle in Palestine, shall be liable to be kept in custody in such manner as the High Commissioner may by the Deportation Order or otherwise direct and whilst in that custody shall be deemed to be in lawful custody.

Article 119

(1) A Military Commander may by order direct the forfeiture to the Government of Palestine of any house, structure, or land from which he has reason to suspect that any firearm has been illegally discharged, or any bomb, grenade or explosive or incendiary article illegally thrown, or any house, structure or land situated in any area, town, village, quarter or street the inhabitants or some of the commit, or abetted the commission of, or been accessories after the fact to the commission of, any offence against these Regulations involving violence or intimidation or any Military Court offence; and when any house, structure or land is forfeited as aforesaid, the Military Commander may destroy the house or the structure or anything on growing on the land.

(2) Members of His Majesty's forces or of the Police Force, acting under the authority of the Military Commander may seize and occupy, without compensation, any property in any such area, town, village, quarter or street as is referred to in subregulation (1), after eviction without com-

pensation, of the previous occupiers, if any.

Article 120
The High Commissioner may by order direct the forfeiture to the Government of Palestine of all or any property of any person as to whom the High Commissioner is satisfied that he has committed, or attempted to commit, or abetted the commission of, or been an accessory after the fact to the commission of, any offence against these Regulations involving violence or intimidation or any Military Court offence.

Article 124
A Military Commander may by order require every person within any area specified in the order to remain within doors between such hours as may be specified in the order, and in such case, if any person is or remains out of doors within that area between such hours without a permit in writing issued by or on behalf of the Military Commander or some person duly authorised by the Military Commander to issue such permits, he shall be guilty of an offence against these Regulations.

Article 125
A Military Commander may by order declare any area or place to be a closed area for the purposes of these Regulations. Any person who, during any period in which any such order is in force in relation to any area or place, enters or leaves that area or place without a permit in writing issued by or on behalf of the Military Commander shall be guilty of an offence against these Regulations.

Source: *The Palestinian Gazette*, no. 1442, Supplement no. 2, 27 September 1945, pp. 1055-109.

BI(1). Eyewitness Testimony

Jerusalem, May 5, 1976.
We, the undersigned Sylvie Garbarz, Eytan Grossfeld and Witold Jedlicki hereby declare that we witnessed the following two incidents, both of which occurred in the city of Jerusalem, on Monday, May 3, 1976, between the hours of 9 and 10 p.m.

(1) We were on Sultan Suleiman Street, walking toward the corner of Nablus Road, when we noticed a strange commotion on and around an army vehicle (a middle-sized personnel carrier not covered by any tarp) stationed on the opposite side of the street, in the close proximity

of Damascus Gate. Intrigued by the sight, we crossed the street and approached the vehicle. Sitting or standing on the platform of the vehicle there were about 12 uniformed soldiers of the Border Guard. Milling around the vehicle there was another group of soldiers, of roughly the same number: it included several paratroopers. Lying on the floor of the platform there were detainees in civilian clothes. We were in the position to see them clearly, but we could not determine their exact number. We can state, however, that there were no less than two and no more than four of them. The detainees were being beaten, kicked and stomped by at least two of the soldiers, relentlessly and with savagery.

Undersigned Grossfeld promptly identified the commanding officer and approached him with the aim of intervening on behalf of the victims. He was rudely told to move away from the scene immediately. Undersigned Garbarz pleaded with another soldier to stop the beatings; with the same effect. Another soldier, apparently more amicably disposed, explained to us that the beatings were a 'matter of (venting) emotions.' One of the two by-standers, siding with the perpetrators of the beatings, attempted to convince us that 'perhaps these Arabs planted a bomb'. He referred to an explosion which had occurred, approximately one hour earlier, in the center of the Jewish part of the city. (Until then, we did not know about this explosion.) When undersigned Grossfeld retorted: 'but perhaps they did not', another bystander said: 'So what; they are Arabs anyway.' All these exchanges took place in Hebrew. While they were taking place, the beatings went on, uninterruptedly.

Source: *The Colonization of the West Bank Territories by Israel*, Hearings before the Subcommittee on Immigration and Naturalization of the Committee on the Judiciary, United States Senate, 17 and 18 October 1977 (Washington, US Government Printing Office, 1978), p. 165.

BII(1)

Your Excellencies and Majesties, the Kings and Presidents in attendance at the Arab Summit Conference in Cairo

From inside the occupied lands, the land of Arab Palestine, the land of perseverance and continuous struggle on the road to Palestinian Arab rights, we affirm our loyalty and allegiance to the Palestine Liberation Organization and its leadership, brother Yassir Arafat, and we consider this Organization, under all circumstances, the sole legitimate representative for the Palestinian people.

We reject any attempt to contain or make the Organization subservient.

We hope that your Conference will support the perseverance of our people inside the occupied territories, both mutually and morally, because we are capable of defeating the plans of the enemy to make our people submit to these plans.

Signed by:

Mayor of Municipality of Anabta
Mayor of Municipality of Nablus
Mayor of Municipality of Qalqilya
Mayor of Municipality of Hebron
Mayor of Municipality of Ramallah
Mayor of Municipality of Tul Karam
Mayor of Municipality of Halhoul
Mayor of Municipality of Beit Jala
Mayor of Municipality of Bethlehem
Mayor of Municipality of Al-Bireh

Source: *MERIP Reports*, no. 70 (September 1978).

BII(2). Who Represents the Palestinian People?

On September 17 and 21, 1977, sixty-six Arab-Palestinian mayors, presidents and members of legislative councils, directors and members of Chambers of Commerce, presidents of social welfare organizations, chairmen and members of municipal councils, chairmen and members of unions, religious and humanitarian societies, youth and women's organizations who are still living in the occupied territories in the West Bank and Gaza Strip addressed the Secretary-General of the United Nations in a petition which was circulated as a United Nations official document A/32/313, 27 October 1977. They spelled out who represents the Palestinian People.

Note Dated 17 September 1977 Addressed to the Secretary-General

'One of the most important items on the agenda of the present session of the United Nations General Assembly is the question of Palestine. While the Assembly is preparing to welcome the delegations of its Member States, Israel is trying to forestall events, in disregard of international covenants, United Nations resolutions and the basic tenets of human rights, by continuing to establish new settlements, to apply Israeli laws in the occupied territory and to torture and humiliate the Arab populations, in order to annex the occupied territories in accordance with expansionist Zionist designs.

We the undersigned representatives of the various sectors of the people of the occupied territories and their national institutions, proclaim the following:

Our attachment to the Palestinian Liberation Organization as the sole legitimate representative of the Arab people of Palestine wherever they may be. We emphasize that we, the inhabitants of the occupied territories, are a part of the Arab people of Palestine, who constitute a single national entity.

We confirm and reiterate the resolutions of the Rabat Arab Summit Conference, and at the same time, denounce and reject the various attempts and strategies aimed at repudiating these resolutions.

We reject any trusteeship or mandate over the Arab people of Palestine, and affirm their right to a homeland, to self-determination and to the establishment of their own independent national State.

We demand complete Israeli withdrawal from all the occupied territories, the implementation of the United Nations resolutions and the guarantee of the legitimate rights of the Arab people of Palestine.

We support the decisions of the Palestine Liberation Organization, including the one rejecting Security Council resolution 242, because it ignores the humane cause of the Arab people of Palestine.

Source: *Washington Post*, 15 December 1977.

BIII(1). Palestinian Political Prisoners in Israeli Jails as Described by the Oppressor

Superficially this is an accidental collectivity of men captured after bombings and murders. This is only the facade, behind it hides a well organized machine, there is a command descending from the 'supreme committee' down to the last soldier, there is discipline. Despite the fact that the saboteurs are tightly crammed, sometimes 80 in one hall, on average 30 to 40 in one cell, you find here cleanliness and order.

Commissioner Haim Levi, who observes the situation says that despite being kept in large groups they manage to maintain their own regime, the hygiene, cleanliness, and mostly – their educational network which we have not probed in depth. 'An educational network which, when fully exposed, will certainly create amazement.'

I could hear this in the talk in cell 4. In order to convince me that the state ought to be a secular state with a Palestinian government they quoted Ze'ev Jabotinsky[1] and the writings of David Ben-Gurion.[2] When they spoke about their rebellion and being revolutionaries serving an emerging nation they uttered quotations from Che Guevara to 'The Rebellion' by Menachem Begin. An immense quantity of written material is hidden in hideouts under the floors of the saboteurs' section of the Beer-Sheva prison. It seems that the problem is not the knives found in one hideout nor a transistor radio which has not yet been proved as a communication means with a command transmitting coded orders. The dangerous material are papers, closely written pages instructing the saboteurs not how to prepare explosives, but containing ideological instructions.

The commissioner says that the imprisoned saboteurs have their own study regime. A firm regime. They know everything related to underground movements throughout the world. They know by heart the writings of Ben-Gurion. They can quote them at length. They know by heart the biography of Prime Minister Begin at the time when he was a leader of an underground movement.[3] They learn by heart the writings of leaders of underground movements, their mode of operation, organization and methods. One of the prisoners undertakes to read a book and is asked to submit a written paper about it as well as his views on the way these conceptions can be applied by the PLO. In a search conducted after the prison riot in Beer-Sheva prison we found a notebook containing an analysis of an article by General (reserves) Meir Amit dealing with the Vietnam war and its implications.

Inspector Levi quotes figures indicating the scope of the intellectually explosive capacity of the imprisoned saboteurs: out of 3,000 imprisoned saboteurs 10% to 15% sit for their A-level examinations every year and their rate of success is between 90% and 95%.

Imprisoned teachers teach the students. Lawyers and other intellectuals chair the meetings, read submitted manuscripts. You sense an atmosphere of activity. Not a moment is lost. You sense a directing hand governing every minute of the prisoners' life – study, athletics, sports, Judo, political propaganda.

The riot in the Beer-Sheva prison raises a problem which commissioner Haim Levi is aware of: 'We treat them as criminals, but they are not. It is unpleasant to compare but in principle there is something which characterizes them as political organizations behind bars.'

Notes

1. Z. Jabotinsky – Founder of the nationalist-militarist wing of Zionism, its political party 'Herut', and its military organization (IZL) 'National Military Organization'. Begin's mentor.
2. D. Ben-Gurion – Leader of Zionist social-democrats (MAPAI), first Prime Minister of Israel, and dominant figure in Israeli politics from 1948 to 1964.

3. The IZL (Irgun Zevai Leumi) – 'National Military Organization'.

Source: Y. Lev, 'Saboteurs behind Bars', *Ma'ariv*, 24 March 1978, as translated in *Prisons and Prisoners in Israel* (Umm al-Fahm and Tel Aviv, Committee for the Defence of Political Prisoners in Israel, 1978), pp. 46-7.

CI(1). The Koenig Report

Top Secret: Memorandum-Proposal – Handling the Arabs of Israel
Proposal no. 1
General:

1. Until a very short while ago it was accepted by those dealing with this part of Israel's population that it had fully come to terms with the establishment of the State of Israel and that most of this (Arab) population had a high degree of identification with the state and had been drawn into its various frameworks. This, at least, was expressed by those who handle them, and by those close to the social centers of Arab residents and citizens of the state.

2. Recently, certain phenomena have occurred which have challenged these assumptions and which have seriously questioned the loyalty of a large part of them to the state and to its very existence.

Even though doubts about the ideas and ways of dealing with the Israeli Arabs have been expressed over the years for reasons that will be mentioned below, these were opposed to the accepted conception of the Arabists and rejected outright. It appears to us that it can no longer be disputed that there is room to discuss these 'preconceptions' which have, until recently, served as guiding principles.

3. With the establishment of the state, the remnants of the Arab population in the country were left without a leadership. A minority was created which had to adapt itself to the reality of a Jewish state waging a war against its neighboring countries and proving its strength against them.

The military government, under whose aegis this population was placed, established the rule of 'notables' and thus entered into the framework of Arab society which was built on family clans. The abolition of the military government caused the undermining of the authority of the 'notables' and those whom they represented. The undermining of the individual's dependence on the establishment – the military government – enabled the younger generation to feel the power that had come into its hands in a democratic society, and this also because of the passage of Arab society from an agricultural society to an industrial one with all the social implications of this.

Moreover, the 'revolt' of the younger generation frequently forced the older generation to join the camp of the rebels and exposed the state as a target for their struggle, since the tools to insure their dependence on Jewish society had not been prepared. Moreover, we encouraged the letting off of steam by attempts to bring the rebels to our side by various 'means'.

In the fifties, the Arab society was dependent from an economic point of view on the Jewish economy which had, in the course of time, been opened to the Arabs as a result of Jewish manual laborers having left it. This situation has created an affluent economic stratum, on which to a large extent, the economy of the country and its well being are dependent.

4. With the abolition of the military government the country put the affairs of the Arab population into the hands of those who spoke Arabic and who pulled out the violent elements and made them leaders while founding their status on their ability to obtain benefits for themselves and their families. This they did while ignoring the social problems in the Arab sector on the one hand, and lacking a long-term plan for the creation of an identity of a loyal Arab citizen on the other.

Those dealing with the Arab sector at all levels, political, military, police and civilian — their test was to familiarize themselves with the Arab mentality. Their thinking and practical ability was not always greater than that of the people with whom they were dealing, and dealing with their interests instead of maintaining their independent thinking and analytical abilities is a phenomenon that causes concern on the one hand, as opposed to the attempt to deal with this from the point of view of objective thought that insures the long-term Jewish National interests on the other hand.

5. In the northern district are concentrated most Israeli Arabs, whose sincerity and involvement among the Jewish population manifestly and prominently put into focus the problems that have already been created and the expectations in the near and distant future. One of the most worrying phenomena is the loss of patience of the average Jew toward the Arab citizen, and in certain cases a hostility can be felt, and any provocation might cause an uncontrollable explosion on both sides whose results might have negative consequences in Israel and especially abroad.

(See the decision of the student organization in Haifa not to perform guard duty because of the possibility given to Arab students to pay a guard fee.)

This catalyst containing powerful emotional residues among the

Jewish population upsets the demographic balance in these areas, and this can be felt by and is a source of fear to each individual.

In the framework of this memorandum we will point to certain critical issues establishing the background, and, in conclusion, recommendations to solve the problems.

The problems to be discussed are: a) The demographic problem and the manifestations of Arab nationalism. b) The Arab leadership and its implications. c) Economy and employment. d) Education. e) Implementing the law.

A. The Demographic Problem and the Manifestations of Arab Nationalism

Suggestions

a) Expand and deepen Jewish settlement in areas where the contiguity of the Arab population is prominent, and where they number considerably more than the Jewish population; examine the possibility of diluting existing Arab population concentrations.

Special attention must be paid to border areas in the country's northwest and to the Nazareth region. The approach and exigency of performance have to deviate from the routine that has been adopted so far. Concurrently, the state law has to be enforced so as to limit 'breaking of new ground' by Arab settlements in various areas of the country.

b) At the same time, a strong and solid Jewish leadership should be fostered in Upper Nazareth and in Acre capable of facing the expected crucial developments.

c) Introduce a policy of reward and punishment (within the framework of the law) for leaders and settlements that express hostility in any way toward the state and Zionism.

d) To deny RAKAH its 'priority' in carrying out a national struggle and representing Israeli Arabs and to provide a valve for communities still sitting on the 'fence,' a sister Labor Party should be established in which the stress will be on ideas of equality, humanism and language, social struggle and on raising the banner of peace in the region. The establishment has to prepare itself to maintain covert presence and control in that party.

e) Invest every possible effort in bringing all Zionist parties toward a national consensus regarding the issue of Israel's Arabs in order to disentangle them from their internal political squabbles.

B. The Arab Leadership and Its Implications

Suggestions

a) We would act courageously and replace all the people who deal with the Arab sector on behalf of government institutions, the police and the parties, including policymakers.

b) We should disassociate ourselves from the present Arab 'leadership' which does not represent the Arab population and stress the establishment's nonsolidarity with them.

c) Those who will be given the job of performing this mission should start immediately to create new figures of high intellectual standard, figures who are equitable and charismatic. They should be helped to establish an Arab party as mentioned above.

d) Special team should be appointed to examine the personal habits of RAKAH leaders and other negative people and this information should be made available to the electorate.

e) Steps should be taken against all negative personalities at all levels and in all institutions.

C. Economy and Employment

Suggestions

a) Appropriate arrangements have to be made with the management of a concern bearing the 'approved investment' label in crucial areas (as noted above). The number of Arab employees should not exceed 20 percent.

b) The tax authorities must adopt immediate steps to intensify tax collection, performing it with firmness and without deviations.

c) Reach a settlement with central marketing factors of various consumer goods that would neutralize and encumber Arab agents, particularly in the northern areas, in order to avoid dependence of the Jewish population of those agents, especially in times of emergency.

d) The government must find a way to neutralize the payment of 'big family' grants to the Arab population, either by linking them to the economic situation or by taking this responsibility from the national insurance system and transferring it to the Jewish Agency or to the Zionist organization, so that the grant is paid to Jews only.

e) Endeavor to have central institutions pay more attention in giving preferential treatment to Jewish groups or individuals rather than to Arabs.

D. Education

Suggestions

a) The reception criteria for Arab university students should be the same as for Jewish students and this must also apply to the granting of scholarships.

A meticulous implementation of these rules will produce a natural selection and will considerably reduce the number of Arab students. Accordingly, the number of low standard graduates will also decrease, a fact that will facilitate their absorption in work after their studies. [sentence as published]

b) Encourage the channeling of students into technical professions, to physical and natural sciences. These studies leave less time for dabbling in nationalism and the dropout rate is higher.

c) Make trips abroad for studies easier, while making the return and employment more difficult – this policy is apt to encourage their emigration.

d) Adopt tough measures at all levels against various agitators among college and university students.

e) Prepare absorption possibilities in advance for the better part of the graduates, according to their qualifications. This policy can be implemented thanks to the time available (a number of years) in which the authorities may plan their steps.

E. Law Enforcement

Suggestions
a) Make clear to everyone dealing with the Arab sector that violation of the law must not be ignored, and that its literal implementation should be carried out firmly.

b) Adopt legal steps against civil servants and institutions not fulfilling their duty in the enforcement of what the law prescribes.

c) Introduce law suits and put into effect a number of court sentences, particularly in the sphere of income tax and illegal building, which will deter the population from any thought about an escape from the hands of the law.

d) Increase the presence of various police and security forces in the Arab streets to deter extremist circles and those who are 'sitting on the fence' and are likely to be drawn into uprisings and demonstrations.

(Signed: March 1, 1976)

Editors' Note: Israel Koenig, the author of this memorandum, has been the Northern District (Galilee) Commissioner of the Ministry of the Interior for the last 14 years. This memorandum was reportedly submitted to the then Prime Minister Rabin as a secret document. Its first publication in Hebrew was in *Al Hamishmar*, 7 September 1976.

Source: Excerpts adapted from *Journal of Palestine Studies*, vol. 6, no. 1 (1976), pp. 190-200, which was reprinted from *SWASIA* (weekly news digest), vol. III, no. 41 (15 October 1976), pp. 1-8 (original in Hebrew).

CII(1). Resolutions of the Convention for the Defence of Arab Lands which was held in Nazareth on 18 October 1975 (excerpts)

The convention condemns the Israeli government's measures whose intent is the expropriation of additional Arab lands in the Galilee, the Triangle, and al-Naqab, and it demands an end to these official schemes which are being executed under the guise of development, population redistribution, and the like.

The convention declares that the Arab citizens in Israel insist on achieving their complete rights on the basis of equality, and that they look forward to a just and stable peace between Israel and the Arab countries. They also extend their hand in cooperation with all Jewish progressive elements in the country. . .

This national, mass-based convention which represents the various trends within the Arab masses, and which is supported by progressive Jewish forces, rejects all plans which aim at depriving Arab peasants of their land, and transforming the Arab people in Israel to a people without a country. . .

The convention rejects, absolutely and categorically, all measures of expropriation and dispossession. It declares, further, that the Arab masses will not tolerate the policies which strangle and impoverish their villages and which result in their dispossession and dispersal. The Arab masses will continue their struggle with vigor to undermine this oppressive policy which threatens their national and daily existence.

Source: *The Black Book on 'Land Day,' 20 March 1976* (Haifa, al-Ittihad Publishing House, September 1976), pp. 152-5. Original in Arabic.

CII(2). Memorandum from the Committee of the Heads of Arab Local Authorities in Israel to the Prime Minister (excerpts)

His Excellency the Prime Minister, Mr. Yitzhak Rabin, Jerusalem

Allow us first to thank your excellency in the name of the Committee of the Heads of Arab Local Authorities for granting us an interview on 24 May 1976.

Allow us also to clarify our positions regarding the answers to our inquiries which we received from your excellency and from the ministers and directors of various departments.

1) Your excellency's candid answer that Israel is a Jewish state whose

goal is the realization of Zionist aspirations in a framework which pre-serves the Arabs with equal religious and cultural rights only:

Your statement makes us fearful about our existence as an Arab people in this country. We fear that such an incomplete view which you have expressed would lead to treating the Arabs of this homeland as subjects, and not as citizens of equal rights. This is what we feel; and we appeal to your excellency to respect our feeling that we must be equal partners in this state, and that Arab-Israeli conflict should not provide any justification for barring the Arabs from full equality and from a recognition of their national existence which is a historical fact.

2) The expropriation of Arab lands:
We believe that equality will not be realized unless there is an end to the policy of Arab expropriation in all its shapes and forms. . .

The government's insistence against declaring a halt to all recent expropriation orders, and its failure to ensure that the Arabs will not be dispossessed of the last remnants of their lands depress us greatly, and make us worry about the future of our Arab villages and our Arab people in this country, and the future of Jewish-Arab brotherhood and peace.

3) The policy which government agencies apply in the Arab sector regarding land-use and zoning gives no real weight to Arab local author-ities or to their jurisdictions. . .

4) We hold an immense confidence in the victory of justice and democ-racy, and we believe that the brotherly and peaceful coexistence between the two peoples of this country is a historical inevitability. And towards achieving this coexistence, we feel that it is imperative to minimize these contradictions.

Most important among these contradictions are the denial of our existence as a national minority, the faiure to recognize our right to maintain our ancestral lands, the lack of serious concern to improve the standard of local services, and the absence of serious coordination with Arab local authorities relating to planning and the agricultural, industrial, and demographic development of our villages. . .

Signed: Committee of the Heads of Arab Local Authorities in Israel—
17 June 1976

Source: *The Black Book on 'Land Day,' 20 March 1976* (Haifa, al-Ittihad Publish-ing House, September 1976), pp. 129-32 (original in Arabic).

CII(3). To the Masses of our Palestinian People (excerpts)

The present Zionist assault on the last remnants of our land is an integral part of the Zionist racist scheme which started around the end of the last century and continues until the present. The goal of this scheme is the Judaization of the entire Palestinian land, and the dispersal of our Arab Palestinian people.

We see no difference between the Zionist colonial settlements at Qadum, Agrabah, al-Khan al-Ahmar, Rafah and al-Khalil, and what is taking place in al-Naqab, the Triangle and Galilee.

The land issue is at the heart of the Palestine question. We reiterate here with resolute determination that the resistance of our Arab Palestinian masses in the occupied areas against Zionist occupation, *and* the struggle of our Palestinian refugee brethren for their sacred right of return, *and* the continued struggle of our Palestinian people within the 'green line' against judaization, expropriation, national oppression and racist discrimination constitute one indivisible struggle.

Down with Zionist occupation and long live the struggle of our people in the occupied areas.

Freedom to all political prisoners.

Halt the expropriation of Arab lands and return the already expropriated lands to its Arab owners.

History has charged us with the responsibility to unify our struggle and to choose our sincere popular leadership so that we can frustrate all Zionist schemes. Unity of all popular forces is the correct path against occupation, oppression and expropriation.

30 March 1976

Source: Arab Students Committee – Jerusalem. Original in Arabic.

CIII(1). A Statement on Sadat's Visit

Public attention in the country and throughout the world is directed today, and justly so, to Sadat's visit to Israel. Many genuinely hope that this visit will open an avenue towards peace, which is now discussed by everybody.

Can this visit realise these hopes?

Our answer is negative for the following reasons:

The root of the conflict in the Middle East is not in the conflict between Israel and Egypt, but rather in the dispossession of the Palestinian Arab people from its homeland, its exile and the denial of its natural right to exist as a people, in addition to the denial of its national and human rights.

Sadat's visit is directed to circumvent 'procedural problems' in order to bypass the recognized representatives of the Palestinian-Arab people, namely the Palestine Liberation Organization (PLO).

Even if Sadat succeeds in getting Begin's consent to the return of the Sinai peninsula to Egypt, or alternatively Begin succeeds to wrest out of Sadat portions of the Sinai, the Palestinian problem will remain unsolved, and therefore peace will not be achieved.

The road to peace must go through the recognition and the realization of the right of the Palestinian-Arab people to self-determination and to return to its homeland. Any settlement reached behind the back of the Palestinian-Arab people or at its expense and without the participation of its recognized representative the Palestine Liberation Organization (PLO) will not bring peace to the peoples of the area. It will rather constitute a prelude to a new war.

So long as the reality of life for the Palestinian-Arab people under Israeli rule is subject to confiscation of lands, destruction of houses, colonization, Judaization of the Galilee, the suppression of basic human rights and the murder of citizens like the murder of the seven Palestinians on the day of the land and in Majd al-Karum — talk about peace in Jerusalem, Cairo, Geneva or any other place is nothing but an illusion and an exercise in deception of the public which is hoping for peace.

The road to peace goes through Palestine — not through Sadat.

— Harakat Abna' al-Balad (The Sons of the Village Movement)
— The Revolutionary Communist League (Matzpen-Marxist)
— The Socialist Organization in Israel (Matzpen)
— The Editorial Board of Key (Miftah)

19-11-1977

Source: *Free Palestine*, 1978.

CIII(2). A Public Statement

Our Palestinian-Arab people, as well as Arab-Israeli relations in general, are currently exposed to the most delicate and dangerous stage in the conflict since the Balfour Declaration.

The Palestinian people have struggled persistently and continue to struggle for its self-evident and natural right, namely, for its right of self-determination and the establishment of its independent state.

This right was recognized by the international community and was established in a series of resolutions of the United Nations Organization during the past 30 years.

It is now established, after the exchange of visits between Sadat and Begin and its aftermath, that the intention is determined to split Arab ranks throughout its great homeland, the Arab world, strike at the Arab

progressive forces, and liquidate the Palestinian problem – which lies at
the heart of the conflict – in order to promote aims that are completely
contrary to the establishment of just and lasting peace.

In the face of the dangerous situation and the intentional Israeli disregard of the Palestinian-Arab people and its right to establish its independent
state alongside the state of Israel, as well as Israel's obstinate disregard of the
civil and national rights of the Palestinian-Arabs within the state of Israel,
we, the Palestinian residents in the state of Israel since its establishment,
wish to call world public opinion, as well as Arab and Israeli public opinion
to the following issues of principle:

1) The Palestinian problem is at the heart of the Arab-Israeli conflict,
and any attempt to ignore this fundamental reality will not lead to the
establishment of a just and true peace. Rather, such attempts will result
in the continuation of the same conflict.

2) The fundamental solution of the Palestinian problem must begin
with securing the right of self-determination of the Palestinian-Arab
people, the establishment of its independent state and the solution of
the refugee problem according to the repeated resolutions of the United
Nations Organization.

3) The only true legitimate representative of the Palestinian-Arab people
is the Palestine Liberation Organization (PLO), and all attempts to create
a substitute for the PLO from among those who are the crutches of the
occupation and Arab reaction are plainly ridiculous.

4) The repeated attempts of the triangle Carter-Begin-Sadat to remove
the PLO and the Soviet Union from their natural role in the pursuit
and the promotion of the just solution aims to serve imperialist strategic,
oil and financial interests, Zionist colonial expansion and the interests
of Arab reaction.

5) Being an inalienable part of the Palestinian-Arab people, we wish to
emphasize that any solution of the Palestinian problem must include
official recognition and international guarantees for the national identity
of the Palestinian residents in the state of Israel, their right to remain in
their homeland, the re-appropriation of their confiscated lands, property,
villages and charitable waqf estates as well as the implementation of
their full cultural, social, civil and political rights.

Nazareth – 24 February 1978

Name	Profession	Address
1. Aziz Shahada	Advocate	Nazareth
2. Samir Qa'war	Engineer	Nazareth

3. Zuhayr Sabbagh	Translator	Nazareth
4. Hasan Nassar	Advocate	Arraba
5. Henry Tutari	Teacher	Nazareth
6. Mansur Kardosh	Merchant	Nazareth
7. Muhammad Taha	Engineer	Nazareth
8. Akram Zu'bi	Teacher	Nazareth
9. Ramiz Jiraysi	Engineer	Nazareth
10. Jamil Ibrahim Haddad	Arabic Typing Center	Nazareth
11. Said Zu'bi	Director of the Health Dept. at the Nazareth Municipal Council	Nazareth
12. Riyad Umar Zu'bi	Contractor	Nazareth
13. Amin Muhammad Ali	Merchant and Member of Nazareth Municipal Council	Nazareth
14. Ahmad Bakr Zu'bi	Clerk	Nazareth
15. Milad Shajrawi	Engineer	Nazareth
16. Muhammad Nimr Mukhim	Chartered accountant	Nazareth
17. Walid Khaliliyya	Advocate	Yafat al-Nasira
18. Salim Ghurayyib	Advocate	Kufr Kanna
19. Suhayl Abu Nuwwara	Writer	Nazareth
20. Ahmad Hasan Habib-Allah	Merchant	Ein Mahil
21. Muhammad Sirhan	Advocate	Mighar
22. Adnan Athamina	Advocate	Rina
23. Shaqib Jahshan	Teacher and poet	Rama
24. Adnan Raja Matar	Merchant	Nazareth
25. Basim Tuma	Dentist and member of the Nazareth Municipal Council	Nazareth
26. Ibrahim Ghanayim	Health Inspector	Baqa al-Gharbiyya
27. Salih Abu Hussein	Advocate	Umm al-Fahm
28. Rashshad Yunis	Engineer	Ara
29. Faruq Mahajina	Advocate	Umm al-Fahm
30. Susan Murad	Clerk	Umm al-Fahm

31. Sabri Muhsin	Advocate	Jatt
32. Abd al-Aziz Abu Usba'	Contractor	Tayyiba
33. Shakir Jabara	Teacher	Tayyiba
34. Miriam Masarwa	Student	Tayyiba
35. Jamal Abu Manna	Advocate	Kufr Qara'
36. Mahmud Abu Zayd	Engineer	Haifa
37. Mustafa Ghanayim	Advocate	Baqa al-Gharbiyya
38. Fuad Masarwa	Merchant	Baqa al-Gharbiyya
39. I'tidal Munwir	Teacher	Umm al-Fahm
40. Muhammad Tawfik Kiwan	Advocate	Umm al-Fahm
41. Taha Muhammad Ali	Merchant and writer	Nazareth
42. Yusuf Azizi	Insurance agent	Nazareth
43. Nabil Hanna Ibrahim	Advocate	Rina
44. Iliyas Zurayq	Dentist	Aylabun
45. Ziyad Huwwari	Advocate	Nazareth
46. Jamal Qa'war	Teacher and poet	Nazareth
47. Muhammad May	Physician	Acre
48. Hasan Amun	Physician	Deir al-Asad
49. Nasr San'allah	Advocate	Deir al-Asad
50. Ali San'allah	Head of the Deir al-Asad Local Municipal Council	Deir al-Asad
51. Musbah Qabbani	Advocate	Kufr Yasif
52. Micha'il Da'ud	Advocate	Kufr Yasif
53. Ibrahim Khuri	Pharmacist	Nazareth
54. Jalal Musmar	Ceramics man-ufacturer	Nazareth
55. Raiq Jarjura	Advocate and Vice-Mayor of the Naz-areth Municipal Council	Nazareth
56. Walid Fahum	Advocate	Nazareth

Source: *Shahak Reports*, 1978.

BIBLIOGRAPHY

al-Abrashi, M. *Woman's Status in Islam* (Cairo, 1970) (Arabic)
Abu Ali, K. *Women's Experience in the Palestine Revolution* (Beirut, 1975) (Arabic)
Abu al-Nur, M. *Sunni Teaching and Marriage* (Cairo, 1972) (Arabic)
Abu-Ghazaleh, A. *Arab Cultural Nationalism in Palestine* (Beirut, 1973)
Abu-Ghosh, S. 'The Politics of an Arab Village in Israel' (unpublished PhD dissertation, Political Science Department, Princeton University, 1965)
Abu-Lughod, I. (ed.) *The Transformation of Palestine* (Northwestern University Press, Evanston, Ill., 1971)
___ 'PNC Maps out Palestinian Strategy', *MERIP Reports*, no. 57 (1977), pp. 10-13
___ and Said, E. *Two Studies on the Palestinians Today and American Policy* (AAUG Information Paper no 17, 1976)
Adams, H. *Modernizing Racial Domination* (University of California Press, Berkeley, 1971)
Adams, M. 'Israel's Treatment of the Arabs in the Occupied Territories', *Journal of Palestine Studies*, vol. 6, no. 2 (1977), pp. 19-40
Allon, Y. *A Curtain of Sand* (Hakibutz Hameuchad, Tel Aviv, 1959) (Hebrew)
Amin, Q. *The New Woman* (Cairo, n.d.) (Arabic)
Anderson, P. *Lineages of the Absolutist State* (New Left Books, London, 1974)
Antonius, G. *The Arab Awakening* (New York, 1939)
al-Aqqad, A.M. *The Woman and the Qur'an* (Cairo, 1959?) (Arabic)
Arkadie, B. *Benefits and Burdens: A Report on the West Bank and the Gaza Strip Economies Since 1967* (New York, 1977)
Aruri, N. 'Jordan: A Study on Political Development 1921-1965' (unpublished PhD dissertation, University of Massachusetts, 1967)
___ *Jordan: A Study in Political Development* (Nijhoff, The Hague, 1972)
Asad, T. 'Anthropological Texts and Ideological Problems', *Economy and Society*, vol. 4 (1975)
Ashrawi, H. 'The Contemporary Palestinian Poetry of Occupation', *Journal of Palestine Studies*, vol. 7, no. 3 (1978), pp. 77-101
Ashtor, E. *Social and Economic History of the Near East in the Middle Ages* (University of California Press, Berkeley, 1976)

Ater, M. 'Autonomous West Bank is Poor Economics', *Jerusalem Post*,
    30 October 1975
Auerbach, A. 'Ibni the doctor', *Jerusalem Post Weekly*, 20 January
    1976
Avineri, S. 'Modernization and Arab Society: Some Reflections' in I.
    Howe and C. Gresham (eds.), *Israel, the Arabs and the Middle East*
    (Bantam Books, New York, 1972)
Badran, N. *The General Picture of the Present State of Palestinian Educat-
    ion* (PLO Planning Center, Beirut, 1971)
Barakat, D., and Daw, H. *The Emigrants: Uprooting and Exile* (Beirut,
    1968) (Arabic)
Barakat, H. *Lebanon In Strife – Student Preludes to the Civil War* (Austin,
    Texas, 1977)
Barry, B. 'Review Article: Political Accommodation and Consociational
    Democracy', *British Journal of Political Science*, vol. 5, part 4 (Oct-
    ober 1975)
Baruch, H. 'Facing the 180,000: How the Military Government Rules',
    reprinted from *Davar* in *Ner*, vol. X, nos. 3-4 (December 1958-Jan-
    uary 1959)
al-Bedeiry, M. 'Arab Labor Movement in Palestine during the British
    Mandate', *al-Jadid*, vol. 10, pp. 25-33 (Arabic)
Beinen, J. 'The Palestine Communist Party, 1919-1948', *MERIP Reports*,
    no. 55 (March 1977)
Ben-Porath *The Arab Labor Force in Israel* (Jerusalem, 1966)
Bill, J. 'Class Analysis and the Dialectics of Modernization in the Middle
    East', *International Journal of Middle East Studies*, vol. 3 (1972), pp.
    41-3.
Boggs, D. 'Gramsci's "Prison Notebooks"', *Socialist Revolution*, vol. 11
    (1971)
Bowden, T. 'The Politics of the Arab Rebellion in Palestine: 1936-1939',
    Middle Eastern Studies, vol. II, no. 2 (1975)
Bregman, A. *Economic Growth in the Administered Areas, 1968-1973*
    (Bank of Israel Research Department, Jerusalem, 1975)
—— *The Economy of the Administered Areas, 1974-1978* (Jerusalem,
    1976)
Bull, V. *The West Bank, is it Viable?* (Lexington, 1975)
Carmi, S., and Rosenfeld, H. 'The Origins of the Process of Proletarian-
    ization and Urbanization of Arab Peasants in Palestine', *Annals of
    the New York Academy of Sciences*, vol. 220, art. 6 (March 1974)
Castles, S., and Kosack, G. *Immigrant Workers and Class Structure in
    Western Europe* (London, 1973)

Christian Science Monitor, 12 February 1970

Cohen, A. *Arab Border-Villages in Israel: A Study of Continuity and Change in Social Organization* (Manchester University Press, Manchester, 1965)

Daalder, H. 'The Consociational Democracy Theme', *World Politics*, vol. XXVI, no. 4 (July 1974)

Davis, F. *Minority-Dominant Relations* (AHM Publishing, Arlington Heights, Ill., 1978)

Davis, U., and Lehn, W. 'And the Fund Still Lives', *Journal of Palestine Studies*, vol. VII, no. 4 (1978), pp. 3-31

Dessouki, A. 'Arab Intellectuals and *al-Nakba*: the Search for Fundamentalism', *Middle Eastern Studies*, vol. 9, no. 2 (May 1973)

Documents on American Foreign Relations, 1957 (New York, 1958)

Dodd, P. 'Family Honor and the Forces of Change in Arab Society', *International Journal of Middle East Studies*, vol. 4 (1973)

Eisenstadt, S.N. 'Convergence and Divergence of Modern and Modernizing Societies', *International Journal of Middle East Studies*, vol. 8 (1972), pp. 1-27

El-Asmar, F. *To be an Arab in Israel* (Frances Printer, London, 1975)

Fanon, F. *The Wretched of the Earth* (New York, 1963)

Farsoun, S. 'South Africa and Israel: A Special Relationship', paper given at Conference on Socio-Economic Trends and Policies in Southern Africa, United Nations African Institute for Economic Planning, Dakar, 29 November-12 December 1975

—— 'Settler Colonialism and Herrenvolk Democracy' in R.P. Stevens and A. Al-Messiri (eds.), *Israel and South Africa* (North American, New Brunswick, N.J., 1977)

—— and Carroll, W. 'The Civil War in Lebanon', *Monthly Review*, vol. 28 (June 1976)

Fershafsky, M. 'Israel's Plan to Annex the West Bank, Gaza, and the Golan', *al-Manar* (London), 14 January 1978 (Arabic)

Financial Times (London), 'Expatriates, No Pot of Gold', 27 February 1978

Fox, G. '"Nice Girl": Social Control of Women Through a Value Construct', *Signs* (Summer 1977)

Free Palestine, vol. 5, nos. 9-10 (1977)

Garrett, P. 'Orphans of Empires: A Case Study of the Palestinian Refugees' (unpublished MA thesis, University of Wisconsin, Madison, 1970)

Giddens, A. *Capitalism and Modern Social Analysis* (Cambridge University Press, London, 1971)

Giele, J., and Smock, A. *Women: Roles and Status in Eight Countries* (New York, 1977)

Ginat, S. 'Days and Nights', *Maariv Supplement*, 21 May 1976 (Hebrew)

Glubb, J. *A Soldier with the Arabs* (London, 1957)

Goitein, S.D. *Studies in Islamic History and Institutions* (E.J. Brill, Leiden, 1966)

Gouldner, A. 'Prologue to a Theory of Revolutionary Intellectuals', *Telos*, no. 26 (Winter 1975/6)

Gramsci, A. *The Modern Prince and Other Writings* (New York, 1968)

Granott, A. *Agrarian Reform and the Record of Israel* (Eyre and Spottis-woode, London, 1956)

Granqvist, H. *Marriage Conditions in a Palestinian Village* (Helsingfors, 1935)

Greenway, H. 'Israelis Ratify Expansion on Bank', *Guardian* (London), 11 January 1978

The Guardian Weekly, 'Israel's Plan for the West Bank and Gaza', 8 January 1978

Haaretz, 14 and 26 February 1976 (Hebrew)

Haaretz, 8 June 1976 (Hebrew)

Habibi, E. *Strange Episodes in the Disappearance of Sa'ad Abu an-Nahs* (Haifa, 1974) (Arabic)

Haddad, Y. 'Traditional Affirmations Concerning the Role of Women as Found in Contemporary Arab Islamic Literature' in J.I. Smith (ed.), *The Role and Status of Women in Contemporary Muslim Societies* (forthcoming, Bucknell University Press)

Hagopian, E., and Zahlan, A.B. 'Palestine's Arab Population', *Journal of Palestine Studies*, vol. 3, no. 4 (Summer 1974)

Hamadeh, S. *Economic Organization in Palestine* (Beirut, 1939) (Arabic)

Harris, G. *Jordan* (New Haven, Conn., 1958)

Hijjawi, S. 'The Palestinians in Lebanon', *Journal of the Center for Palestine Studies* (Baghdad), no. 22, May/June 1977 (Arabic)

Hilal, J. *The West Bank: the Socio-Economic Structure, 1948-1974* (Beirut, 1975) (Arabic)

—— 'Class Transformation in the West Bank and Gaza', *MERIP Reports*, no. 53 (December 1976)

—— *The Palestinians of the West Bank and the Gaza Strip* (Beirut, 1976) (Arabic)

Hindess, B., and Hirst, P.Q. *Pre-Capitalist Modes of Production* (Routledge and Kegan Paul, London, 1977)

Hoare, Q., and Smith, G.N. *Selections from the Prison Notebooks of Antonio Gramsci* (New York, 1971) al-Husseini, M. *Social and Economic Development in Arab Palestine* (Jerusalem, *c.* 1946) (Arabic)

Iraqi Chronicles, no. 530, 1 June 1961 (Arabic)

Iraqi Chronicles, no. 1772, 28 August 1969 (Arabic)

Ismail, T. *The Arab Left* (Syracuse, 1976)

Israel, Central Bureau of Statistics (CBS), *Demographic Characteristics of the Population* (Jerusalem, Population and Housing Census 1961, Part II, 1962) (Hebrew)

Israel (CBS) *Statistical Abstract of Israel 1975* (Jerusalem, no. 26, 1976) (English and Hebrew)

Israel, Ministry of the Interior, Arab Department 'Elections for Eight Local Authorities in the Arab Sector in the Years 1971, 1972', June 1972 (Hebrew)

Israel and Palestine, 'Israeli colonialism in 1975' (Paris), December 1976

Israel Economist, 'Two Approaches to the Administered Territories' (Tel Aviv), August 1972 and January 1973

Israel Economist, 'Green Revolution in Judea and Samaria' (Tel Aviv), October-November 1975

Israeli, A., 'The Employment Revolution among the non-Jewish Minorities of Israel', *Hamizrah Hehadash*, vol. 26, nos. 3-4 (1976), pp. 232-9 (Hebrew)

Israleft, Biweekly News Service, nos. 78, 79 and 81

al-Ittihad (Haifa), 12 September 1977 (Arabic)

al-Ittihad, 'an interview with Hanna Naqqara' (Haifa), 27 January 1978 (Arabic)

al-Ittihad (Haifa), 16 and 20 June 1978 (Arabic)

Jabber, F. 'The Arab Regimes and the Palestinian Revolution, 1967-71', *Journal of Palestine Studies*, vol. 2, no. 2 (Winter 1973), pp. 79-101

Jerisati, J. 'The Palestinian People: Figures and Pointers', *Shu'un Filastiniya* (Jan./Feb. 1976), pp. 123-44 (Arabic)

Jerusalem Post (Jerusalem), 'Mahmoud Yunis vs. Ministry of Finance', 16 March 1954

Jerusalem Post (Jerusalem), 21 January 1962

Jiryes, S. *The Arabs in Israel*, 2nd ed (Institute for Palestine Studies, Beirut, 1973)

───── *The Arabs in Israel* (Monthly Review Press, New York, 1976)

Jordan, Department of Statistics *Population Census and Internal Migration for Amman, Jerusalem, Ruseifa, Irbid and Aqaba* (Amman, 1967) (Arabic)

Jordan, Kingdom of *Proceedings of the Jordan House of Representatives*

(Amman, 1954-55) (Arabic)

Jordan, Kingdom of *The Bases of the Jordanian Position: The National Declaration Presented by King Hussein at the Rabat Summit Conference* (Press Department, Amman, October 1974) (Arabic)

Kanaana, S. *Socio-Cultural and Psychological Adjustment of the Arab Minority in Israel* (R. and E. Research Associates, San Francisco, 1976)

Karmi, G. 'Palestinian Women: a Force for Liberation', *Palestine Digest*, vol. 8, no. 4 (July 1978)

Katnelson, I. 'Comparative Studies of Race and Ethnicity', *Comparative Politics*, vol. V, no. 1 (October 1972)

al-Kayyali, A. (comp.) *Documents of Palestinian Arab Resistance* (Beirut, 1968) (Arabic)

Kazziha, W. *Revolutionary Transformation in the Arab World* (New York, 1975)

Kerr, M. *The Arab Cold War, 1958-1970* (London, 1971)

Khalifah, I. *The Woman and the Palestine Question* (Cairo, 1974) (Arabic)

al-Khalili, G. *Palestinian Women and the Revolution* (Beirut, 1977) (Arabic)

al-Khatib, A., *et al. The Role of the Jordanian Woman in the Fields of Education, Social and Medical Care* (Amman, 1976)

Khouri, E. *Palestinian Statistics* (PLO Research Center, Beirut, 1974) (Arabic)

al-Khuli, A.B. *Islam and the Contemporary Woman* (Kuwait, 1970) (Arabic)

King Hussein *Uneasy Lies the Head* (London, 1962)

Koenig, I. 'Koenig Memorandum', *SWASIA* (weekly news digest), vol. III, no. 41 (15 October 1976)

Konikoff, A. *Transjordan: An Economic Survey* (Jerusalem, 1946)

Kuper, L., and Smith, M.G. (eds.) *Pluralism in Africa* (University of California Press, Berkeley, 1971)

Kuwait, Ministry of Guidance and Information *Kuwait Today: A Welfare State* (Nairobi, Kenya, n.d.)

Kuwait Today: The National Gazette, no. 84 (18 May 1965) (Arabic)

Landau, J. *The Arabs in Israel* (Oxford University Press, London, 1969)

Langer, F. *With My Own Eyes* (London, 1975)

____ *These are my Brothers: Israel and the Occupied Territories* London (forthcoming)

Laroui, A. *The Crisis of the Arab Intellectual, Traditionalism or Historicism*, translated from French by D. Cammell (Berkeley, 1976)

Layish, A. 'Women and Succession in the Druze Family in Israel', *Asian and African Studies*, vol. 11, no. 1 (1976)

Le Monde, 9 September 1976, p. 5

Lenczowski, G. *The Middle East In World Affairs* (Ithaca, NY, 1962)

Lenin, V.I. *What is to be Done?* (Moscow, 1964)

Lesch, A. 'A Survey of Israeli Settlements', *MERIP Reports*, no. 60 (September 1977)

___ 'Israeli Settlements in the Occupied Territories', *Journal of Palestine Studies*, vol. VII, no. 1 (1977), pp. 26-47

Lijphart, A. *The Politics of Accommodation* (University of California Press, Berkeley, 1968)

Litani, Y. 'Cabinet Hears Statistics on Jewish Settlements', *Haaritz* (Tel Aviv), 12 May 1976 (Hebrew)

Loftus, P. *National Income of Palestine, 1944* (Government Printer, Palestine, 1946), no. 5 of 1946

Lustick, I. 'Israeli Arabs: Built-in Inequality', *New Outlook*, vol. 17, no. 6 (1974)

___ 'Israeli Arabs' in A. Cottrell and J. Ross (eds.), *The Mobilization of Collective Identity: Comparative Perspectives* (University Press of America, Washington, DC, 1978)

Lutfiyya, A. *Baytin, A Jordanian Village* (The Hague, 1966)

Maariv (Tel Aviv), 7 June 1976 (Hebrew)

Machover, M., and Orr, A. 'The Class Nature of Israeli Society' in A. Bober, *The Other Israel* (New York, 1972), pp. 91-3

al-Majali, H. *Memoirs* (Amman, n.d.) (Arabic)

Mansour, S. 'Identity among Palestinian Youth: Male and Female Differentials', *Journal of Palestine Studies*, vol. 6, no. 4 (1977), pp. 71-89

Mansur, G. *The Arab Worker in the Palestine Mandate* (The Commercial Press, Jerusalem, 1936)

Ma'oz, M. 'The "Moderation" of the PLO and Israeli Policies', *Maariv*, 12 December 1975 (Hebrew)

Mar'i, S. *Arab Education in Israel* (Syracuse University Press, Syracuse, NY, 1978)

Mar'i, S., and Dharir, N. *Facts and Levels in the Development of Arab Education in Israel* (Haifa, 1976) (Hebrew)

Marx, K., and Engels, F. *Communist Manifesto* (New York, 1933)

___ *The German Ideology* (New York, 1947)

McRae, K. (ed.) *Consociational Democracy* (McClelland and Stewart, Ottawa, 1974)

Mendis, H. *Labor and Laborers in the Palestinian Camp* (Arabic)

MERIP Reports 'Likud Plan for Settlements in the West Bank', no. 59 (August 1977), p. 23

Mernissi, F. *Beyond the Veil* (New York, 1975)

Middle East International, no. 67 (January 1977), p. 24

Middle East International, no. 76 (October 1977), p. 22

Migdal, J. 'Urbanization and Political Change: "The Impact of Foreign Rule"', *Comparative Studies in Society and History*, vol. 19, no. 3 (1977), pp. 328-49

Miliband, R. *Marxism and Politics* (Oxford, 1977)

Mogannam, M. *The Arab Woman and the Palestine Problem* (London, 1936)

Monroe, E. *Britain's Moments in the Middle East* (Baltimore, 1963)

al-Mufti, I. *Department of Women's Affairs: A Working Paper Setting Forth the Aims and Functions of the Department* (Amman, 1977)

al-Mustaqbal, no. 40 (1977), pp. 35-40 (Arabic)

Naffar, A., *et al.* 'The Role of Mass Media in Attracting Women for Development', unpublished typescript (Amman, 1976)

al-Nahar (Beirut) 20 April 1970 (Arabic)

Nakhleh, K. 'Cultural Determinants of Palestinian Collective Identity: the Case of the Arabs in Israel', *New Outlook*, vol. XVIII, no. 7 (October-November 1975), pp. 31-40

_____ 'On the Cure of Nazareth: A Reply', *New Outlook*, vol. XIX, no. 2 (February-March 1976), pp. 62-3

_____ 'Anthropological and Sociological Studies on the Arabs in Israel: a Critique', *Journal of Palestine Studies*, vol. 6, no. 4 (1977), pp. 41-70

_____ *Nationalist Consciousness and University Education* (Wilmette, Illinois, 1978)

Ner, vol. XXII, no. 11-12 (July-August 1962), p. 26 (Hebrew)

New Outlook (Tel Aviv), vol. 20, no. 4 (June-July 1977), pp. 66-7

New York Times, 26 April 1957

New York Times, 26 April 1968

New York Times, 3 August 1969

New York Times, 13 February 1970

New York Times, 16 February 1970

New York Times, 12 September 1970

New York Times, 15 March 1972

New York Times, 11 June 1973

Nordlinger, E. *Conflict Regulation in Deeply Divided Societies* (Harvard University Center for International Affairs, Occasional Paper, no. 29, January 1972)

Oded, Y. 'Land Losses among Israel's Arab Villagers', *New Outlook*, vol. VII, no. 7 (September 1964)

Orni, E. *Agrarian Reform and Social Progress in Israel* (Ahva Cooperative Press, Jerusalem, 1972)

Owen, R. 'Economic History of 19th Century Palestine: Some Points and Some Prpblems' (prepared for the Tenth Annual Convention of the American Arab University Graduates, October 1977)

Palestine, Department of Statistics *Statistical Abstract of Palestine, 1944-1945* (Jerusalem, 1946) (English ed.)

Palestine, Government of *A Survey of Palestine* (prepared in December 1945 for the information of the Anglo-American Committee of Inquiry) (Government Printer, Jerusalem, 1946), Vol. II

Palestinian Documents. (PLO Research Center, Beirut, 1969)

'The Palestinian Resistance and Jordan', *Journal of Palestine Studies*, vol. 1 (Autumn 1971), p. 162

Perara, J. 'West Bank', *The Middle East* (London), no. 36 (October 1977)

Peretz, D. 'Palestinian Social Stratification: the Political Implications', *Journal of Palestine Studies*, vol. 7, no. 1 (1977)

Peristiany, J. (ed.) *Honor and Shame: The Values of Mediterranean Society* (Chicago, 1966)

Pinner, W. *How Many Arab Refugees?* (London, 1959)

Porath, Y. 'The Land Problem in Mandatory Palestine', *The Jerusalem Quarterly*, no. 1 (1976), pp. 18-27

—— 'The National Liberation League', *Asian and African Studies* (Jerusalem), vol. 4 (1968)

—— *The Palestinian Arab National Movement 1929-1939: From Riots to Rebellion* (Frank Cass, London, 1977)

Preuss, W. *The Labour Movements in Israel* (Jerusalem, 1965)

Qahwaji, H. *The Arabs under Israeli Occupation since 1948* (PLO Research Center, Beirut, 1972) (Arabic)

Rabie, W. *et al. Turmusayya, A Study in Palestinian and Folk Heritage* (Beirut, 1973) (Arabic)

Rekhess, E. *A Survey of Israeli-Arab Graduates from Institutions of Higher Learning in Israel (1961-1971)* (American Jewish Committee, Shiloah Center, Jerusalem, 1974)

Robinson, M. *Islam and Capitalism* (Pantheon Books, New York, 1973)

Rosenfeld, H. 'The Contradictions between Property, Kinship and Power, as Reflected in the Marriage System of an Arab Village' in J. Peristiany (ed.), *Contributions to Mediterranean Sociology* (Athens, 1963)

Rothschild, D. 'Ethnicity and Conflict Resolution', *World Politics*, vol. XXII, no. 4 (July 1970)

Ryan, S. *Israeli Economic Policy in the Occupied Areas: Foundations of a New Imperialism* (Middle East Research and Information, Washington, DC, Project Report no. 4)

Sakhnini, 'The Palestinians in Iraq', *Shu'un Filastiniya*, no. 13 (September 1972)(Arabic)

Samara, A. *The Economy of the Occupied Territories: Underdevelopment Reinforces Annexation* (Jerusalem, 1975) (Arabic)

Samed, A. 'Entering the Proletariat', *Journal of Palestine Studies*, vol. VI, no. 1 (1976)

Sarhan, B. 'Family and Kinship among Palestinians in Kuwait', Workshop on Family and Kinship (Kuwait, 27-30 November 1976)

Sayigh, R. 'Sources of Palestinian Nationalism', *Journal of Palestine Studies*, vol. 6, no. 4 (Summer 1977)

Schiff, Z., and Rothstein, R. *Fedayeen* (London, 1972)

Schmelz, U. *Late Foetal and Infant Deaths in Israel 1948-1972* (CBS, Jerusalem, Special Series no. 453, 1976)

Selznick, P. *TVA and Grass Roots* (Harper and Row, New York, 1966)

Shaath, N. 'High Level Palestinian Manpower', *Journal of Palestine Studies*, vol. 1, no. 2 (1972), pp. 80-95

Shahak, I. *Le Racisme de L'Etat d'Israel* (Editions Guy Authiers, Paris, 1975)

Sharabi, H. *Nationalism and Revolution in the Arab World* (Princeton, 1966)

___ *Arab Intellectuals and the West: the Formative Years, 1875-1914* (Baltimore, 1969)

___ 'A Talk on the "Political Dimensions of Palestinian Identity"', 31st Annual Meeting of the Middle East Institute (Washington, 30 September-1 October 1977)

al-Sha'rawi, N. *The Naked Face of the Arab Woman* (Institute of Arab Studies and Publications, Beirut, 1977) (Arabic)

Shils, E. 'The Intellectuals in the Political Development of the New States', *World Politics*, vol. 11 (1960)

Silver, E. 'Cool Reception for General with a Dream', *Observer* (London), 11 September 1977

Smilianskaya, I.M. 'From Subsistence to Market Economy, 1850's' in C. Issawi (ed.), *The Economic History of the Middle East* (University of Chicago Press, Chicago, 1966), pp. 222-47

Snow, P. *Hussein: A Biography* (Washington, DC, 1972)

Social Conflict in Jordan (al-Ittihad Publishing House, Haifa, March 1972) (Arabic)

Suleiman, M. 'Origins of the Lebanese Civil War' in N. Aruri and F. Moughrabi (eds.), *Lebanon: Crisis and Challenge in the Arab World*

(Association of Arab American University Graduates, Detroit, 1977), pp. 2-4

Sussman, Z. *Wage Differentials and Equality Within the Histadrut* (Massada Press, Israel, 1974) (Hebrew)

SWASIA (weekly news digest), 21 May 1976, p. 7

Syrian Arab Republic, Central Bureau of Statistics *Statistical Abstract 1977*, vol, 30

Tamari, S. 'Notes on the Composition of the Labor Force in the West Bank', *Al-Quds* (Jerusalem), 4 December 1973 (Arabic)

Tibawi, A. *Arab Education in Mandatory Palestine* (London, 1956)

—— *A Modern History of Syria* (New York, 1969)

The Times (London), 28 September 1970

Totah, K. 'Education in Palestine', *The Annals of the American Academy of Political and Social Science*, vol. 164 (1932)

Turner, B. 'Avineri's View of Marx's Theory of Colonialism: Israel', *Science and Society*, vol. XL, no. 4 (1976-7), pp. 385-409

—— *Weber and Islam* (Routledge and Kegan Paul, London, 1974)

Tzidkone, D. 'Colonial Policy in the Territories', *New Outlook* (Tel Aviv), July-August 1975

United Nations Documents

Economic Commission for Western Asia (ECWA), *Reports on the Third Session 10-15 May 1976* (ECOSOC, 61 Session Supplement no. 12, New York, 1976)

ECWA *Demographic and Related Socio-Economic Data Sheets for Countries of the Economic Commission for Western Asia*, no. 2 (Beirut, January 1978)

Final Reports of the U.N. Survey Mission for the M.E., AAC 256 (New York, 1949), Part 1

International Conference on Population, *Proceedings of the Conference in Bukharist* (August 1974)

International Survey of Fertility

Report of the High Commission for Aid, June 1968

UN Relief and Works Agency (UNRWA) *Report* (July 1966-June 1967)

UNRWA Report of the Commissioner-General of the UNRWA for Palestine Refugees in the Near East, 1 July 1971-3 June 1972

UNRWA's Area of Operations, 30 June 1977

UN Special Committee on Palestine (UNSCOP) *Report*, vol. I, p. 54

Vance, V., and Lauer, P. *Hussein of Jordan: My War With Israel* (Peter Owen, London, 1969)

van den Berghe, P. *Race and Racism* (Wiley, New York, 1967)

Waines, D. *A Sentence of Exile* (Medina Press, Wilmette, Ill., 1977)

Weigert, G. *Ploughing New Fields: the Story of West Bank Farmers, 1970-1975*

Weinstock, N. 'The Impact of Zionist Colonization on Palestinian Arab Society Before 1948', *Journal of Palestine Studies*, vol. 2, no. 2 (1973)

—— 'Introduction' in A. Leon, *The Jewish Question* (Pathfinder Press, New York, 1970)

Weitz, J. 'Land Ownership' in *Immigration and Settlement* (Keter Publishing House, Jerusalem, 1973)

Yaacov, A. 'The Uprooted and the Abandoned', *Haaretz* (Tel Aviv), 7 January 1955 (Hebrew)

Yalgin, M. *The Muslim House as it Should Be* (Cairo, 1972) (Arabic)

Yasin, A. *The Struggle of the Palestine People before 1948* (PLO Research Center, Beirut, 1975) (Arabic)

Yusef, S. *Palestinian Reality and the Labor Movement* (Beirut, 1973) (Arabic)

Zahlan, A. and R. 'The Palestinian Future: Education and Manpower', *Journal of Palestine Studies*, vol. 6, no. 4 (Summer 1977)

Zarhi, S. 'The Occupied Territories – Economic Liability', *New Outlook* (January-February 1977)

Zeine, A. *The Emergence of Arab Nationalism* (Beirut, 1966)

Zoo Haderech (Tel Aviv), 3 September 1975 (Hebrew)

Zoo Haderech (Tel Aviv), 13 September 1975 (Hebrew)

Zoo Haderech (Tel Aviv), 22 April 1976, p. 5 (Hebrew)

Zureik, E. *The Palestinians in Israel, A Study in Internal Colonialism* (Routledge and Kegan Paul, London, 1979)

—— 'Toward a Sociology of the Palestinians', *Journal of Palestine Studies*, vol. 6, no. 4 (Summer 1977)

—— 'Transformation of Class Structure among the Arabs in Israel: from Peasantry to Proletariat', *Journal of Palestine Studies*, vol. 6, no. 1 (1976)

NOTES ON CONTRIBUTORS

Naseer Aruri teaches political science at Southeastern Massachusetts University, North Dartmouth, Massachusetts, USA.

Samih Farsoun teaches sociology at American University, Washington, DC, USA.

Yvonne Haddad teaches at Colgate University, Hamilton, New York, USA.

George Kossaifi is a demographer with the United Nations Economic Commission for Western Asia, Beirut, Lebanon.

Ian Lustick teaches political science at Dartmouth College, Hanover, New Hampshire, USA.

Khalil Nakhleh teaches anthropology at St John's University, Collegeville, Minnesota, USA.

Salim Tamari teaches sociology at Bir Zeit University, Bir Zeit, occupied West Bank, Palestine.

Elia Zureik teaches sociology at Queen's University, Kingston, Ontario, Canada.

INDEX

The following pages list the people, places, and events about which a pertinent statement is made in this book. By no means should this index be considered a complete listing of the people, places, and events recorded in this book.

For Product Safety Concerns and Information please contact our EU
representative GPSR@taylorandfrancis.com
Taylor & Francis Verlag GmbH, Kaufingerstraße 24, 80331 München, Germany

* 9 7 8 1 0 3 2 7 6 9 4 6 2 *